Strengthening International Courts

As goods, information, capital, and people flow across borders in ever-increasing volume, states sign agreements establishing laws to protect property rights, human rights, and national security. In many cases, states delegate authority to resolve disputes regarding the interpretation or violation of these laws to an independent institution, such as a court, whose power depends upon its ability to enforce its rulings. Leslie Johns uses the term *court* to refer to any institution that resolves disputes about the interpretation or application of an international agreement. Using detailed case studies of the International Court of Justice and the transition from the General Agreement on Tariffs and Trade to the World Trade Organization, she investigates the ways in which the court's strength, in turn, affects dispute settlement, compliance, and the stability of the international economic and political system. Johns finds that a court's design has nuanced and mixed effects on international cooperation. A strong court encourages litigation because, uncertain of the forthcoming ruling, states are reluctant to accept a pre-trial settlement. Yet a strong court, by increasing the expected cost of litigation, makes states more likely to comply with cooperative agreements when compliance is easy and withdraw from an agreement when compliance is difficult. These mixed effects suggest that a weak court is optimal when law is imprecise and states can easily exit agreements. A strong court, however, is optimal when it rules on precise laws and is nested in a political structure, such as the European Union, that makes exit costly. Johns concludes the book with a discussion of the ways in which creating more precise international laws and increasing both delegation and obligation to international courts can promote cooperation.

Leslie Johns is an Assistant Professor of Political Science at UCLA and a term member of the Council on Foreign Relations.

Michigan Studies in International Political Economy

SERIES EDITORS: Edward Mansfield, Lisa Martin, and William Clark

Michael J. Gilligan
Empowering Exporters: Reciprocity, Delegation, and Collective Action in American Trade Policy

Barry Eichengreen and Jeffry Frieden, Editors
Forging an Integrated Europe

Thomas H. Oatley
Monetary Politics: Exchange Rate Cooperation in the European Union

Robert Pahre
Leading Questions: How Hegemony Affects the International Political Economy

Andrew C. Sobel
State Institutions, Private Incentives, Global Capital

Roland Stephen
Vehicle of Influence: Building a European Car Market

William Bernhard
Banking on Reform: Political Parties and Central Bank Independence in the Industrial Democracies

William Roberts Clark
Capitalism, Not Globalism: Capital Mobility, Central Bank Independence, and the Political Control of the Economy

Edward D. Mansfield and Brian M. Pollins, Editors
Economic Interdependence and International Conflict: New Perspectives on an Enduring Debate

Kerry A. Chase
Trading Blocs: States, Firms, and Regions in the World Economy

David H. Bearce
Monetary Divergence: Domestic Policy Autonomy in the Post–Bretton Woods Era

Ka Zeng and Joshua Eastin
Greening China: The Benefits of Trade and Foreign Direct Investment

Yoram Z. Haftel
Regional Economic Institutions and Conflict Mitigation: Design, Implementation, and the Promise of Peace

Nathan M. Jensen, Glen Biglaiser, Quan Li, Edmund Malesky, Pablo M. Pinto, Santiago M. Pinto, and Joseph L. Staats
Politics and Foreign Direct Investment

Yu Zheng
Governance and Foreign Investment in China, India, and Taiwan: Credibility, Flexibility, and International Business

Leslie Johns
Strengthening International Courts: The Hidden Costs of Legalization

Strengthening International Courts
The Hidden Costs of Legalization

Leslie Johns

University of Michigan Press
Ann Arbor

Published in the United States of America by the
University of Michigan Press
Manufactured in the United States of America

♾ Printed on acid-free paper

2018   2017   2016   2015   4   3   2   1

A CIP catalog record for this book is available from the British Library.

ISBN 978-0-472-07260-6 (hardcover)
ISBN 978-0-472-05260-8 (paperback)
ISBN 978-0-472-12101-4 (e-book)

Library of Congress Cataloging-in-Publication Data

Johns, Leslie Nicole, 1979– author.
    Strengthening international courts : the hidden costs of legalization / Leslie Johns.
        pages cm. — (Michigan studies in international political economy)
        Includes bibliographical references and index.
        ISBN 978-0-472-07260-6 (hardcover : alk. paper) — ISBN 978-0-472-05260-8 (pbk. : alk. paper) — ISBN 978-0-472-12101-4 (e-book)
        1. International courts.   2. International law.   3. General Agreement on Tariffs and Trade (Organization)   4. World Trade Organization.   5. Dispute resolution (Law)   6. Judgments, Foreign.   I. Title.
    KZ6250.J64 2015
    341.5′5—dc23   2014038351

Contents

List of Tables

List of Figures

Acknowledgments

This book developed from innumerable discussions about international organizations with Mike Gilligan and Peter Rosendorff. Components of the theoretical argument build on our collaborative work, and I am grateful to them for their support over the years both as collaborators and as friends.

I also thank my many friends and colleagues at UCLA, including Kathy Bawn, Michael Chwe, Lorrie Frasure-Yokley, Tim Groseclose, David Kaye, Kal Raustiala, Marc Trachtenberg, and Rob Trager. I am even more grateful to those who read portions of the book, including Jeff Lewis, Barry O'Neill, Ron Rogowski, and Art Stein. Lauren Peritz, Andrea Vilan, and Maya Wilson all provided excellent research assistance.

A generous fellowship from the Niehaus Center for Globalization and Governance at Princeton University allowed me to revise the original manuscript. While there, I received valuable feedback and encouragement both from Princeton faculty—including Christina Davis, Joanne Gowa, Bob Keohane, and Helen Milner—and from other fellows, especially Yon Lupu, James Morrisson, and Rachel Wellhausen. The Burkle Center for International Relations at UCLA provided financial support while I completed this book. I also owe a huge debt to Cliff Carrubba, who has been a wonderful mentor, always providing constructive advice.

I am especially grateful to Bill Clark, Ed Mansfield, and Lisa Martin, the series editors for the Michigan Studies in International Political Economy series, as well as Melody Herr and the other excellent staff members at the University of Michigan Press. Two anonymous reviewers provided very helpful feedback on the project.

A few close friends provided unending support. This book would never have been completed without the friendship and camaraderie of Miriam Golden, Krzysztof Pelc, and Lynn Vavreck.

Finally, I must return to the beginning. My career as an academic began when I was hired to answer telephones in the Department of Social and Decision Sciences at Carnegie Mellon University. Kiron Skinner saw something special in me that no one else did. She hired me as her research assistant, mentored me, gave me piles of articles and books to read, and listened to my endless thoughts and questions about them. And then she sent me to Bruce Bueno de Mesquita at New York University. Bruce's generosity with his time, encouragement, and research money allowed me to become a scholar. To these two—Kiron and Bruce—I will always be grateful.

1

Introduction

In October 2007, Jose Ernesto Medellin waited on death row while his lawyers pled before the United States Supreme Court. Medellin, a Mexican national, had been sentenced to the death penalty in a Texas court without assistance from the Mexican government. After exhausting the appeals process in Texas, Medellin's lawyers went to the Supreme Court with a new argument. A recent ruling by the International Court of Justice, they argued, entitled Medellin to further judicial review because the United States had violated international law. Medellin had an unlikely ally in his case: President George W. Bush.

Medellin's Supreme Court hearing came after three cases and six years of litigation at the International Court of Justice (ICJ) in the Hague.[1] Multiple countries sued the United States, arguing that it violated international law by arresting, convicting, and sentencing foreign nationals to the death penalty without notifying their home consulates. In a series of rulings, the ICJ progressively strengthened its own authority and imposed stricter requirements. The United States government tried to implement the initial rulings, but these efforts did not appease the ICJ. After the third lawsuit, the ICJ ordered the United States to provide new judicial reviews of all the criminal cases. President Bush took two unexpected steps: he ordered state courts to reopen the criminal cases and then, seven days later, he withdrew the United States from ICJ jurisdiction.

Just as the ICJ pushed Bush too far, Bush pushed Texas too far. Texas refused to obey either Bush's executive order or the ICJ ruling. Texas ultimately prevailed. The United States Supreme Court found that ICJ rulings are not enforceable in United States courts and that President Bush lacked the authority to order state courts to review the

1

cases. Medellin was executed a few months later.

Years later, this case continues to raise provocative questions. Why did country after country sue the United States on the same legal questions? Why did President Bush act so dramatically against his own ideology—by ordering state courts to reopen death penalty cases— to comply with international law? Why did Bush work so hard to follow the court's ruling, only to exit its jurisdiction seven days later? The unlikely alliance of Medellin and Bush drew extensive media attention, but this case is just one small example of the many ways in which international law and courts shape politics.

Globalization and transnational social movements have made the world more connected. In recent years, foreign investment has surged to new heights and domestic economies have become tightly enmeshed.[2] And money isn't the only thing that is traveling across borders. There has been dramatic growth in the trade of goods and services, and international migration has expanded to unprecedented levels.[3] At the same time, individuals and interest groups have growing social concerns that cross borders, including environmental regulation and respect for both human rights during times of peace and humanitarian law during times of war.

This growing interconnectedness has created new opportunities for international cooperation, but it has also destroyed the good fences that make good neighbors. More foreign investment creates more temptation for a government to expropriate private property. More financial integration opens the door to contagion, in which the financial problems of one country spill over to others, snowballing in size and importance. More international trade can provoke more trade disputes. And more respect for human rights and humanitarian law puts more pressure on leaders to prevent and punish violations that are committed by the leaders of other sovereign nations.

States have responded to these global opportunities and challenges by legalizing international relations. In the economic realm, states have written a plethora of bilateral investment treaties and created institutions to protect intellectual property rights. Many countries are now coordinating financial regulation through international agreements like the Basel III Accord. And states use international law to promote and regulate trade, both through the World Trade Organization and preferential trade agreements. These trade agreements also promote social objectives, such as human rights, environmental regulation, and labor protection. In the social realm, the international community has created the International Criminal Court to prosecute war crimes and human rights violations. States have also begun to use civil courts, like the International Court of Justice, to challenge military actions in the former Yugoslavia, Rwanda, and the Democratic Republic of the Congo. The list goes on and on.

International law is a body of rules that creates expectations about appropriate behavior. These rules specify how a government should behave in its interactions with other governments, foreign firms and individuals, and, increasingly, its own citizens. These rules vary in their precision, ranging from informal understandings to detailed international agreements.

Many written agreements have dispute settlement procedures (DSPs), which specify how states should resolve disputes about the interpretation or application of the agreement. We can describe these DSPs along two dimensions.[4] First, dispute settlement procedures vary in *delegation*, which is the authority of a third party to adjudicate disputes. At one extreme, some DSPs don't grant any authority to a third party. States are still expected to negotiate in good faith, but they do so without any third party assistance. DSPs with some delegation allow a third party to serve as a mediator, and DSPs with even more delegation allow an individual or panel of third parties to hear facts and legal arguments and issue recommendations. DSPs have the highest level of delegation when they grant jurisdiction to an international court.

Second, dispute settlement procedures vary in *obligation*, which is the normative or instrumental pressure to abide by a DSP ruling. From a legal perspective, international agreements can vary in their "binding-ness." Some agreements are hortatory and specify what members should do without creating a legal commitment, while others create legally binding commitments about what a state must do. From a political perspective, international agreements and courts elicit varying levels of political pressure on leaders to comply. This pressure can be created by both international and domestic actors. Of course, the anarchic nature of international politics ensures that a state can never be forced to comply with a treaty rule or implement a court ruling. Compliance is always a challenge in international cooperation (Simmons 2010). Some scholars argue that states have an inherent propensity to comply with rules (Chayes and Chayes 1993), while others argue that states comply when they are pressured to do so by domestic interest groups or other states (Johns 2012; Simmons 2009). Regardless of why states comply (or don't), DSPs vary in their ability to change state behavior through normative and instrumental pressure.

Scholars and policy-makers use many different names to describe dispute settlement procedures, often with little rhyme or reason. They are sometimes called courts, adjudicatory bodies, arbitral bodies, quasi-judicial bodies, legal bodies, dispute settlement bodies, legalized dispute settlement bodies, dispute settlement mechanisms, dispute settlement systems, ... this list too goes on and on. Additionally, many institutions without "court-like" names perform "court-like" functions. For example, the Human Rights Committee hears disputes about alleged violations of the International Covenant on Civil and Political Rights, a human rights treaty, and then writes a document that contains its own interpretation of the facts and legal arguments. The proliferation of international agreements and institutions and the lack of consistency in their names means that there are no standard labels that we can use to organize and distinguish between these DSPs. Legal scholars have only recently begun to create taxonomies for these institutions (Romano 1998, 2011).

Rather than trying to impose order where there is little, I use the term "court" to refer to any institution that resolves disputes about the interpretation or application of an international agreement. I adopt this convention because all of these institutions differ in their powers, but not their purpose, and it is the simplest way to present my argument to readers who are not international law experts. Under this schema, we can think about how changes in the design of a court lead to changes in state behavior. In this book, a "weak court" has limited authority to rule (low delegation) and elicits little pressure on states to implement its rulings (low obligation), while a "strong court" has clear authority to rule (high delegation) and elicits intense pressure to implement rulings (high obligation). A court grows stronger if delegation or obligation increases, while a court becomes weaker if delegation or obligation decreases.

The legalization of international politics has drawn fire from some critics. In 2001 former United States Secretary of State Henry Kissinger described legalization as a "revolution" in the Westphalian conception of state sovereignty. He argued: "advocates [of international courts] trust jurists more than they do statesmen. The advocates of the Westphalian principles trust statesmen more than jurists" (Kissinger 2001, 235, 237). Kissinger does not stand alone. Other critics of legalization believe that strong courts can hinder cooperation by constraining sovereignty and creating a backlash against international cooperation (Goldstein and Martin 2000; Helfer 2002; Posner and Yoo 2005; Rosendorff 2005; Rosendorff and Milner 2001). They can point to the experience of the International Court of Justice (ICJ). Since its creation in 1946 as the main judicial body of the United Nations, the ICJ has been a relatively weak institution. As jurists have asserted stronger powers for the ICJ, many countries, including the United States, have left the Court's jurisdiction or withdrawn from their treaty obligations rather than follow the Court's rulings.

In contrast, supporters of legalization believe that it facilitates cooperation by enhancing compliance with international law. Some also argue that legalization is inherently good because it makes international politics more fair (Franck 1998), and a few believe that legalization will ultimately create a system of global justice that upholds liberal values (Slaughter 1992, 1995). Supporters can point to the multilateral trade regime. From the 1947 General Agreement on Tariffs and Trade (GATT) to the contemporary World Trade Organization (WTO), international trade has grown more legalized. At the same time, tariffs have fallen, trade flows have become less volatile, and the membership of the GATT/WTO has expanded (Goldstein, Rivers and Tomz 2007; Mansfield and Reinhardt 2008; Tomz, Goldstein and Rivers 2007). While states do not always fully comply with WTO law, the dispute settlement system of the WTO is arguably the most successful international court ever.[5]

1.1 My Argument

In this book, I take an intermediate stance and show that there is truth in the arguments of both critics and supporters of legalization. I believe that as globalization and social movements make our world more connected, states have more opportunities to cooperate, benefitting both themselves and the global community. However, cooperation creates opportunities for conflict. International law and courts can play an important role in resolving these conflicts, but this does not mean that international law is an unmitigated good. Legalization comes with hidden costs.

At its core, my argument is about uncertainty. Suppose two states are involved in a dispute. Regardless of the design of an international court, there will always be some uncertainty about how the court will rule. This uncertainty can come from disagreements about what a law requires or the facts of a given case. For example, GATT/WTO members are allowed to raise tariffs if a domestic industry is harmed by a subsidized import. Yet two members may disagree about the legal interpretation of the term "subsidy" or how much harm the industry must experience. Even if two members agree about the interpretation of the law, they may be uncertain about basic facts of the case, such as the actual magnitude of harm to the industry.

When there is low delegation to a court, it is unlikely to issue a substantive ruling. Uncertainty about the law and facts therefore plays a small role in state decision-making. When delegation increases, the court is more likely to rule on a case and uncertainty about how the court will rule becomes more important.

Similarly, when there is low obligation to the court, winning or losing a ruling will only generate slight pressure, so the stakes of a trial are relatively small. But when obligation increases, a substantive court ruling will elicit more pressure and thus have a larger impact on final political outcomes, so the stakes of a trial increase. Once again, uncertainty about how the court will rule becomes more important.

Uncertainty creates bargaining failure. When two disputants know how a court will rule, they can negotiate a settlement that they both prefer to litigation. However, if states are uncertain about how a court will rule, then they are less likely to reach a pre-trial settlement. As a court grows stronger, through higher delegation or obligation, uncertainty about how the court will rule becomes more important and it is harder for states to negotiate an early settlement. This is the first hidden cost of legalization: when a dispute occurs, delegation and obligation magnify the importance of uncertainty and states are less likely to reach pre-trial settlements.

The design of an international court also affects the likelihood of disputes. When a state decides whether to comply with a cooperative agreement, it knows that other states that are harmed by noncompliance can use the agreement's dispute settlement procedures. States decide whether to comply in the shadow of international law. When delegation or obligation increase, the expected cost of violating a cooperative agreement increases. If a state wants to benefit from future cooperation, compliance becomes more attractive relative to noncompliance. Supporters of legalization are partly correct because strong courts facilitate compliance. This is the primary benefit of legalization: delegation and obligation increase compliance with cooperative agreements.

However, sometimes a political leader will face tough times and be unable or unwilling to comply with her state's legal commitments. Dispute settlement procedures provide such states with an escape mechanism: they can temporarily violate their commitments and then engage in dispute settlement. But delegation and obligation increase the cost of this tactic. When leaders face tough times, it may be easier to simply leave the cooperative regime than to bear the cost of formal dispute settlement. Critics of legalization are also partly correct because strong courts reduce stability. This is the second hidden cost of legalization: delegation and obligation increase the likelihood that a state will exit a cooperative agreement, which reduces stability.

Strong courts have a mixed impact on international cooperation. The optimal design of a court is ultimately determined by how an institutional designer evaluates the trade-offs between promoting compliance, on the one hand, and reducing settlement and stability, on the other. Nevertheless, my argument has two major implications for the design of strong courts. First, an institutional designer can offset the negative effect of delegation and obligation on pre-trial settlement if she reduces uncertainty about how the court will behave. So increased delegation or obligation to a court should be accompanied by increased precision of the law. Second, an institutional designer can ameliorate a strong court's impact on stability if she raises the cost of exit from the treaty regime. One way to do this is to nest a strong court in a political context that makes exit difficult, such as the European Union and the World Trade Organization.

1.2 Assessing the Theory

To assess my theory, we need to take two steps. The first step is to ask: is the theory accurate? Namely, do states behave in a manner that is consistent with the theory? To answer this question, we must examine whether changes in court strength led to the changes in settlement, compliance, and stability that are identified in my model. We should also examine whether a key implication of my model holds: have attempts to strengthen courts been accompanied by enhanced precision of the law? The second step in assessing my theory is to ask: is this theory useful? Does it provide new insight on an important topic? Can its findings and implications be used to promote international cooperation? To show my theory's usefulness, I include a chapter that discusses the broad implications of my argument for contemporary topics in international law.

Accuracy

Answering the first question—is the model accurate?—requires that we first identify cases in which the design of a legal regime varies. Making structured comparisons *across* two different legal regimes is difficult because courts vary along a multitude of dimensions. We cannot truly isolate the impact of delegation, obligation, and precision unless we control for all other possible sources of variation. Ideally, we would compare outcomes from two institutions that are identical in all respects except for one dimension of legal design. However, the international system lacks enough institutions to make such comparisons. I adopt the alternative approach of examining variation *within* legal regimes. Suppose that we examine a single court and identify a point in time at which the strength of the court changes. If all other aspects of the court and its environment remain the same, then we can be confident that the change in court strength caused—or at least was strongly associated with—any observable changes in state behavior.

After presenting my theory, I include chapter-length case studies of the International Court of Justice and the GATT/WTO dispute settlement system. These case studies are intended to play two complimentary roles. First, they serve as detailed illustrations of my arguments. Namely, they demonstrate how the design of legal regimes can change, how these changes affect state behavior, and how rational states can design courts to better promote cooperation. Second, they help us to assess the explanatory power of my theory. Qualitative case studies are commonly used to assess the accuracy of formal models (Lorentzen, Fravel and Paine 2013). While these case studies cannot test hypotheses with the same rigor as statistical analysis, they can help us to assess whether the assumptions, results, and implications of a model are consistent with real world examples.

It is not my intention to make comparisons between the ICJ and the GATT/WTO. The institutions that I consider are drastically different in many ways that make such comparison vacuous. Instead, I examine how variation within an individual court affects settlement, compliance, and stability. This variation can come about in two ways. First, international judges can change delegation or obligation through their jurisprudence. I call this *internal change* because actors within an institution enact change. Second, member-states can change delegation or obligation by renegotiating rules or treaty texts. I call this *external change* because actors outside of an institution enact change.

Table 1.1 shows some of the many contemporary courts. A handful of courts were created in the years following World War II and there was a resurgence in new courts after the end of the Cold War. Not all of these courts are well-functioning institutions; many of the newer courts are still nascent. But this list demonstrates that any lessons learned from my theory can be applied to many different institutions. The main benefit of focusing on the ICJ and the GATT/WTO is that they both have a long history, but they differ dramatically in their design and the type of change they have experienced.

Table 1.1: A Sample of International Courts

Name	Subject-matter	Date created
International Court of Justice	General	1946
World Trade Organization Dispute Settlement System	Trade	1947/1995*
European Court of Justice	Regional	1952
European Court of Human Rights	Human Rights	1959/1998**
Benelux Court of Justice	Regional	1974
Inter-American Court of Human Rights	Human Rights	1979
Andean Court of Justice	Regional	1984
International Criminal Tribunal for the Former Yugoslavia	Criminal	1993
Economic Court of the Commonwealth of Independent States	Regional	1993
Court of the European Free Trade Association	Regional	1994
Central American Court of Justice	Regional	1994
International Criminal Tribunal for Rwanda	Criminal	1995
International Tribunal for the Law of the Sea	Law of the Sea	1996
Court of Justice for the Common Market for Eastern and Southern Africa	Regional	1998
Court of Justice for the East African Community	Regional	2001
Court of Justice for the Economic Community of West African States	Regional	2001
International Criminal Court	Criminal	2004
African People's Court of Human Rights	Human Rights	2006

* The WTO dispute settlement system was formed in 1995 as the successor to the GATT dispute settlement system.

** European Court of Human Rights was formed in 1998 as the successor to the European Commission on Human Rights.

Data from: PiCT (2004) and Alter (2012).

The International Court of Justice is the oldest international court that is still in existence. The ICJ has adjudicated a broad range of international disputes since its creation in 1946. The Statute of the ICJ is a component of the bundle of legal documents that created the United Nations and there have been no changes to this text. However, the Court has struggled over its history to define its role in the international system. There have been key points at which the Court has redefined its role through significant changes in its jurisprudence. These are examples of internal change. I examine two such turning-points in the history of the ICJ: the *South West Africa* case of 1960–1966, and the recent string of consular relations cases against the United States. As I discuss at greater length in chapter 4, these two turning-points allow us to examine whether changes in the ICJ's strength led to changes in settlement, compliance, and stability.

The WTO's dispute settlement system is the second oldest international court because it evolved from the 1947 General Agreement on Tariffs and Trade. The GATT encouraged diplomatic negotiations between states and contained few dispute settlement procedures. Over time, states developed informal norms and procedures that were increasingly legalized. These norms were codified in the late 1970s and remained stable during the mature GATT period of 1980 to 1994. During this time period, the GATT dispute settlement system was a well-functioning institution that heard many cases and had clear procedural rules. However, dissatisfaction with these rules is one of the major reasons why states created the new World Trade Organization in 1995. The GATT dispute settlement system was replaced by new procedures that are specified in the WTO's Dispute Settlement Understanding. These procedures were created through intense, prolonged, inclusive, and deliberative negotiations. This is an example of external change. The nature of these negotiations makes it reasonable for us to assume that the resulting dispute settlement system was designed by mostly (if not completely) rational actors with an eye to the system's expected effect on international trade. As I discuss in chapter 5, the transition from the mature GATT to the WTO gives us an opportunity to consider the key implication of my argument: that attempts to strengthen courts should be accompanied by enhanced precision of the law.

Finally, this book uses the European Court of Justice (ECJ)—the third oldest court—to illustrate some of the implications of my theory. The ECJ is the judicial institution of the European Union. This relationship ensures that the cost of exiting the ECJ is extremely high because when a violator decides whether to participate in dispute settlement, it is implicitly choosing whether to remain a member of the EU as a whole. My theory should still apply to this institution, but we are unlikely to observe much of the behavior that my theory explains simply because the cost of exit is so high. Nevertheless, this court is an ideal example for the second implication of my theory: that a strong court should be nested in a political context that makes exit difficult. I therefore return to the example of the ECJ at various points in the book.

Usefulness

After I assess the accuracy of my arguments in the ICJ and GATT/WTO dispute settlement system, I show that my findings and implications can be used to improve international cooperation. Chapter 6 applies the lessons learned from my theory to other contemporary institutions and issues.

I first argue that stronger courts aren't always better at promoting international cooperation. Strong courts increase the likelihood of exit during tough times, which decreases the long-term stability of cooperation. States experiencing tough times are less likely to exit from regimes with weak courts. This should make states more willing to join the cooperative regime in the first place if they anticipate future instability.

Second, I argue that one way to reduce the negative impact of strong courts on stability is to nest them in broader political institutions. A regime becomes more stable when the cost of exit increases. States can achieve this objective if they link court membership to other institutions that provide benefits to their members. I illustrate this argument using the design of the ECJ.

Third, I explain why stronger courts need more precise laws. One of the negative effects of strong courts is that they exacerbate the impact of uncertainty during trade disputes. Instead of peacefully resolving disputes through diplomatic negotiations, states are more likely to resort to costly litigation. This effect can only be offset by increasing the precision of the body of law that the court oversees.

Fourth, I argue that specialized courts, which oversee law for a single issue-area, should be more effective than general courts, which oversee many different issue-areas. Specialization helps a court to reduce imprecision by building up a large body of jurisprudence on a narrow set of legal questions. Over time, precedent can create precision, even if the underlying treaty text is vague or ambiguous. General courts will develop less precise law since they must rule on a larger and more diverse set of questions. They are thus less able to enhance precision through precedent.

Finally, I show that my arguments suggest that limited membership agreements—such as bilateral and regional agreements—may harm cooperation more than they help. The proliferation of these agreements ensures that states often have overlapping and conflicting legal commitments. This creates uncertainty about legal rights and obligations, which hinders the early settlement of disputes and fuels costly litigation.

***

In the rest of this book, I explore the theoretical relationships that link the design of a legal regime to its effectiveness in resolving conflicts and promoting cooperation. Chapter 2 develops and illustrates the key concepts in my argument. In Chapter 3, I present my theoretical arguments in a verbal, rather than a mathematical, framework. Readers who wish to see the mathematical details of my analysis can consult the Appendix. I then evaluate the accuracy of my theory through two chapter-length case studies of courts that have changed over time. Chapter 4 examines the International Court of Justice and Chapter 5 examines the 1995 transition from the General Agreement on Tariffs and Trade to the World Trade Organization. Finally, Chapter 6 demonstrates that my theory is useful by applying my arguments to contemporary debates over the design of international law and courts.

2

Rational Institutions and International Law

2.1 Introduction

As the modern world grows more interconnected through globalization and social movements, there is a greater need for states to cooperate in areas like foreign investment, international trade, financial regulation, environmental protection, human rights, and other issue-areas. International organizations can help states to capture the benefits of cooperation. For states to cooperate, they must first have common expectations about appropriate behavior and the consequences for inappropriate behavior. International law and organizations help states to articulate and uphold these expectations.

There has long been a divide between scholars of international relations and international law, which has only recently been bridged (Burley 1993; Keohane 1997). Most international law scholars analyze legal texts and judicial rulings (Brewster 2003; Diehl and Ku 2010). Many of these scholars are driven by normative concerns and support the expansion of international law because they view it, either implicitly or explicitly, as more fair and legitimate than international politics (Franck 1998; Helfer and Slaughter 1997–1998). In contrast, many political scientists and some legal scholars now use modern social science tools—such as game theory and statistical analysis—to examine international law from a rational choice perspective (Gilligan and Johns 2012).[1] Rather than describing law or advocating for legalization, rational choice theorists seek to understand why states write and comply with laws, and how legal institutions shape state behavior.

This chapter provides an overview of rational choice perspectives on international law and shows how my argument builds on and relates to previous research. I begin by examining the ways in which international law can help states cooperate. Since a key premise of this book is that policy-makers can and should design institutions to facilitate cooperation, I then provide a brief summary of previous accounts of how international courts are created and changed. Finally, I introduce the key components of my theory, first by discussing my theory's key outcome variables—settlement, compliance, and stability–and then by examining its explanatory variables—delegation, obligation, and precision.

2.2 What Does International Law Do?

The simplest way in which law and courts can promote cooperation is by solving coordination problems (Snidal 1985; Stein 1982, 1990).[2] Suppose that each individual in a society must decide whether to drive his car on the left or right side of the street. Once the drivers collectively adopt the norm of driving on the right side, no individual will want to drive on the left. Law and courts can facilitate such coordination by creating common beliefs about appropriate behavior. These common beliefs are called focal points. States may have conflicting preferences over which norm to adopt. However, once a norm is chosen, no one gains from violating that norm.

In a coordination problem, international courts can change state behavior even if states feel no normative obligation to abide by the court's ruling. Every state will want to comply if it believes that other states will comply too. Coordination problems are amenable to judicial lawmaking—the creation of rules by judges, rather than treaties—because a judge knows that states will follow her ruling (Helfer 2008b). Many legal scholars believe that coordination problems drive a large portion of international law.[3]

These arguments are persuasive, but they stack the deck in favor of effective courts. If we ask a court to choose rules that everyone will automatically follow, then we are not asking the court to do much: we have only picked the low-hanging fruit. States could solve a coordination problem just as easily by flipping a coin because any public signal can serve as a focal point. My theory does not model international cooperation as a coordination problem because I want to explore a more difficult strategic interaction: collaboration problems.

In a collaboration problem, states can benefit from joint cooperation but each state is tempted to not cooperate (Snidal 1985; Stein 1982, 1990).[4] For example, all states can benefit from reduced carbon emissions, but each state prefers that others bear the cost of environmental protection. Similarly, free trade can benefit society as a whole, but it harms import-competing industries. Each state wants others to remove their trade barriers so that its own exporters can sell their goods abroad. However, each state also wants to keep its own trade barriers in place so that its industries are protected from foreign competition.[5]

Some legal scholars argue that states can solve collaboration problems if they use coercion to change the costs and benefits of cooperation and defection (Goldsmith and Posner 2005; Guzman 2007). However, these arguments are unsatisfying from a theoretical perspective because they amount to assuming that states don't have a collaboration problem. The more satisfying, albeit more complex, solution to a collaboration problem is to create a system in which each state is willing to bear its own cost of cooperation to ensure access to the benefits of cooperation. If states repeatedly interact over time, they can promote cooperation by using reciprocity, such as reverting to uncooperative behavior if any player breaks the cooperative agreement (Keohane 1986).[6] Reputational accounts of cooperation are not without their critics, yet they dominate rational choice studies of collaboration problems (Brewster 2009; Mercer 1996).

International law and courts can help states to overcome collaboration problems. First, they can create expectations about appropriate behavior. These expectations are clear in a simple collaboration problem, where states have two choices: cooperate or defect. However, what exactly does cooperation entail in a complex policy area such as international trade? Treaties and courts clarify legal commitments, and help "states to come to a common understanding regarding relevant facts or law" (Guzman 2007, 51–52).[7] Second, courts can provide information about the prior actions of states (Keohane 1982, 1984). If each state can perfectly observe the behavior of all relevant actors, then states can sustain a system of cooperation based purely on reciprocity (Morrow 2001, 2002, 2007). Courts are thus most needed when states cannot observe the behavior of relevant actors (Koremenos 2007, 2008).

Information about state behavior facilitates the enforcement of law by third parties. For example, during the medieval era, no central authority enforced contracts, but traders developed an informal legal regime to promote cooperation (Milgrom, North and Weingast 1990). When a merchant violated a contract, his victim reported the violation to an individual known as the law merchant who kept a public record of all violations. Each merchant could then go to the law merchant prior to making a trade to see if his potential partner was a violator. If merchants refused to trade with violators, then merchants had no incentive to cheat. A system based on reciprocity can therefore reduce the temptation to violate because violators are excluded from future cooperation (Keohane 1986).

This argument can be pushed even further. Suppose that instead of refusing to cooperate with a cheater, third parties impose punishments that are costly to both the punisher and the state being punished. For example, third party states might impose sanctions or take military action. A third party will enforce another state's contracts if it believes that other states will later enforce its own contracts (Johns 2012). However, both this regime and the law merchant system only work if an institution, such as a court, provides public information about whether a state has violated an agreement. Courts can promote cooperation if they are information-clearinghouses that collect and provide information about past actions (Carrubba 2005; Carrubba and Gabel 2013).

My theoretical model does not explicitly model how court rulings translate into final political outcomes. However, I do assume that states prefer winning a ruling to losing. One way to interpret this assumption is that a negative court ruling brands a state as a treaty violator. If other actors in the international system are willing to enforce the court ruling, then the loser has a disadvantage in post-trial bargaining. So a court ruling will benefit the winner and harm the loser. The litigation process as a whole is thus a costly punishment for a state that violates a cooperative agreement.

Other rational choice accounts of international law focus on commitment problems. This area of research is somewhat muddled because scholars use two different definitions of the term. Under a strict definition, a commitment problem occurs when a state with fixed and known information and preferences cannot credibly commit to a plan of action that is optimal *ex ante*.[8] Consider the example of foreign direct investment. If I am the leader of a developing country, then I benefit if a foreign investor decides to build a shoe factory in my country. The factory will increase employment, generate tax revenue, and develop infrastructure. Before the investment is made, it is optimal for me to woo the foreign investor by promising to respect his property rights. However, after the factory is built, I have less incentive to abide by my prior promise. I may want to seize his factory and make it a government-run enterprise. Or I may wish to increase taxes or regulation to secure a larger share of the factory's profits (Guzman 1998; Sornarajah 2004). The foreign investor should be able to anticipate these temptations and he will not build the factory if he believes that my promise will be broken. So I can only lure in foreign investment if I can find a way to make my promise credible. I must find a way to "tie my hands" so that the investor knows I can't later grab his property. International law and courts can ameliorate such commitment problems if they credibly constrain or change the actions of political leaders. For example, Gilligan (2006) argues that the existence of the International Criminal Court allows states to credibly commit to refuse asylum to repressive leaders. Commitment can be particularly valuable to powerful states that are most likely to break their earlier promises (Goldstein and Gowa 2002*a*). My arguments don't apply to this strict definition of a commitment problem because my model is driven by uncertainty about the law (information) and changes in the cost of compliance (preferences).

Under the looser definition, a commitment problem occurs when a change in information or preferences affects a state's most preferred action.[9] Consider the example of human rights. Governments that respect human rights under normal circumstances sometimes violate human rights during economic or political emergencies (Hafner-Burton, Helfer and Fariss 2011). A government's action changes because the costs and benefits of violating a human rights agreement change (Hathaway 2003). Similarly, a political leader who is under intense domestic pressure— such as an economic recession or a tight reelection campaign—has an increased incentive to violate her international trade commitments (Johns and Rosendorff 2009; Rosendorff 2005). International law and courts can solve this kind of commitment problem if they increase the cost of a treaty violation.[10] My arguments apply to this kind of a commitment problem because I assume that states are uncertain about the meaning of law and the cost of cooperation fluctuates over time.

There are two other possible roles for international courts. First, courts can fill holes in incomplete contracts (Ayres and Gertner 1989). If two states wish to cooperate on a complex issue, it can be prohibitively costly to write an agreement that precisely specifies how each state should behave under all possible contingencies. States may sometimes want to write an incomplete contract that is vague or silent on an issue and then grant the court authority to fill these holes. This is most likely to occur if the court can develop the expertise to fill these holes in a way that matches the regime's objectives (Maggi and Staiger 2011). In my model, I assume that the plaintiff files a case because it believes that the defendant has violated its legal obligations. Under this interpretation of the model, the litigants are uncertain about whether the court will find the defendant guilty. However, another way to interpret the model is to assume that the plaintiff and defendant are uncertain about the proper interpretation of a law that is vague or silent. Each player has its own interpretation of what the law should require, but the court ultimately possesses the authority to fill the hole in the contract.

Finally, an international court can be a tool for power politics. While many scholars believe that law is inherently fairer than power politics, others believe that powerful states can use international law to coerce the weak (Goldsmith and Posner 2005). For example, a powerful state may pressure a weaker state to sign a trade agreement, even if the agreement harms the weaker state. Similarly, some scholars believe that the International Criminal Court was created, at least in part, so that middle powers, like France and Germany, could limit the actions of more powerful states, like the United States (Goldsmith 2003). Interest groups can also use international law and courts to entrench their preferred domestic policies (Brewster 2003). For example, Moravcsik (2000) argues that after World War II, new democracies supported the European Convention on Human Rights because they wanted to prevent fascism and communism by constraining future politicians. Legalization can also promote the growth of interest groups that support compliance (Dai 2005; Hollyer 2010; Simmons 2009).

My theory doesn't explicitly address power politics. I show that delegation, obligation, and precision provide both costs and benefits, but I do not make predictions about optimal levels of delegation, obligation, and precision. States may vary in how they assess the costs and benefits of legalization. Power politics would then presumably influence the chosen institutional design by privileging the preferences of some states and discounting the preferences of others.

2.3 How Are Courts Created and Changed?

Just as international law and institutions can solve many different problems, they can emerge and evolve in many different ways. Some scholars argue that the nature of the underlying cooperation problem affects the design of an international organization (Koremenos 2013; Koremenos, Lipson and Snidal 2001). For example, Rosendorff and Milner (2001) suggest that states will be most likely to write flexible agreements, which allow occasional violations, when they are very uncertain about the future costs and benefits of cooperation. These scholars believe that institutions are designed by rational actors who are acting in their own self-interest to solve a specific cooperation problem (Carrubba 2005; Carrubba and Gabel 2013).

Other scholars believe that diffusion, rather than rationality, drives institutional design. They argue that institutional design depends heavily on context because states often create new institutions by copying the design of existing ones, even if these designs are not appropriate for the new context. For example, Elkins, Guzman and Simmons (2006) argue that the spread of bilateral investment treaties is explained by states mimicking the prior practice of other states, rather than rationally designing individual treaties. Similarly, Alter (2012, 2014) argues that many new international courts closely resemble the European Court of Justice because regional organizations, such as the Andean Community, have simply copied the design of a preexisting court that they believe is effective. If states simply mimic the practice of others, then the cost of creating new treaties and organizations is small because states do not need to negotiate every detail of institutional design. However, diffusion can lead to markedly irrational outcomes if states copy an institutional design that is not appropriate for their particular political context.

One final group of scholars emphasizes the importance of an organization in shaping its own design. After an organization is created, it becomes an actor in the international system that can push for institutional change (Hawkins, Lake, Nielson and Tierney 2006). Keohane (1989, 5) writes that "International organizations ... evolve partly in response to their interests as organizations and partly in response to the ideas and interests of their leaders; and in this evolution they may also change the nature of the regimes in which they are embedded." The preferences of actors within an organization do not always perfectly align with the preferences of its members (Johns 2007). This is particularly apparent in international courts, where jurisprudence can dramatically expand or contract a court's authority to rule and change the interpretation of existing rules. States that dislike this evolution can always leave the treaty regime. States that continue to participate in these institutions give their tacit acceptance of the institution's redefined role. Over time, this evolution can change the beliefs of states about their own interests and appropriate behavior (Carrubba 2009; Keohane 1989).

Institutional change—changes in the "rules" of international interactions and the consequences for rule violations—can thus occur in two ways. States can collectively change existing institutions through a deliberative process. I refer to this as *external change* because states, which are external to the organization, impose changes on an existing organization. Alternatively, actors within an existing organization, such as bureaucrats and judges, can attempt to redefine the organization's authority and objectives. I refer to this as *internal change* because individuals within the existing organization are seeking to change its design. There will of course be limits on both kinds of change. External change is difficult because it requires a group of states to renegotiate an agreement and build a consensus for a new institutional design. Internal change is difficult because if it occurs too quickly or dramatically, members will be more likely to leave the institution.

***

Supporters of legalization believe that international law and courts promote cooperation and benefit the international system, while many critics believe that international law and courts are unimportant. These critics argue that law and courts are epiphenomenal and any apparent changes in behavior are driven by coercion and power politics (Goldsmith and Posner 2005). While I do believe that laws and courts can promote cooperation, my theory shows that courts can sometimes play an darker role by harming international cooperation.

When states attempt to cooperate, they create new opportunities for conflict. Every state must sometimes violate its legal commitments for political or economic reasons. When this occurs, those states that comply with their commitments are hurt. Not only do they lose the anticipated benefits of joint cooperation, but they can become worse off than if they had never cooperated in the first place. In a coordination problem, if one state deviates from the prescribed behavior, its partner is worse off than if it had never signed an agreement and had instead randomized its behavior. In a collaboration problem, each state prefers mutual defection to being the sucker who unilaterally cooperates. In a commitment problem, one state's commitment induces its partner to take an action that it would not have otherwise taken. Breaking the commitment makes the partner worse off than if the commitment had never been made.[11]

Such treaty violations can quickly transform into international disputes. When a regime becomes more legalized, dispute settlement shifts from the diplomatic to the legal realm (Burley and Mattli 1993; Johns and Pelc 2014b). By increasing the importance of a formal institution, legalization increases the importance of uncertainty about how the institution will behave. Courts can raise the cost of treaty violations by helping the victim to secure compensation from the violator. But they also increase the likelihood that states must spend their time and resources on litigation. International law and courts come with negative consequences. This book identifies some of these negative consequences and examines ways in which states can promote cooperation while minimizing the hidden costs of legalization.

2.4 Elements of Cooperation

To be effective institutions, legal regimes must solve fundamental problems of both conflict and cooperation. Courts must resolve disputes that arise over the interpretation and application of the law. Since litigation is costly, effective legal regimes will provide incentives for states to settle their disputes prior to trial. Additionally, courts must promote short-term compliance with the law and the long-term stability of the regime. I discuss each of these aspects of state behavior—settlement, compliance, and stability—in turn.

Settlement

International cooperation creates two different opportunities for conflict. First, states must allocate the costs and benefits of cooperation. Since all states prefer to extract the maximum benefit at the minimal cost, cooperation creates a distributional problem (Fearon 1998; Morrow 1994; Schneider 2007, 2009). The regulation of international fishing is a prime example (Jo 2008). Each country would prefer that fishing be limited to ensure that there are adequate fish-stocks for the future. States can create rules to protect fishing-stocks, but these rules must allocate fishing rights across the states. How should states allocate these rights? Should all states be treated equitably and be given the same share? Should states that are economically dependent on fishing be given a larger share? Should landlocked states have fishing rights? Similar distributional questions plague environmental negotiations. The international community wishes to protect the environment by restricting carbon emissions. However, states have conflicting preferences over how these restrictions should be allocated. Should larger countries be allowed to pollute more than smaller countries? Should developing countries be allowed to pollute more than developed countries? Even if states negotiate a cooperative agreement, they can continue to have distributional conflicts after the treaty is implemented. For example, the Organization of Petroleum-Exporting Countries (OPEC) helps oil-producing states to cooperate by restricting the supply of oil in the global market. However, each OPEC member wants to obtain the largest possible share of the aggregate restricted production (Blaydes 2004).

Second, a cooperative regime creates opportunities for a state to cheat or free-ride on the efforts of others. Consider international trade. Countries differ in the products that they produce and trade. Each state benefits from liberalization that opens foreign markets to its own exporters. However, liberalization can harm domestic import-competing industries. Politicians, who face pressure to protect such industries, can resort to many different forms of protectionism: they can subsidize domestic industries, impose safeguard measures or antidumping duties, and create nontariff barriers to trade. While all states would benefit from an agreement that eliminated protectionism, each state is tempted to violate such an agreement by protecting its own import-competing industries. This opens the door to conflict. The temptation to cheat or free-ride grows even larger if it is difficult to observe the actions of individual states.

International courts are key to the resolution of such conflicts. When states experience principled disagreement about the content of the law, courts can interpret and clarify a treaty text. Courts can also both help states to distribute the costs and benefits of cooperation, and provide information about member behavior by serving as a forum in which allegations of cheating can be made, investigated, and adjudicated by a third-party (Brewster 2006; Guzman 2007).

However, litigation is itself a costly process. Both the plaintiff and defendant must collect evidence and present legal arguments, and then judges must deliberate and rule. Litigants must often repeat this process multiple times before a case is resolved. In the International Court of Justice, states can argue about provisional measures, jurisdiction and admissibility, the merits of a case, and the interpretation of a court ruling. In the World Trade Organization, states can hold formal consultations, present their case before a panel, and then challenge a panel ruling by arguing before the Appellate Body. Most cases at the ICJ and WTO take many years, if not decades, to resolve. When states spend their time and resources on litigation, they reduce the value of cooperation. If the existence of a court means that diplomatic conflicts are replaced with prolonged legal battles, then the court isn't enhancing international cooperation. It is merely changing the form of the costs of a dispute.

A key indicator of the effectiveness of a court is not just its ability to adjudicate legal disputes, but also its ability to prompt the early settlement of disputes prior to costly litigation (Brewster 2011a). As Hudec (1993, 360) argues, "No functioning legal system can wait until [the final verdict] to exert its primary impact." Legal scholars have argued that one benefit of strong courts is that they will hasten settlements between disputants, resulting in a reduction in costly litigation (Bilder 1987).

Many international courts actively encourage pre-trial settlement. For example, the dispute settlement system of the World Trade Organization, which is one of the most legalized bodies currently in existence, is explicit that settlement is always preferred to litigation. The WTO's Dispute Settlement Understanding (DSU), which contains the institution's dispute settlement rules, states that "The aim of the dispute settlement mechanism is to secure a positive solution to a dispute. A solution mutually acceptable to the parties to a dispute and consistent with the covered agreements is clearly to be preferred."[12] The WTO's training module—which is used to train lawyers, diplomats, and other representatives of WTO members—adds that "The preferred objective of the DSU is for the Members concerned to settle the dispute between themselves in a manner that is consistent with the WTO Agreement."[13] The importance of settlement is also reflected in the WTO's formal procedures. After a complaint is filed, the WTO requires states to conduct negotiations, called "consultations," before litigation begins. Also, the complainant can withdraw its complaint at any point if it reaches a mutually agreed solution with the defendant.

Litigation is surely less costly than armed conflict and it may yield fairer outcomes, but it is not costless. International courts reduce the value of cooperation if they prolong disputes that could be settled through diplomatic negotiations. So when we evaluate the effectiveness of a court, we should consider the court's impact on the early settlement of disputes.

Compliance

Courts also play a key role in deterring disputes by promoting compliance with international agreements. The design of a cooperative agreement determines the extent to which a treaty requires a state to change its behavior. *Ceteris paribus*, an agreement will be more effective when it imposes deep obligations for a broad scope of issues on many members. However, rules can only be effective if member states actually change their behavior.[14] In the short-term, an agreement will be more effective when members comply with its rules.[15]

Scholars disagree about why states comply with their international commitments. Henkin (1979, 47) echoed the views of many international lawyers when he wrote that "almost all nations observe almost all principles of international law and almost all of their obligations almost all of the time." These scholars often view compliance as a managerial problem (Chayes and Chayes 1993). They believe that states genuinely want to comply, but sometimes break their legal commitments because they are uncertain about what compliance entails or lack the capacity to comply. For example, a country may be genuinely committed to reducing carbon emissions, yet nonetheless violate its international commitments if it is uncertain about the environmental effect of a technology or if it cannot afford to adopt an environmentally friendly technology. In contrast, scholars who adopt the rational choice paradigm argue that a state's willingness to comply will depend on the expected costs and benefits of compliance, relative to noncompliance. States will differ in how they assess the short- versus long-term effects of cooperation. If it is relatively easy for a state to comply, then the state will bear the short-term cost of compliance in exchange for the long-term benefit of cooperation.

A state's incentive to comply with an agreement can change over time. Difficult political or economic situations—such as a pending election, a poor economy, or even a natural disaster—can make compliance more costly for a leader. For example, in spring 2002 the Bush administration prepared for upcoming Congressional elections. The administration feared that poor economic conditions in politically important states, like Ohio and Pennsylvania, would harm Republican candidates at the polls. To bolster Republican support, it announced that it would raise tariffs on imported steel to protect the domestic steel industry—which is primarily located in Ohio and Pennsylvania—from foreign competition. The action was widely viewed as a blatant violation of WTO rules and provoked litigation and threats of retaliation, but the administration refused to back down until after the midterm election passed (Davis 2012).

The design of a legal regime can affect compliance with an agreement if it changes the costs or benefits of compliance. A court should have little impact on compliance rates if imposes only a small cost on treaty violators. But if the court has authority to rule on the disputes and if its rulings impact political outcomes, then the prospect of litigation can make noncompliance more costly, thereby increasing the likelihood of compliance.

Stability

A final way in which legal design can affect state behavior is by changing the stability of a cooperative regime. States are sovereign in the international system, so each state always has the option of leaving an international regime (Johns 2007; Voeten 2001). The ability of states to exit from agreements means that institutions must be self-enforcing to be effective. States must want to join an agreement and remain as members in order for the regime to survive and have a long-term impact on cooperation.

States often exit from legal regimes. The most visible and extreme form of exit is to withdraw completely from treaty membership. Helfer (2005) examined membership data from the multilateral treaties registered with the United Nations. He found that from 1945 to 2004, states exited from these multilateral treaties 1,547 times. While dramatic, this figure understates the overall incidence of treaty exit since it does not include bilateral or many regional agreements. Additionally, many legal scholars now suggest that states can exit from customary international law (Gulati and Gulati 2010*a,b*; Helfer 2010).

One example of treaty exit occurred in the late 1990s. At that time, multiple Caribbean nations were members of the International Covenant on Civil and Political Rights (ICCPR), a major human rights treaty. Many individuals who were sentenced to the death penalty argued that their ICCPR rights had been violated and appealed their cases to a British Commonwealth court that served as a *de facto* constitutional court for many Caribbean nations.[16] In 1993, the Commonwealth court ruled that Jamaica had violated the ICCPR because of excessive delays in imposing the death penalty. Jamaica initially implemented the ruling by commuting the death sentences for 105 prisoners, and many other Caribbean nations that also belonged to the ICCPR mimicked Jamaica's behavior.[17] However, these states were troubled by the court's ruling, which imposed many new procedural constraints on death penalty cases, thereby raising the cost of future compliance with the treaty. In subsequent years, three Caribbean nations—Guyana, Jamaica, and Trinidad and Tobago—withdrew from the ICCPR because they believed that membership in the regime had grown too costly.

A state can also exit a legal regime in a more subtle way if it continues to accept a treaty's rules, but exits the treaty's dispute settlement procedures. This type of partial withdrawal is common in large multilateral agreements that consist of multiple legal texts. For example, the Vienna Convention on Consular Relations (VCCR), which is discussed in Chapter 4, has a main text that creates state rights and responsibilities and a separate optional protocol that gives the ICJ jurisdiction to hear disputes over the treaty's interpretation and application. A state can be a member of the VCCR without being a member of the optional protocol. This legal structure allows a state to accept legal rights and responsibilities, but reject court jurisdiction to adjudicate treaty disputes. Just as states can exit from treaties, they can also exit from optional protocols. As mentioned at the beginning of Chapter 1, the United States withdrew from the optional protocol of the VCCR after it was sued three times at the ICJ. The United States continues to be bound by the legal commitments in the VCCR, but the ICJ can no longer rule on alleged VCCR violations by the United States.

A final option that is available to states is to place limits on their treaty membership by imposing a reservation, which is "a unilateral statement ... [that] purports to exclude or modify the legal effect of certain provisions of the treaty."[18]   International law places some constraints on reservations and reservations are often criticized within the legal community.[19] Nevertheless, states often use reservations to respond to political and economic changes.

For example, Australia accepted jurisdiction of the ICJ in 1975 by making a unilateral declaration. This declaration had relatively few constraints, allowing the ICJ to hear a broad variety of cases. In 1991, Portugal sued Australia at the ICJ over maritime delimitations.[20] At that time, both Portugal and Indonesia claimed legal authority over East Timor. Australia had previously negotiated an agreement with Indonesia that delimited a maritime border between the two countries so that both could extract mineral resources from the continental shelf. This area included the Timor Gap, a section of the continental shelf near East Timor. Portugal made two main legal arguments to the ICJ. First, Portugal alleged that the agreement violated its own rights as the administering authority for East Timor. Second, Portugal argued that by negotiating exclusively with Indonesia, Australia had violated the self-determination rights of the people of East Timor.

The case was resolved relatively quickly because the ICJ refused to rule on the merits of the dispute. The ICJ argued that it could not rule on either of Portugal's legal arguments without first determining the legal status of East Timor. Since Indonesia also claimed authority over East Timor, the ICJ refused to rule unless Indonesia was also a litigant. Indonesia, which had not accepted ICJ jurisdiction, refused to participate.

In 1999, East Timor voted to become an independent nation. Australia feared that this would revive ICJ litigation over the Timor Gap because an independent East Timor could sue on its own behalf. Shortly before East Timor's official date of independence in 2002, Australia added a reservation to its ICJ declaration. This reservation stated that Australia did not accept ICJ jurisdiction for "any dispute concerning or relating to the delimitation of maritime zones ... [or] the exploitation of any disputed area."[21] Australia exited from ICJ jurisdiction for all maritime delimitation disputes.

These three mechanisms for treaty exit—complete withdrawal from treaty membership, withdrawal from dispute settlement procedures, and reservations—all provide states with ways to leave a cooperative regime. Of course, exiting a treaty is never costless. States that exit a treaty can be excluded from the future benefits of cooperation and lose their influence in the development of future policy (Helfer 2005, 2010). Additionally, treaty members may punish a state if its exit is perceived as aggressive unilateralism (Quigley 2009). North Korea's withdrawal from the Nuclear Non-Proliferation Treaty in 2003 is one prominent example in which treaty exit imposed significant reputational costs on an exiting state. Nonetheless, states often exit from treaties, reducing the stability of cooperation.

2.5 Elements of Legal Design

Any legal regime must have two components. First, the regime must have rules that specify appropriate behavior. Second, regime members must have a shared understanding of how they will respond to a violation of the rules. This understanding is often embedded in an institution that oversees dispute settlement. I generically refer to this institution as a court. Legal regimes vary along three separate dimensions.[22] Courts vary with respect to delegation and obligation. A court grows stronger if its ability or willingness to rule increases (delegation) or if the impact of its rulings of final political outcomes increases (obligation). Rules vary with respect to precision. Rules grow more precise if members can anticipate more accurately how the court will rule on the merits of a case. I discuss each of these dimensions in turn.

Delegation

In the 1990s, the United States and many Latin American countries were going bananas. The European Community (EC) adopted a trade policy that lowered tariffs on bananas imported from former European colonies. The United States and its allies, which were subject to higher banana tariffs, believed that the EC's policy violated WTO law, and filed a complainant against the EC at the WTO dispute settlement system.[23] During litigation, the EC tried to convince the WTO panel to dismiss the case. The EC argued that the United States lacked a direct legal interest in the trade policy because the United States did not export bananas to the EC. Therefore, the EC argued, the panel should not rule on the merits of the dispute. The WTO panel disagreed and adopted a permissive view of what constituted a legal interest. It ruled that the United States had a legal interest in the case because the United States could potentially export bananas to the EC and the

United States domestic banana market might be affected indirectly by EC tariffs. The panel was thus willing and able to rule on the merits of the case, and ultimately ruled against the EU policy.

As the *Bananas* dispute shows, one frequent question in international litigation is whether a court will make a ruling on the merits. Like a domestic court, an international court may refuse to rule on a legal claim because it believes that a case is inadmissible. However, unlike a domestic court, international courts often refuse to rule on a case because they do not believe that they have the authority to rule. The likelihood that a court will actually rule is thus one attribute of a legal regime: *delegation* refers to the likelihood that a court will be willing and able to issue a substantive ruling on the merits of a case.

One way to think about delegation is to imagine that a court is an agent of its member-state principals. In principal-agent theories of politics, a political actor (the principal) can grant authority to another actor (the agent) to take certain actions. In the international context, the difficulty of international cooperation often compels states to grant authority to technocratic institutions, such as courts (Johns and Pelc 2014*b*; Kahler 1992). The ability of a court to make a substantive ruling is thus a function in part of the court's relationship with its political principals.

Another way to think about delegation is to consider the authority that a court asserts for itself. A court is the final interpreter of a treaty, so an international court can, and usually does, decide for itself whether it can hear and rule on substantive arguments. These decisions can be affected by both legal and political considerations. The ICJ must routinely rule on whether it has jurisdiction to hear cases.[24] Other international courts, like the WTO's dispute settlement system and the European Court of Justice, have clear jurisdiction over their members, but sometimes refuse to rule on the merits for other reasons. As in the *Bananas* case, international courts play an active role in establishing the boundaries of their own authority. An individual ruling can create precedent about whether the court will rule in future cases and can even dramatically transform the understanding of international actors about how the court functions. This is particularly apparent in the history of the European Court of Justice. Alter (2000, 491) writes: "Although member states created an unusual supranational court, the advanced state of legalization in Europe is in no small part a result of the court's own efforts. The ECJ was not designed as a tool for domestic actors to challenge national policies; these powers the ECJ created for itself, despite the intention of member states." Courts are therefore key actors in determining their willingness and ability to issue a substantive ruling on the merits of a case.

Courts vary greatly in delegation. In a court with low delegation, such as the International Court of Justice, judges routinely fail to make rulings on the merits. Only 53 percent of ICJ cases have resulted in a ruling on the merits. Other courts, such as the WTO dispute settlement system (DSS), have high delegation. After WTO members submit a case to the DSS, it will proceed to a judicial ruling unless the disputants negotiate an early settlement. Even a court with high delegation, such as the DSS, can exercise judicial economy and decline to rule on important legal questions (Busch and Pelc 2010). Legal advisors can help disputants to prepare their cases and anticipate likely outcomes of their legal arguments, but they cannot fully remove uncertainty about whether a court will rule.[25] As Pomerance (1997, 308) writes:

> [the] line dividing ... the "non-justiciable" from the "justiciable" remains undefined and probably undefinable except by some of the tautological and circuitous formulae which tend to be quoted and requoted unthinkingly.

States are thus always somewhat uncertain about whether an international court will rule. However, courts vary in the likelihood that they will rule on the merits.

This variation in delegation is often apparent in how a court interprets general legal principles. For example, one principle of international law is that in order for a plaintiff to sue a defendant, the plaintiff must have a legal interest in the case. Neither the WTO nor the ICJ has precise legal texts that establish criteria for a legal interest. These courts rely on the same set of general principles of international law when deciding whether to hear cases, but they differ in their interpretation of these principles. The WTO adopted a permissive interpretation of a legal interest in the *Bananas* case because it allowed the United States to sue the EC even though the United States was not directly affected by EC policy. However, ICJ jurisprudence has established a relatively strict interpretation. The ICJ will only rule on the merits of a case if the plaintiff has a direct legal interest in the dispute.[26]

Courts can provide a variety of reasons for refusing to rule on the merits of a given case, which fall under the general rubric of what legal scholars call the justiciability of a case. First, the court can find that it lacks jurisdiction to rule in a given dispute. Second, even if jurisdiction exists, the court can find that the given claims are inadmissible for reasons such as excessive delay in initiating a lawsuit or non-exhaustion of local remedies. Finally, even if jurisdiction exists and a case is admissible, a court may decline to issue a ruling on the basis of judicial economy or propriety.[27] As illustrations, consider the following three well-known examples from the docket of the International Court of Justice.

In 1984, Nicaragua filed a complaint against the United States alleging that it had illegally mined Nicaraguan harbors and engaged in other acts of conflict. Nicaragua based its case in part on a unilateral declaration from 1946 in which the United States accepted the jurisdiction of the Court.[28] However, the United States declaration was subject to reservations, one of which specified that the United States recognized ICJ jurisdiction for cases involving a multilateral agreement only if all other affected members of the agreement were also impleaded. The United States argued that jurisdiction did not exist for the dispute with Nicaragua because the Court had excluded El Salvador, an affected party under the agreement in dispute, from the proceedings.[29] Nonetheless, the court ruled that it did have jurisdiction under customary law—a startling claim to many legal scholars at the time.[30]

The *South West Africa* case illustrates a similar situation with an opposite result. In 1960, Ethiopia and Liberia filed cases with the ICJ alleging that South Africa had violated its UN mandate over the South West Africa territory (present-day Namibia) by introducing a policy of apartheid. The court initially ruled in 1962 that it had jurisdiction over the case. However, the court dismissed the case in 1966 as inadmissible, stating that Ethiopia and Liberia had no "legal right or interest in the subject-matter."[31] This latter judgment came as an unexpected "*volte-face*" in light of the Court's earlier 1962 ruling stating that Ethiopia and Liberia did have a legal interest in the dispute.[32]

Finally, consider the lawsuit brought by the Republic of Cameroon against the United Kingdom in 1961. Cameroon alleged that the United Kingdom had violated its duties under a UN Trusteeship Agreement as the Administering Authority for the Northern Cameroons territory. Shortly after the lawsuit was filed, Northern Cameroons joined the independent state of Nigeria and the relevant trusteeship agreement was dissolved. The Court refused to hear the case, reasoning that:

> even if the Court ... finds that it has jurisdiction, the Court is not compelled in every case to exercise that jurisdiction. There are inherent limitations on the exercise of the judicial function which the Court, as a court of justice, can never ignore. There may thus be an incompatibility between the desires of an applicant, or indeed, of both parties to a case,

on the one hand, and on the other hand the duty of the
Court to maintain its judicial character. The Court itself,
and not the parties, must be the guardian of the Court's
judicial integrity.[33]

The key claim made by the Court was that ruling on the merits of
the *Northern Cameroons* case would violate judicial propriety. Since
the relevant agreement was no longer in effect, any ruling "would be
inconsistent with [the Court's] judicial function" because its judgment
would be "devoid of purpose."[34]

   While the ICJ made different legal arguments in the three cases
above, the arguments all had the same effect. No substantive ruling
was made on the merits of the case. Because a plaintiff usually files a
case to challenge the behavior of a defendant, the defendant usually
benefits politically when a court refuses to rule. A decision by a court
about the justiciability of a case can affect a plaintiff's ability to secure
remedies and may even cause litigants to believe that the court will
refuse to rule in future cases. Additionally, absent a condemnation
of the court, a defendant and third party observers may continue to
believe that the defendant's actions are permissible under the existing
law. However, just as a willingness to rule does not imply that a
plaintiff has won a case, a refusal to rule does not imply that the
defendant's interpretation of the law is correct. When a court refuses
to intervene, litigants are unable to learn new information about the
court's interpretation of substantive legal obligations. All three of the
factors above—jurisdiction, admissibility, and judicial propriety—limit
the ability and willingness of a court to rule on the merits of a dispute.
In this sense, all three issues capture the concept of delegation to the
court.

Obligation

In the early 1970s, Australia and New Zealand grew incensed at France
for testing its nuclear weapons in the South Pacific. They filed a lawsuit
at the ICJ in May 1973, and sought provisional measures. A few weeks
later, the ICJ ordered France to cease all future tests until the dispute
had been resolved.[35] France quickly announced that it would not
follow the ICJ order and would continue its nuclear tests. France faced
formal opposition from governments all over the world, including the
United Kingdom and numerous countries in the South Pacific and Latin
America. Domestic constituency groups exerted pressure internally
and externally. The French government had to contend with political

pressure from environmental organizations, religious groups, and trade unions. The French clergy attacked military policy, while British trade unions boycotted French goods. Additionally, France was highly criticized within international organizations. France soon bowed to the pressure and pledged to refrain from any future atmospheric nuclear tests. Even powerful states can find that abiding by an international court ruling is less costly than blatant defiance.[36]

Many scholars argue that states follow court rulings for normative reasons: states may believe that a ruling is fair or that it upholds moral values to which they are committed (Franck 1998; Kelley 2007). While some rules and institutions are believed to create legally binding commitments, others are hortatory or suggestive. For example, Raustiala (2005, 586) argues that there is immense variation in the "legality" of the rules that make up the canon of international law. He argues that "[c]ontracts create legally binding obligations for states, while pledges create only moral or political obligations." Abbott and Snidal (2000) make a similar distinction between covenants and contracts.

Other scholars believe that states follow court rulings for instrumental reasons. International courts rarely have explicit enforcement powers. Some courts, such as the WTO dispute settlement system, have well-established mechanisms to authorize punishments for states that do not implement court rulings. Others, such as the ICJ, do not.[37] Even courts that believe their rulings are binding have "no bail bondsmen, no blue helmets, no truncheons or tear gas" to enforce their rulings (Bello 1996, 417). International courts rely on external enforcement of their rulings.

Obligation refers to the normative or instrumental pressure to abide by a court ruling. Obligation varies dramatically in international law. If we wish to understand the politics of international law, we must understand how obligation shapes final political outcomes. A finding of a court need not automatically result in the full implementation of the ruling. Disputants can continue to negotiate with each other even after a court rules (Fischer 1982). However, a judicial ruling on the merits of a case opens the door to both normative and instrumental pressure from international and domestic actors. This pressure can change political outcomes.

When litigation ends, political negotiations begin. Consider the 1995 WTO dispute between the United States and Venezuela regarding gasoline. In 1994, the United States mandated restrictions on imported gasoline that it did not apply to domestically refined gasoline. Venezuela argued that this policy violated WTO law, and the WTO dispute panel agreed with Venezuela.[38] After the ruling, the United

States reopened negotiations with Venezuela to find regulations that were mutually acceptable, and the United States ended up weakening its regulations.[39] More generally, even if a finding of the WTO's dispute settlement system authorizes compensation or the suspension of concessions, the WTO encourages the reopening of negotiations to find a mutually acceptable outcome.

Similarly, ICJ cases usually consist of two countries making competing claims over which legal principles should hold in allocating an asset. Once the Court has ruled on such principles, the disputants must subsequently return to the bargaining table in order to negotiate a final settlement.[40] ICJ judgments often contain explicit provisions that require states to return to negotiations and reach a new settlement in accordance with the principles established by the Court.[41] Third parties can facilitate these post-trial negotiations (Johns 2012). Post-trial bargaining is not only the norm, but is also encouraged by courts and states as a method of settling disputes.

International court rulings usually don't result in immediate and full implementation. Nevertheless, the normative and instrumental pressure that is triggered by a court ruling changes the bargaining power of the disputants (Busch and Reinhardt 2000; Fang 2010; Johns 2012). The loser of a court ruling knows that leaving the bargaining table can result in punishment by third parties. This makes an exit from negotiations less attractive and weakens his bargaining position (Johns 2007; Voeten 2001). As third parties exert more pressure on the loser to abide by a court ruling, the winner of adjudication has a better bargaining position in subsequent negotiations. Increasing the strength of obligation thus has the effect of increasing the bargaining power of the winner of a ruling, relative to the loser. Of course, powerful states will probably gain more than weak states during international negotiations both before and after rulings. But as long as a state feels some obligation to implement a court ruling, even a weak state can secure better negotiated terms than it would in the absence of litigation (Davis 2006).

In addition to normative beliefs, obligation can come from international or domestic pressure to follow court rulings. At the international level, affected states can threaten retaliation if a defendant state is ruled against and fails to abide by the ruling. Retaliation can come in the form of trade sanctions and restrictions, the withdrawal of cooperation on other policy dimensions, reductions in loans and foreign aid, and even military conflict and coercion. For example, the Bush administration's announcement in spring 2002 that it was raising tariffs on steel provoked outrage from the European Union, Brazil, and other steel-producing countries.[42] The European Union responded by initiating litigation at the WTO. A favorable ruling would allow the EU to secure compensation by imposing retaliatory tariffs if the United States refused to remove the steel tariffs. EU leaders made it clear that they would punish the Bush administration by imposing these retaliatory tariffs on exports from Republican-controlled states, including Florida orange juice and South Carolina cotton.[43] This threat of targeted retaliation prompted the United States to back down on steel tariffs and comply with relevant WTO law.

Retaliation can also occur via multilateral agencies. The United Nations Commission on Human Rights lacks the authority of a court, but it has the power to issue resolutions that "shame" human rights violators (Lebovic and Voeten 2006). These resolutions have a significant impact on multilateral aid—when a country is shamed, it loses access to aid—even though there is no association between measures of human rights and foreign aid (Lebovic and Voeten 2009). This suggests that the institution has an independent effect because its resolution triggers retaliation via the withholding of aid, while a human rights violation does not.

We can see the influence of international political pressure to follow a court ruling in the ICJ's *Bakassi* case. The Bakassi peninsula lies on the border of modern-day Nigeria and Cameroon. When this region was under British colonial rule, Anglo-German diplomatic exchanges specified that Bakassi was part of the Southern Cameroons territory. However, the land was controlled and administered by a regional government in southern Nigeria. As part of the decolonization process, Southern Cameroons voted in 1961 to form the independent state of Cameroon. This new state claimed sovereignty over Bakassi, but the land remained under *de facto* Nigerian control. This led to a long-standing and bloody border dispute. After decades of conflict, the dispute was submitted to the ICJ. The pre-trial bargaining positions of the disputants were clear. Both Cameroon and Nigeria claimed exclusive rights to the Bakassi peninsula, and each was willing to fight for the territory.

In 2002, the Court ruled that Bakassi belonged to Cameroon, which provoked intense domestic opposition in Nigeria and Bakassi.[44] The Nigerian government immediately increased its military deployment to the territory. Local and regional politicians refused to implement the ICJ ruling, and militant groups spread violence throughout the region.[45] Responding to intense domestic political pressure, Nigerian President Olusegun Obasanjo refused to accept the Court's ruling and surrender Bakassi immediately. He insisted that further negotiations must take place: "We want peace, but the interest of Nigeria will not be sacrificed ... [W]hat may be legally right may not be politically expedient."[46] However, the ICJ ruling severely limited Nigeria's bargaining power. According a Nigerian diplomat: "No matter the situation, Nigeria's position has been weakened even before such negotiations start."[47]

Nigeria's initial defiance triggered international pressure to reach a peaceful settlement. UN Secretary-General Kofi Annan intervened and oversaw negotiations between the two countries. We cannot be sure of what specific threats were issued (and perhaps imposed) by diplomats behind closed doors. However, the United Kingdom, France, Germany and the United States pressured Nigeria to withdraw from Bakassi.[48]

Post-trial bargaining resulted in two key outcomes. First, the parties created a neutral body of technical experts that oversaw the drawing of final boundaries along the contested territory.[49] Second, UN-led negotiations resulted in the signature of the Greentree Agreement of June 12, 2006 in New York. This agreement set a two-year timeline for the phased withdrawal of Nigerian military and political authorities. In exchange, Cameroon agreed to provide economic and political protection for Bakassi residents.[50] Multilateral involvement in treaty negotiations resulted in a peaceful (if belated) transfer of Bakassi to Cameroon, an outcome that had not been possible prior to or immediately after the ICJ's ruling.[51] Multilateral attention to an issue can thus lead to outcomes that would not otherwise be possible (Davis and Oh 2007).

Obligation to court rulings can also be created by domestic political pressure. Domestic interest groups can be effective in pressuring governments to comply with international agreements (Conrad and Ritter 2013; Dai 2005; Hafner-Burton and Tsutsui 2005; Simmons 2009). They can similarly punish leaders if they fail to implement court rulings (Allee and Huth 2006a; Carrubba and Zorn 2010; Johns and Rosendorff 2009). International court rulings can even generate political pressure from individual citizens. Many scholars argue that an important function of international legal institutions is that they provide information to individual citizens about the behavior of political leaders (Johns and Rosendorff 2009; Mansfield and Milner 2012; Mansfield, Milner and Rosendorff 2000, 2002). For example, Pelc (2013b) shows that when a trade dispute is filed at the World Trade Organization, there is a statistically significant increase in Google web searches for information that is related to the dispute. Even in the highly technical area of trade law, international adjudication can increase voter information about government policies.

If interest groups or voters believe that their state has an obligation to comply with international law, then court rulings can provide leaders with political cover to adopt policies that are unpopular at the domestic level. Allee and Huth (2006*a*,*b*) argue that international court rulings can reduce the audience costs that a leader faces when he backs down during an international dispute.[52] They provide statistical evidence that politicians are more likely to resort to arbitration or adjudication during territorial disputes if they face strong domestic opposition. This suggests that leaders use international courts in part because the domestic public's belief in obligation to a court ruling allows a leader to blame the court for unpopular actions. Similarly, in her analysis of the 2002 Bush steel safeguards, Davis (2012) argues that the WTO Appellate Body ruling that the safeguards were impermissible gave the Bush administration political cover to remove the policies, which were only intended to be temporary measures.[53] Domestic political pressure can thus be key in promoting cooperation if voters believe that their state has an obligation to abide by international law or legal rulings.

However, domestic constituencies can also pressure a government to violate international law and ignore court rulings (Pollack and Shaffer 2009; Rosendorff 2005; Rosendorff and Milner 2001). This is often apparent in international trade. For example, the WTO dispute settlement system ruled in 2005 that United States cotton subsidies violated WTO law.[54] As a WTO member, the primary obligation of the United States under the ruling was to remove the offending measure by eliminating domestic cotton subsidies. However, cotton growers had so much political power that it was infeasible for the United States government to fully comply with its legal obligations. Rather than removing the cotton subsidies and facing the wrath of its agricultural lobby, the United States government provided annual payments of $147.3 million to a technical assistance fund that compensated Brazil and other cotton exporters. The domestic pressure to violate the WTO law and ruling was so large that the United States chose to subsidize cotton production in foreign countries rather than to implement the ruling.[55] Overall, it is not clear whether voters and interest groups either increase or decrease obligation to international courts. In some issue-areas, such as human rights and environmental policy, domestic political pressure appears to strengthen the impact of international courts and law on political outcomes. However, in other issue-areas, such as trade policy, domestic political pressure can weaken obligation.

A final factor that affects obligation to court rulings is the relationship between international and domestic legal systems. The general principle of good faith requires that states abide by their international legal commitments. Yet this principle does not ensure that a domestic court will uphold or enforce an international legal commitment. States vary in the extent to which they embed international law and court rulings within their domestic legal systems. Some countries, such as the United States, have a dualist legal system in which international commitments are distinct from domestic law. Other countries, such as Germany, have a monist legal system in which international commitments automatically become sources of domestic law.

One way to strengthen obligation to international law and courts is to embed them more deeply into domestic legal systems. This can occur via constitutional reforms that give international rulings direct effect in domestic law (Elkins, Ginsburg and Simmons 2012; Gabel, Carrubba, Ainsley and Beaudette 2012; Ginsburg, Chernykh and Elkins 2008). Alternatively, a more feasible and common method is to use judicial doctrine to change societal understandings of the relationship between domestic and international law (Helfer and Slaughter 1997–1998; Slaughter 1995). This tactic is most apparent in the historical development of the European Court of Justice (Alter 1998, 2001; Pollack 2003). When the ECJ was first created, there was not a political consensus about how its rulings would impact the domestic law of its members. Over time, the ECJ used its jurisprudence to develop two important doctrines. First, the supremacy doctrine requires that European law take precedence over domestic law when the two conflict. Second, the direct effect doctrine requires that domestic courts must recognize and enforce ECJ rulings, even in the absence of domestic legislation. Obligation to ECJ rulings increased as member-states began to respect and abide by these two doctrines, showing that international judges can change obligation to their rulings via the slow accumulation of jurisprudence (Carrubba 2009).

The United States is far from accepting the supremacy of international law over domestic law. Recall from Chapter 1 that the United States Supreme Court ruled in the *Medellin* case that United States domestic courts are not required to implement ICJ rulings.[56] However, the Supreme Court has become somewhat amenable to using international law to interpret the contemporary meaning of the United States Constitution. The Court invoked international law in recent cases that challenged the constitutionality of sodomy laws and the juvenile death penalty.[57] International law was not determinative in these cases, but when the Supreme Court ruled that the juvenile death penalty was unconstitutional, it was keen to note that "[t]he opinion of the world community, while not controlling our outcome, does provide respected and significant confirmation for our own conclusions."[58]

One key attribute of a legal regime is thus its impact on subsequent political outcomes. Obligation can be generated by the belief that a state has a moral duty to abide by international law, but it can also be created by instrumental political pressure to implement a ruling. In my theoretical argument, I focus on the general impact of obligation on state behavior, rather than the specific mechanisms of normative beliefs and political pressure. I model obligation as the extent to which a ruling of the court affects bargaining outcomes. This is represented by the difference between the plaintiff's share of the asset if he wins a ruling on the merits, and his share if he loses. If there is no obligation to the court's ruling, then the ruling has no impact on subsequent political outcomes. As obligation increases, the benefit of winning a ruling and the cost of losing both increase. The winner of the court's ruling should receive an advantage in post-trial bargaining, but she may need to make concessions in order to reach a settlement with the loser. When obligation is at its highest, court judgments are always fully implemented and litigation is a winner-takes-all system.

Precision

The final dimension of legalization is precision. Consider the *North Sea* case, which was heard by the International Court of Justice in the late 1960s.[59] In this case, Germany, Denmark, and the Netherlands could not agree on maritime delimitations in the North Sea. All three states had a common interest in avoiding conflict. However, each state wanted to secure the largest possible share of the territory. This led the states to have differing opinions about which legal principles should govern delimitation. Denmark and the Netherlands, which have projecting coastlines, favored the equidistance principle, which privileges states with projecting coastlines over states with recessing coastlines. Germany, which has a recessing coast line, argued that the principle of equity, not equidistance, should prevail to ensure that each state received a "just and equitable share" of the North Sea shelf.[60] Each side made complex arguments in favor of its preferred principle. The Court ultimately ruled that "equitable principles" should prevail.[61] Once the Court clarified that equity should trump equidistance, all parties were able to reach a post-trial settlement on precise boundaries (Gill 2003, 165).

   Precision refers to the clarity of a legal regime's rules for appropriate behavior. The content of international law can vary greatly from vague principles that regulate state behavior—such as the principles of equidistance and equity—to highly precise legal texts that clearly articulate a set of legal obligations—such as the rules of the World

Trade Organization. One important characteristic of a legal regime is the precision of its rules.

All areas of international law have some imprecision. However, some legal regimes have less precise laws than others. For example, the International Court of Justice is notorious for overseeing an unwieldy and imprecise body of law. The court has no inherent subject-matter limitations. Additionally, states and judges can invoke a hodgepodge of different legal principles and documents in order to support their case. ICJ judges usually give the most deference to plain text readings of written treaties. However, if such a treaty does not exist or its meaning is unclear, states can appeal to a broad diversity of other sources, including diplomatic exchanges between political leaders, unilateral public statements of political leaders, the negotiating history of relevant documents, resolutions adopted by international organizations, the history of state practice, and even general principles of law such as equidistance and equity. As seen in the *North Sea* case, states often disagree about which principles should take precedence and how these principles translate into tangible legal commitments.

In contrast, the dispute settlement system of the WTO adjudicates on the basis of a precise set of legal texts (WTO 1999). To be sure, some imprecision remains. States that use the WTO dispute settlement system to resolve trade conflicts have principled disagreements regarding the interpretation of their commitments and appropriate remedies for violations. Additionally, WTO jurists must balance the institution's commitment to trade liberalization against other competing values.[62] As argued below in Chapter 5, the precision of GATT/WTO law has changed significantly over time. Nonetheless, the body of law that is covered by the WTO dispute settlement system is much more precise than the panoply of legal sources used by the ICJ.

2.6 Conclusion

A legal regime is a complex system of rules about appropriate behavior and understandings of how to respond to violations of these rules. These understandings are usually embodied in a legal institution that oversees disputes about the interpretation and application of the law. These institutions come in many forms. Some regimes create bodies that hear disputes and issue non-binding rulings. For example, the Optional Protocol to the International Covenant on Civil and Political Rights creates a body known as the Human Rights Committee. This Committee can hear disputes brought by individuals against states and then "forward its views" about the legal claims of both parties.[63] Other legal regimes allow their members to submit cases to institutions with the authority to hear cases and issue legally binding rulings, such as the International Court of Justice. These institutions vary dramatically in both their ability to hear cases and the political impact of their rulings. This variation is captured by the concepts of delegation and obligation. As I discussed in Chapter 1, I refer to all of these legal institutions as courts because they all oversee disputes about alleged treaty violations. They vary in their powers, but not in their purpose.

Legal regimes also vary in the precision of their rules. Some regimes, such as the World Trade Organization, have complex and highly developed rules. Other regimes rely upon less precise sources of law, including general principles and custom. As in the *North Sea* case, the International Court of Justice must sometimes rule on the basis of vague concepts like equity and equidistance if no treaty text applies to the dispute.

The design of a treaty regime affects the behavior of its members. States often have opportunities and incentive to violate their legal commitments. They can choose to either comply with their commitments, or to break them. When a state refuses to comply, it must then decide whether to participate in the regime's dispute settlement process. Since participation is voluntary, a state always has the option to exit the treaty regime. This exit can occur through formal withdrawal from the entire treaty regime, renunciation of optional dispute settlement procedures, or reservations to its membership in the regime. If a treaty violator does want to remain a member by participating in dispute settlement, it must then engage in bargaining and litigation. Disputants benefit from pre-trial settlements because they can avoid litigation costs.

The next chapter demonstrates the precise mechanisms by which the design of a legal regime affects state behavior. Delegation, obligation, and precision all have complex effects on compliance, settlement, and stability. Strong courts promote compliance, but they also come with hidden costs: they reduce stability and make settlement more difficult. Precise laws can ameliorate, but never fully remove these costs. While courts can promote short-term compliance, their overall impact is not always an unmitigated good.

3

Theoretical Argument

3.1 Introduction

An international legal regime can have complex effects on state behavior. Members must decide whether to comply with a regime's rules given the anticipated consequences of violating these rules. However, if an actor decides not to comply, then the anarchic nature of international politics ensures that a rule-violator can decide whether to remain a member of the legal regime by participating in dispute settlement, or to exit the legal regime and forgo the future benefits of international cooperation. Since international institutions must be self-enforcing, a rule-violator cannot be compelled to appear before a court. Membership in the legal regime is a voluntary choice.

This chapter constructs a theoretical account of how the design of a legal regime affects state behavior.[1] I divide my argument into two parts that address the dual problems of cooperation and conflict. I begin with a conflict model that examines how the design of a legal regime affects the ability of its members to resolve their disputes prior to litigation.[2] I assume that one player believes that another has harmed it by violating a rule. Both players are uncertain about how the court will behave if the case goes to trial and the court rules on the merits, but I assume that one player has private information about its ability to win a legal ruling. These two players can try to resolve their conflict by negotiating in the shadow of a court. But if the two players cannot reach a negotiated settlement, the case then goes to litigation. I ask how delegation, obligation, and precision each affect the likelihood of pre-trial settlement.

I first show that delegation and obligation hinder settlement. If a court is unlikely to rule on a dispute or if its rulings are unlikely to

41

change political outcomes, then uncertainty about how the court will rule on the merits is relatively unimportant. Uncertainty thus has only a small impact on pre-trial negotiations. However, as delegation or obligation increase, uncertainty about how the court will rule becomes more important. Since uncertainty can lead to bargaining failure, states are less likely to reach a settlement as delegation or obligation grow larger. Precision has the opposite effect: as rules become more precise, players face less uncertainty about how the court will behave, and are more likely to resolve their disputes without resorting to costly litigation. Precision thus promotes the settlement of conflicts. Finally, I examine the distributional impact of delegation and obligation. I show that both delegation and obligation increase the *ex ante* expected utility of the plaintiff at the expense of the defendant. Strong courts—with high levels of delegation and obligation—benefit the plaintiff and harm the defendant.

Given these initial results, I nest the conflict model within a larger model of interstate cooperation. I use this cooperation model to analyze how the design of the legal regime affects the willingness of each member to comply with the regime's rules. If a member is not willing to comply, it can choose between participating in dispute settlement or exiting the legal regime. If each regime member either complies or participates in dispute settlement, then the regime is stable and its members can continue to cooperate in the future. However, if a member violates the regime's rules and then refuses to participate in dispute settlement, the regime is unstable and the player that exits does not participate in future cooperation. The model thus examines the indirect influence of delegation and obligation on compliance and stability of the treaty regime.

Delegation and obligation increase the cost of dispute settlement for a rule-violator because they both harm the defendant in the conflict model. These higher costs increase the likelihood of both compliance and exit in the cooperation model. When the cost of dispute settlement increases, those states that find it relatively easy to cooperate are more likely to comply. However, states that cannot afford to fully comply with the regime's rules are less likely to engage in dispute settlement and more likely to exit the treaty regime.

The design of a legal regime thus has complex effects on both conflict and cooperation. Delegation and obligation promote compliance, but do so at the cost of reducing institutional stability. Additionally, delegation and obligation make it more difficult for states to settle their disputes because they exacerbate the impact of uncertainty on pre-trial negotiations. Since precision reduces uncertainty about court behavior, precision promotes the early settlement of court disputes. The three dimensions of legalization—delegation, obligation, and precision—can therefore have differing effects on state behavior, and we cannot reduce the design of legal regimes to a unilateral measure that varies from soft to hard law (Abbott and Snidal 2000).

The design of a legal regime can change over time for many reasons. Sometimes these changes come from forces that are internal to the legal regime, such as idiosyncratic rulings that limit or expand judicial authority. However, my theoretical results have two implications for how rational external actors, such as member states of the regime, should design courts. First, institutional designers can try to capture the benefits of a strong court while mitigating its costs if they increase the precision of the regime's rules. Increased delegation or obligation to a legal institution should be paired with more precise rules. Second, institutional designers can ameliorate some of the costs of a strong court if they increase the cost of exit from the treaty regime. This can sometimes be achieved by linking a court to a broader political institution, such as the European Union. If exit from the court means that a state will be excluded from more benefits, the court becomes more stable.

My theoretical models are intentionally spare and strip away much of the detail and nuance of real-world international conflict and cooperation, such as power, judicial precedent, and the nesting of courts within broader political organizations such as the European Union. I do not ignore these factors because I believe that they are unimportant. Rather, I present simple models so that we can more easily understand some of the mechanisms that drive cooperation and conflict. After I present each basic model and its arguments, I discuss whether and how my arguments continue to hold as layers of nuance are added back into my account of the world. Finally, I discuss the implications of my theory for institutional design.

3.2 Conflict

Model Framework

Suppose that two players are involved in a dispute. The plaintiff believes that the defendant has taken an illegal action that harmed the plaintiff. For example, a state may allege that the defendant violated a border agreement, a foreign company may argue that the defendant violated a bilateral investment treaty, or an individual may believe that the defendant violated her human rights. The plaintiff wants the defendant to provide compensation for its prior actions. Compensation is any action that is costly to the defendant and beneficial to the plaintiff. Compensation may occur via a land concession in a border dispute, a monetary payment in an investment dispute, a change in government policy in a human rights dispute, a tariff reduction in a trade dispute, or any other action that that benefits the plaintiff at the expense of the defendant. The defendant prefers to provide no compensation, while the plaintiff wants full compensation for its alleged loss.

It is difficult for the two players to agree on whether and how much the plaintiff should compensate the defendant because they have differing beliefs about how the court will rule if the case goes to trial. They may disagree in their interpretation of the law, with the defendant believing that its action was legally permissible and the plaintiff believing otherwise. This often happens when a state tries to use a flexibility mechanism in a treaty. Alternatively, they may agree that the plaintiff has violated a treaty, but disagree about appropriate compensation. This occurred in the consular relations cases discussed in the next chapter. My model is agnostic about how disputants form their beliefs about how the court will rule. These beliefs can be shaped by the court's past jurisprudence on similar cases (Busch and Pelc 2010; Huth, Croco and Appel 2011). However, past jurisprudence does not eliminate uncertainty altogether. Judges often write rulings that are deliberately vague (Fox and Vanberg forthcoming; Staton and Vanberg 2008). And even if prior rulings are clear, states can still be uncertain about how past rulings will apply to current circumstances. Figure 3.1 shows the structure of the conflict model.

The game begins when the plaintiff learns the quality of his case, which is his expected probability of success at trial if the court rules on the merits.[3] We can refer to the case quality as the plaintiff's "type." A higher type is more likely to win a ruling on the merits than a lower type. The defendant does not know the plaintiff's type, but has prior beliefs about the likelihood of each type.[4] If the law is imprecise, then the defendant is very uncertain about the plaintiff's private information. The defendant has more accurate beliefs about the case quality if the law is more precise. The term "case quality" is most easily interpreted as the quality of legal arguments, but it can include other factors such as access to information about the facts of the case or the plaintiff's ability to prove his case in court.

One possible interpretation of the information structure is that the defendant's political elites know their own past transgressions, but do not know what evidence the plaintiff can produce in court. For example,

Figure 3.1: Structure of the Conflict Model

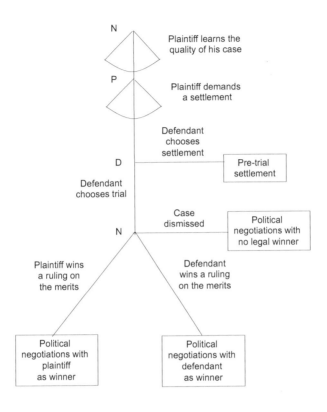

when Nicaragua sued the United States at the International Court of Justice (ICJ) in 1984, it argued that the United States violated international law by supporting paramilitary groups in Nicaragua. The United States foreign policy and military elite surely knew the extent of United States involvement in Nicaragua during the early 1980s. However, they were probably uncertain about whether Nicaragua could present evidence that would prove its allegations. Lawsuits with well-documented violations of international law can fall apart if the plaintiff cannot meet the evidentiary demands of a court. For example, in a recent case between Bosnia and Serbia, the ICJ refused to subpoena war archive records held by the International Criminal Tribunal for the Former Yugoslavia (ICTFY).[5] This led to a controversial judgment in which the ICJ ruled that Serbia was not guilty of genocide, even though the ICTFY held extensive evidence that Serbia had committed genocide.

After the plaintiff learns the quality of his case, he can demand a settlement from the defendant. This settlement specifies how much compensation the defendant must provide. The defendant must then decide whether to accept the plaintiff's demand. If she accepts, then she compensates the plaintiff, and the dispute ends in a pre-trial settlement. Settlement and litigation are complimentary events in this model. So if the defendant rejects the demand, then the dispute goes to trial and both disputants must pay litigation costs.[6] The design of the legal regime affects whether states settle or litigate. So delegation, obligation, and precision all affect the probability that disputants pay litigation costs in equilibrium. However, they do not affect the size of the litigation costs. Regardless of the design of the court, litigation consumes time and resources that the disputants could spend elsewhere.

Both players are uncertain about whether the court will rule on the merits of the case, but they have common beliefs about the level of delegation. As delegation increases, the court is more likely to rule on the merits, rather than dismiss the case. If the court dismisses the case, then there is no legal winner. The plaintiff and defendant can continue political negotiations, but the international legal process is over. If the court agrees to hear the case, then the quality of the plaintiff's case determines who wins the ruling. The disputants can then conduct further political negotiations, but the court's ruling affects the outcome of these negotiations.[7]

As obligation increases, the benefit of winning a ruling on the merits, relative to losing, grows larger because the loser faces more pressure to implement the ruling. I do not assume that players fully abide by the ruling. For example, if a foreign company wins an investment dispute, the defendant state might still not fully compensate the company for its losses. However, I assume that the foreign company will receive more compensation if it wins a ruling than if it loses. As obligation increases, the difference between winning and losing the ruling increases: the benefit of a legal victory grows larger. Even though an international court cannot directly enforce its rulings, the design of the legal regime can affect the impact of a court ruling on final political outcomes through the many mechanisms discussed in Chapter 2.

Equilibrium and Comparative Statics

International courts hear disputes over important issues, and states are most likely to use these courts when litigation costs are low relative

Figure 3.2: Better Cases Yield Higher Demands

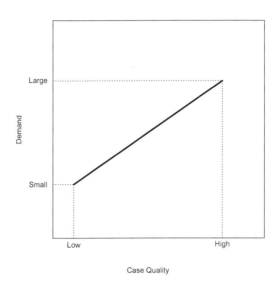

to the expected benefits of litigation. After all, if litigation costs are excessive, then disputants can address their conflict in other ways. I therefore focus on situations in which litigation costs are relatively small or the plaintiff's loss is relatively large, which generate a fully separating equilibrium.[8] In this equilibrium, each plaintiff type makes a unique offer, which allows the defendant to infer his type.

The better the plaintiff's case, the more likely he is to win a court ruling on the merits. Since winning a court ruling is always better than losing, the litigation process is more appealing to the plaintiff if he has a better case. The opposite holds for the defendant. If the plaintiff is a high type, then the defendant is likely to lose a ruling on the merits and thus wants to avoid litigation. So high quality cases give the plaintiff a bargaining advantage: the better the plaintiff's case, the more he will demand in pre-trial negotiations. This relationship is shown in Figure 3.2. The horizontal axis represents the plaintiff's type, while the vertical axis represents the plaintiff's optimal demand. When the plaintiff has a low quality case, he makes a relatively small demand.

However, when the case is of higher quality, the plaintiff makes a larger demand.

After the defendant hears the plaintiff's demand, she must decide whether to accept. By accepting the demand, the defendant is choosing to settle the case. However, if the defendant rejects the demand, the case will go to trial at the international court. Recall that the defendant does not know the quality of the plaintiff's case. The defendant must try to infer the plaintiff's type based on the size of his demand. As shown in Figure 3.2, large settlement demands indicate that the plaintiff has a high quality case. So one might expect that the defendant will be more likely to accept large demands in order to avoid litigation of cases that she will probably lose. However, such a strategy would allow the plaintiff to take advantage of the defendant. If the defendant is more likely to accept larger demands, then the plaintiff would always have incentive to bluff, even if he has a low quality case, by making the highest possible demand. By asking for more, a low type plaintiff would avoid a trial that he would probably lose and he would receive an even larger benefit from settlement. However, if the plaintiff behaved this way, the plaintiff's demand would not communicate any credible information. If all types make the largest possible demand, then the defendant would no longer be willing to accept it. The conflict game thus cannot have an equilibrium in which larger demands are more likely to be accepted.[9]

In equilibrium, as the plaintiff's demand grows larger, the defendant will be more likely to reject it and the probability of trial will thus increase. This relationship is shown in Figure 3.3. The horizontal axis represents the size of the plaintiff's demand, while the vertical axis represents the equilibrium probability of trial. As the demand goes from small to large, the probability of trial increases. Note that the line in Figure 3.3 is flat for both very low demands and very high demands. These regions are made up of demands that are off-the-equilibrium-path: they are demands that the defendant never expects to hear. Nonetheless, she must know how to respond to any possible demand that could be made. Unexpectedly small demands ask the defendant to give up almost nothing, and are thus demands that the defendant will always accept. However, unexpectedly large demands require the defendant to give up too much, so the defendant will always choose trial over settlement.[10]

Figure 3.3: Higher Demands Increase the Probability of Trial

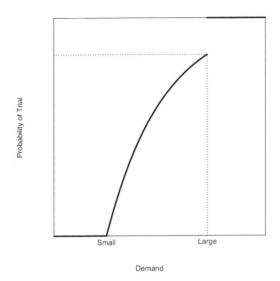

We can state the behavior illustrated in Figures 3.2 and 3.3 in a simple proposition about equilibrium behavior.

Proposition 1. *In equilibrium:*
(a) As the quality of the plaintiff's case increases, he demands more in pre-trial negotiations.
(b) As the plaintiff's demand increases, the defendant is more likely to reject it.

We can now examine how the design of a legal regime affects state behavior. A court grows stronger when delegation or obligation increase. While delegation and obligation are different concepts, they exert a similar impact on how states behave during pre-trial negotiations. When the plaintiff chooses his demand, he takes into account what he believes will happen if the case goes to trial. Better cases always make trial more appealing to the plaintiff and less appealing to the defendant. However, the magnitude of this effect is moderated though the level of delegation and obligation to the court.

To understand the intuition behind this logic, first consider the impact of delegation. When delegation is low, the court is unlikely to rule on the merits. The most likely outcome is that the court will dismiss the case by finding that it lacks jurisdiction or that the case is inadmissible. Case quality thus has a relatively small impact on how the plaintiff and defendant assess trial. After all, case quality is of little relevance if the court is unlikely to rule on the case. In contrast, case quality becomes more important if delegation increases because the court is more likely to rule on the legal merits. The higher the level of delegation, the greater the importance of case quality on each player's assessment of litigation.

Obligation has a similar effect. A low level of obligation means that a court ruling elicits little pressure, so the ruling has only a small impact on final political outcomes. While winning a legal ruling is always better than losing, the benefit of victory is small when there is low obligation to the court. The quality of the case thus plays a small role in how the players assess litigation. Uncertainty about legal claims has only a small impact if the political consequences from winning or losing a ruling are small. However, if obligation increases, the benefit of a legal victory increases. Obligation therefore heightens the stakes of a trial by ensuring that the legal ruling has a bigger impact on political outcomes, and thus increases the importance of case quality.

Both delegation and obligation magnify the importance of case quality. So the impact of case quality on pre-trial demands grows larger if a court grows stronger. Figure 3.4 shows the impact of court strength on plaintiff demands. If the court is relatively weak, because it has low delegation and obligation, then case quality has a small marginal effect on demands. This is shown in Figure 3.4 by the solid line. This line, which represents equilibrium demands under a weak court, is increasing in case quality, but only at a moderate rate. However, increasing the strength of the court, by increasing delegation or obligation, heightens the importance of case quality. An increase in case quality thus has a larger marginal effect on demands if the case is strong than if it is weak. This is shown by the dashed line in Figure 3.4, which increases at a much higher rate than the solid line.

How will the defendant respond to these demands? It is important to note in Figure 3.4 that changes in the strength of the court affect *variation* in the plaintiff's demands. A plaintiff with a weak case will make a small demand under a strong or weak court. But as case quality increases, the plaintiff's demand increases more quickly when the court is strong than when it is weak. When the plaintiff has a very high quality case, the size of his demand is much larger if the court is stronger. So stronger courts lead to more variation in demands. The distance between the largest and smallest equilibrium demand is wider under a stronger court than under a weaker one.

As argued above, the defendant must always reject larger demands

Figure 3.4: Strong Courts Increase Variation in Demands

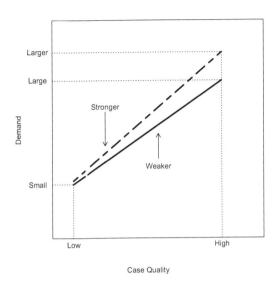

with a higher probability in order to deter bluffing. Under a weak court, there is relatively little variation between the lowest and highest demand, so the temptation to bluff is relatively small. Even if the plaintiff has the worst possible case, mimicking the behavior of the highest type only increases his demand modestly. However, the plaintiff's temptation to bluff is much larger under a strong court because there is more variation in equilibrium demands. Mimicking the behavior of the highest type dramatically increases the demand of a player with the worst possible case. Holding the defendant's behavior constant, the temptation for a low type plaintiff to bluff—by acting as though he is a high type—grows larger as a court grows stronger.

When a court grows stronger, case quality becomes more important in how players assess trial. This increase in importance means that the marginal benefit of case quality grows larger, and the variation in demands grows larger. This increase in variation provides the plaintiff with additional incentive to bluff. To offset this effect, the defendant must be more likely to reject the demand, which increases the probability of trial.

This relationship between court strength and trial is shown in Figure 3.5. When the court is relatively weak, the plaintiff will only

Figure 3.5: Strong Courts Increase the Probability of Trial

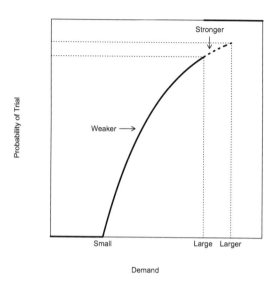

make demands in the interval from "Small" to "Large." But when the court is relatively strong, the interval of equilibrium demands expands from "Small" to "Larger." To remove the temptation for the plaintiff to bluff about his case when the court is strong, the defendant must increase the probability of trial for the demands between "Large" and "Larger." The aggregate impact of this change is that both delegation and obligation increase the *ex ante* probability of trial. If we hold precision constant, strong courts are more likely to generate litigation, rather than pre-trial settlement.

Proposition 2. *Delegation and obligation increase the probability of trial and decrease the probability of settlement.*

This model framework is analogous to bargaining models of war (Fearon 1995). In these models, two states must decide how to divide a valuable resource. If they cannot reach an agreement, they fight a costly war. When both states have the same information about the likely outcome of war, there always exists a set of bargaining outcomes that both players prefer to war. However, if states have asymmetric information—about factors like military capabilities or resolve—then each state is uncertain about how much it can extract from the other during negotiations. It is difficult for states to credibly communicate their private information because each state has incentive to bluff in order to get a larger share of the asset. Legal scholars have long used this analytical framework to analyze bargaining in the shadow of the law because litigation is costly and actors are uncertain about how judges will rule (Bebchuk 1984; Reinganum and Wilde 1986). The analysis above shows that both delegation and obligation increase the importance of uncertainty about trial outcomes. This exacerbates the fundamental difficulty of bargaining under asymmetric information. Holding other factors constant, stronger courts are more likely to induce bargaining failure and litigation.

Precision has the opposite effect on state behavior, but this effect is created by the same basic mechanism.[11] Precision describes the amount of uncertainty that states have about how the court will behave if it rules on the merits. It is unlikely that any state will ever be able to perfectly anticipate how judges will rule on the merits of a case. History is replete with unexpected rulings, including those in the *South West Africa* and consular relations cases that are discussed in Chapter 4. It is also unlikely that two states will begin the dispute settlement process with identical beliefs about how the court will behave. The negotiating process can allow states to converge in their beliefs, as they do in the equilibrium of this model. By the time that the case goes to trial, both the plaintiff and the defendant have the same beliefs. However, this convergence in beliefs does not exist when the game begins. One player has relevant information that the other player does not. When a legal regime has low precision, there are a broad range of possible interpretations and applications of the law. Players are thus very uncertain about how the court will rule. As the law grows more precise, players will have less uncertainty about trial outcomes because there will be less variation in case quality.

Figure 3.6 shows a simple example of how uncertainty can affect plaintiff demands. As always, the plaintiff will demand more when he has a higher quality case. The solid line shows these demands when case quality varies between "Low" and "High." When uncertainty grows larger, the case quality region expands. Figure 3.6 shows the impact of expanding the case quality interval to include higher quality cases. The dashed line shows that these better cases will lead to even larger plaintiff demands. So when uncertainty increases, a wider variety of demands are made in equilibrium. Uncertainty thus plays a role that is similar to delegation and obligation: more uncertainty leads to more variation in plaintiff demands.

By increasing the variety of demands that are made in equilibrium, uncertainty provides the plaintiff with more incentive to bluff about

Figure 3.6: Uncertainty Increases Variation in Demands

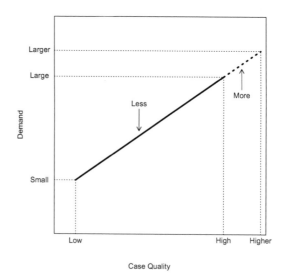

Case Quality

the true strength of his case. When the plaintiff is a low type, his temptation to bluff grows larger because the distance between his own demand and the demand of the highest possible type grows larger as uncertainty increases. The defendant can only deter such bluffing if she rejects larger demands with a higher probability. Once again, more variation in plaintiff demands leads to more litigation and less settlement. This behavior is shown in Figure 3.7.

When laws are more precise, the case quality interval contracts. This reduces uncertainty about how the court will rule, and thus reduces variation in plaintiff demands. Precision therefore lowers the incentive of the plaintiff to bluff, so the defendant can reduce the probability that she rejects the plaintiff's demands.

Proposition 3. *Precision decreases the probability of trial and increases the probability of settlement.*

Note that the dimensions of legalization have differing effects on state behavior. While both delegation and obligation increase the *ex ante* probability of trial, precision reduces it. Previous research has emphasized that increases in any of the three design attributes—delegation, obligation, and precision—correspond to enhanced legalization (Abbott,

Figure 3.7: Uncertainty Increases the Probability of Trial

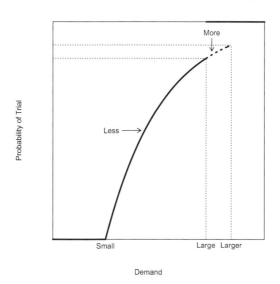

Keohane, Moravcsik, Slaughter and Snidal 2000; Goldstein, Kahler, Keohane and Slaughter 2000). The implicit belief that all three design attributes have the same effect on state behavior has led many scholars to treat legalization as a unidimensional attribute, varying from soft to hard law (Abbott and Snidal 2000). Propositions 2 and 3 demonstrate that this simplification is not always appropriate; different dimensions of legalization can have different effects on state behavior. We must therefore be cautious when we discuss the implications of legalization as a whole.

Finally, we must consider how the design of the legal regime affects the incentives of players to use the dispute settlement process in the first place by examining the *ex ante* expected utility of the conflict game for the plaintiff and defendant.[12] If the legal regime imposes only a low expected cost on the defendant, then she has more incentive to take actions that can later be challenged in court. However, if the regime imposes a high expected cost, then she may avoid disputes with other actors.

Delegation and obligation increase the importance of uncertainty in how the disputants assess litigation. When a court becomes stronger, uncertainty about how the court will rule has a bigger impact on the player's expected utility from trial. This increases the informational advantage that a plaintiff has over the defendant. Overall, the design of the legal regime has a distributional effect. By making uncertainty more important, delegation and obligation benefit the plaintiff at the expense of the defendant.

Proposition 4. *Delegation and obligation both increase the plaintiff's expected utility from dispute settlement and decrease the defendant's expected utility.*

Precision does not have a clear impact on each player's expected utility from the conflict game. When the law becomes more precise, the range of possible types contracts and there is less uncertainty about the plaintiff's type. Recall that the plaintiff's type is the probability that he wins a ruling on the merits. If enhanced precision eliminates low values of case quality, then precision benefits the plaintiff because it increases the *ex ante* probability that the plaintiff wins a ruling. But if enhanced precision eliminates high values, then precision benefits the defendant because it decreases the *ex ante* probability that the plaintiff wins a ruling. Stated another way, when the content of the law changes, so do expected outcomes from trial. An increase in precision can eliminate legal interpretations that privilege the plaintiff, the defendant, or some mixture of the two. The level of precision thus has no clear distributional effect.

***

Law and courts place an emphasis on the settlement of disputes. International agreements and institutions usually require states to make good faith efforts to resolve their dispute via negotiation before they can submit their case to a court. Litigation in any given international dispute is usually viewed as a failure of diplomatic negotiations. Many scholars argue that a primary benefit of legal institutions is that they allow disputants to reach negotiated settlements in the shadow of the law.[13] The conflict model shows that in the international context, settlement is less likely as the shadow of an international court grows larger. Strengthening international courts, by increasing delegation or obligation, does not facilitate negotiated settlements; it makes negotiations more difficult. As shown in Table 3.1, both delegation and obligation decrease the likelihood of pre-trial settlement. Precision has the opposite effect: precise laws increase the likelihood of pre-trial settlement.

Now that we understand the impact of delegation, obligation, and precision on dispute settlement, we can consider the indirect impact

Table 3.1: The Impact of Legal Design on State Behavior

	Settlement	Compliance	Stability
Delegation	Decreases	Increases	Decreases
Obligation	Decreases	Increases	Decreases
Precision	Increases	–	–

of these factors on compliance and stability. That is, we can nest the conflict model within a larger model of cooperation. If a state complies with the rules of a cooperative regime, then there is no dispute between the players. However, if a state does not comply, then a dispute exists and the states must choose whether to participate in the dispute settlement process; that is, the states must decide whether to enter into the conflict model above. This approach allows us to consider the impact of legal design on the dual problems of conflict and cooperation.

3.3 Cooperation

Model Framework

Suppose that two states can cooperate over an infinite number of periods, but the cost of cooperation changes each period for each player.[14] That is, sometimes a state can cooperate at relatively little cost, while at other times the cost of cooperation is very large. In each period, each state must choose an effort level. This effort is costly to the individual state, but creates benefits for all members of the regime. For example, a state may promote free trade by reducing its trade barriers. This action is costly because it limits the government's ability to protect domestic industries from foreign competition, but it creates an aggregate increase in social welfare across all members of the trade regime. Each state wants the other regime members to cooperate, but is tempted to provide less effort itself.

The game begins when each state learns its cost of cooperation for the given period. This is the state's private information. Each state knows its own cost of cooperation for the given period, but does not know the other state's cost. Additionally, since the cost of cooperation is stochastic, neither state knows how much cooperation will cost in future periods.[15] After learning its cost for the current period, each player simultaneously chooses a level of effort. More effort creates more cooperation, which increases each state's utility. However, I assume that each state has diminishing marginal utility from each additional unit of effort.[16] A state's one-period utility is the sum of the utility it gains from every player's effort, less its own cost. This basic game is then repeated over an infinite number of periods.

This model assumes that the two states are investing costly effort, but the results are equivalent to a model in which states are prohibited from taking a beneficial action. For example, we can conceptualize a human rights treaty in two ways. We can say that the treaty requires the government to invest effort in protecting human rights, or we can say that the treaty prohibits the government from violating human rights. Similarly, we can say that a trade agreement requires a state to promote trade liberalization, or we can say that it prohibits a state from imposing trade restrictions (Johns 2014). Under either interpretation, I assume that the cost of cooperation varies randomly over time, and states can change their level of cooperation in response to this cost.

How will states behave in the absence of a cooperative agreement? If players have not made a cooperative agreement, then each player will maximize its one-period utility. It will choose a level of effort for which its marginal cost equals its individual marginal benefit. From a social welfare perspective, this is sub-optimal because each player disregards the benefit that its effort gives to the other player. Both players would be better off if each player increased his effort so that the marginal cost equals the total marginal benefit for both players. However, such cooperation can create conflict. Each player will be tempted to provide less effort and free-ride on the contributions of the other player.[17] Any cooperative agreement must be self-enforcing. No external authority can compel a state to take a particular action, so an agreement can only be sustained if each state wants to comply with the agreement and remain a member of the cooperative regime.

In this model, an agreement has two components. First, an agreement specifies a minimum level of effort. A treaty member violates the agreement if it provides less than this mandated minimum. Given the mandated level of cooperation, we can calculate the losses that a state suffers when the other state violates the agreement. More severe violations create larger losses for the victim. Second, an agreement specifies dispute settlement procedures (DSPs). A victim can attempt to use these procedures to receive compensation for its loss. Many agreements allow their members to adjudicate their disputes before an external body, such as the International Court of Justice or the International Center for the Settlement of Investment Disputes. Other agreements create internal bodies (often called treaty-based bodies), such as the Human Rights Committee, which oversees the International Covenant on Civil and Political Rights. Most previous work on DSPs analyzes how the inclusion of these procedures in a treaty affects state behavior, relative to a treaty with no procedures (Rosendorff 2005; Rosendorff and Milner 2001). However, agreements vary in the precision of their rules, and the level of delegation and obligation that they grant to their dispute settlement bodies. One major theoretical contribution of this book is to examine this variation.

Recall from Proposition 4 that delegation and obligation increase the plaintiff's expected utility and decrease the defendant's expected utility from the conflict game. Because both design attributes have the same effect on the expected utility of dispute settlement, we can refer simply to the strength of the court. A court grows stronger as delegation or obligation increase. I model court strength as the expected share of losses that a treaty violator will pay in dispute settlement. The stronger the court, the larger the cost of dispute settlement to a treaty violator.

The overall cost of dispute settlement is thus determined by two factors. First, the severity of the violation affects how much the defendant is harmed by the plaintiff's action. If the plaintiff only commits a small violation—provides only slightly less cooperation than is required—the defendant suffers only a little harm. Holding all else constant, the cost of dispute settlement will be relatively small. However, if the plaintiff commits a severe violation—provides significantly less cooperation than is required—the defendant suffers more harm, and dispute settlement will be more costly. Second, the strength of the court affects the cost of dispute settlement. A weak court is relatively permissive of occasional defections and imposes only small costs on the defendant, while a strong court imposes higher costs.

Just as a state chooses whether to comply with the agreement, it also chooses whether to participate in dispute settlement. A violator will only be willing to participate if it believes that dispute settlement will provide future cooperative benefits. So in order for a self-enforcing agreement to be effective, cooperation in future periods must decrease if a member violates the agreement and refuses to participate in dispute settlement.

Equilibrium and Comparative Statics

This is an infinitely repeated game, so a huge range of state behaviors can be supported in equilibrium (Fudenberg and Tirole 2000). For example, there exists an equilibrium in which each state always chooses the effort that maximizes its one-period utility. This is the noncooperative behavior that leads to the underprovision of effort. In this noncooperative equilibrium, any agreement is irrelevant because effort is not affected by the treaty minimum, and states never participate in dispute settlement. A state will still contribute to the collective good, but it will provide less than the socially optimal level because it does not fully internalize the benefits that its effort creates for the other state.

However, the interesting theoretical question is how the design of a legal regime can promote cooperation between states. I consider an equilibrium in which each member conditions its behavior on whether any member previously violated the agreement and refused to participate in dispute settlement. In the Appendix, I solve the model by assuming grim trigger punishment. Suppose that a state violates the agreement and refuses to engage in dispute settlement. Under a grim trigger, the cooperative regime collapses and there is noncooperative behavior in all future periods.[18] States will still invest effort that creates benefits for others, but they will invest less than they would under the treaty regime.

I examine an equilibrium in which each state has three options under the agreement. First, a state can comply by providing at least the minimal level of effort. I refer to this as "compliance" (*C*). Second, it can violate the agreement and then engage in dispute settlement. I refer to this as "dispute settlement" (*S*). Finally, a state can violate the agreement, refuse to engage in dispute settlement, and leave the cooperative regime. I refer to this as "exit" (*X*).[19]

In the Appendix, I show that in each period states choose between compliance, dispute settlement, and exit based upon their current cost of cooperation:

Proposition 5. *In equilibrium:*
(a) If a state has a low cost of cooperation, then it complies with the agreement (C).
(b) If a state has a moderate cost of cooperation, then it violates the agreement and participates in dispute settlement (S).
(c) If a state has a high cost of cooperation, then it violates the agreement and exits the legal regime (X).

Figure 3.8: Equilibrium Behavior in the Cooperation Model

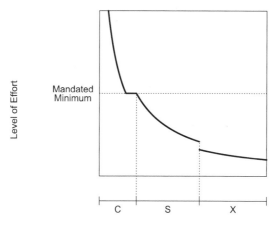

Note: In region C, the state complies with the cooperative treaty. In region S, the state violates the treaty, participates in dispute settlement, and remains a member of the regime. In region X, the state violates the treaty, refuses to participate in dispute settlement, and exits the treaty regime.

Figure 3.8 shows the equilibrium behavior. The horizontal axis is the state's cost of cooperation in the current period. The vertical axis is the level of effort. The dotted horizontal line indicates the mandated minimum effort. The solid line indicates equilibrium effort levels. Suppose that the government has a very low cost. If the government chooses its optimal effort without regard to the treaty, then it would choose an effort level that is higher than the mandated minimum. In such a situation, the state is not constrained by the legal regime and complies with the agreement.[20] However, as the cost increases, the government is tempted to lower its effort. To comply with the agreement, the government must increase its effort to the treaty minimum. This is indicated by the flat portion of the solid line. As the cost of cooperation grows even larger, the benefit of violating the agreement and then participating in dispute settlement outweighs the benefit from compliance. The optimal effort in these circumstances is shown by the middle portion of the solid line. Equilibrium effort

Figure 3.9: Compliance and Stability in Equilibrium

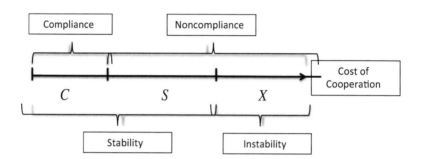

decreases as the cost of cooperation grows larger, but effort is always larger than the effort that the state would choose without an agreement. Finally, if the cost of cooperation becomes very large, then exit becomes the optimal action. The state will violate the agreement by reverting to its ideal effort and will not participate in dispute settlement. This is shown by the right portion of the solid line.

Figure 3.9 shows how each of the actions (C, S, and X) relate to compliance and stability. Compliance will occur when the cost of cooperation is low (region C). However, the state will not comply for larger costs (regions S and X). Similarly, the regime is stable for low or moderate costs (regions C and S). Even if a state violates the treaty, it will engage in dispute settlement to ensure that it can remain a member of the regime in the next period. However, for very high costs a state will prefer to exit the regime (region X). This exit generates instability.

We can now explore how changes in the court's strength affect state behavior. As a court grows stronger, the expected cost of dispute settlement increases. This means that if a state is deciding between either full compliance or dispute settlement, then the state is more likely to choose compliance if delegation or obligation grow larger. Increasing the strength of the court raises the likelihood of compliance.

Proposition 6. *Stronger courts—courts with higher levels of delegation and obligation—increase the probability of compliance.*

To demonstrate this result graphically, Figure 3.10 shows how equilibrium behavior changes as the design of the court varies. The solid line shows state behavior when a court is weak. The dashed line

Figure 3.10: The Impact of Strengthening the Court

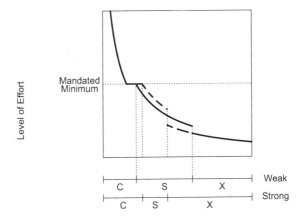

Cost of Cooperation

Note: The solid line shows equilibrium behavior under a weak court. The dashed line shows equilibrium behavior under a strong court. In region C, the state complies with the cooperative treaty. In region S, the state violates the treaty, participates in dispute settlement, and remains a member of the regime. In region X, the state violates the treaty, refuses to participate in dispute settlement, and exits the treaty regime.

shows state behavior when a court is strong. The compliance region (C) is larger when the court is strong, so there is a higher *ex ante* probability of compliance.

Note also in Figure 3.10 that an increase in court strength raises a state's level of cooperation, conditional on the state remaining a member of the agreement (regions C and S). Recall that the expected cost of dispute settlement is affected by both the design of the legal regime, and the size of the plaintiff's loss. Suppose a state has a moderate cost of cooperation. This cost is large enough that the state will violate the treaty, but low enough that the state will engage in dispute settlement to remain a member of the agreement in the future. If the court grows slightly stronger, then the expected cost of dispute settlement increases. To offset this increase, a violator will want to decrease its partner's loss, so the violator must increase its effort level slightly in order to lower the overall cost of dispute settlement. For example, examine the settlement region for the strong court in Figure 3.10. The dashed line (for a strong court) is higher than the solid line (for a weak court). So when a state has a moderate cost of cooperation, it will contribute more as the court grows stronger. Even though these states will violate their commitments, the size of their violations will be smaller. If we consider only the issue of compliance, we might conclude that strong courts are always a good idea. As advocates of legalization argue, strong courts do indeed promote short-term compliance by states. This relationship is summarized in Table 3.1.

However, the design of a legal regime also affects the long-term stability of the regime. If a state has a high cost of cooperation, then it will choose between either dispute settlement or exit. Delegation and obligation both increase the cost of dispute settlement. So when a court grows stronger, the state is less likely to choose dispute settlement, and more likely to exit.

Proposition 7. *Stronger courts—courts with higher levels of delegation and obligation—decrease the stability of the cooperative regime.*

Strong courts harm the stability of cooperative regimes. When a state has a moderate or high cost of cooperation, the short-term cost of full compliance outweighs its long-term benefit. The state must then decide whether to engage in dispute settlement, or exit the treaty regime. As a court grows stronger, the cost of dispute settlement increases, and a violator will be more likely to exit. For such states, the cost of settling today's dispute exceeds the long-term benefits from being a member of the regime.[21]

The impact of court strength on stability can be seen by examining the exit regions (X) in Figure 3.10. When the court is weak, a state exits if the cost of cooperation is very high. However, there are many cost levels at which a violator would engage in dispute settlement under a weak court, but exit the regime under a strong court. As the court grows stronger, region X expands and stability decreases. This result is listed in the last column in Table 3.1.

3.4 Discussion

The models above illustrate that a strong court is a double-edged sword. After a violation has occurred, both delegation and obligation exacerbate the impact of uncertainty during pre-trial negotiations. Their overall effect is to reduce the likelihood of settlement. Precision can offset this effect and increase the likelihood of settlement. Both delegation and obligation make legal uncertainty more important, which benefits the plaintiff and harms the defendant. So as a court grows stronger, the cost of dispute settlement rises for a state that violates a treaty.

When the cost of dispute settlement increases, states that wish to remain within the treaty regime are more likely to comply with their commitments. This is the primary benefit of legalization. However, a treaty member can choose whether to bear the costs of dispute settlement or to exit the treaty. As the cost of dispute settlement increases, a state that must violate its treaty commitments because of political or economic pressure is less likely to remain a treaty member. If the cost of dispute settlement is too high, then the state will exit the treaty. So legalization can harm the long-term stability of cooperation by increasing the likelihood that states will leave the agreement during tough times.

These models are intentionally sparse and simple because I want to clearly demonstrate the mechanisms at work. An important next step is to then ask: how robust are the model results? Do they continue to hold as layers of nuance are added back in? How do additional factors affect my arguments?

Power

One factor that is not included in the model. Few scholars of international relations would contest the claim that power increases a state's ability to achieve its goals, both under anarchy and within institutions (Steinberg and Zasloff 2006; Waltz 1979). International institutions are often designed to reflect power because more powerful states often have a more prominent role in institutional decision-making (Johns 2007; Stone 2011; Voeten 2001). While the model above does not explicitly include power and other non-legal factors, the model is consistent with the argument that power shapes the design of international law and institutions. Namely, power can influence both the choice of an institutional design and how the institution functions for certain actors and disputes.

First, the conflict model shows the consequences of changes in legal design, but it does not provide any predictions about which legal design states will actually choose when creating international courts. If a powerful state generally dislikes international litigation for practical or ideological reasons, we might expect to observe weak courts with low delegation and obligation. Nevertheless, that choice does not invalidate the arguments above, which provide insight into how states will behave if the design of an institution is altered. Power can shape the choice of institutional design without changing the impact of this choice on state behavior.

Second, all of the design elements above can be conditioned on which specific states are involved in litigation. For example, we might imagine that more powerful states have less obligation to court rulings because domestic and international constituencies place less pressure on a more powerful state to implement an adverse ruling (Stone 2011). Alternatively, negotiations that occur after litigation may be biased towards one player, regardless of the legal outcome. Courts may also be more hesitant to rule on cases in which a powerful state is a defendant, legal outcomes may be biased in favor of a powerful state, or litigation costs may be larger when a weak state is challenging a stronger one (Davis and Bermeo 2009; Goldstein and Gowa 2002b; Guzman and Simmons 2005). All of these possibilities can be easily incorporated into the model without changing my arguments.

Similarly, the model can accommodate variation in dispute attributes. For example, Davis and Shirato (2007) argue that industry attributes shape the willingness of states to litigate trade disputes in the WTO because some industries are better able to bear the cost of delay during litigation. So we might imagine that the cost of litigation can vary across players or types of disputes. As long as we can hold the litigation cost for a given case constant, the results above about the impact of changes in delegation, obligation, and precision will all continue to hold.

Risk Aversion

Another factor that we should consider is the role of risk.[22] The analysis above treats all states as risk-neutral actors. However, actors in the international context may be risk-averse if an international dispute threatens state security or the survival of a government in office. In the 1980s and early 1990s, many international relations scholars debated whether states are motivated by absolute or relative gains (Grieco 1988; Powell 1991; Snidal 1991). Under the former account, each state will make choices to maximize its own expected utility, regardless of the impact of these choices on other states in the international system. Under the latter, a state will be hesitant to take an action that benefits others, even if this action increases the state's own utility, because others might use these benefits to threaten the security of the state. For example, even if it is in a state's own economic self-interest to promote free trade, a state may be unwilling to liberalize if its trading partners can use their profits to build up their military capacity (Gowa 1994; Gowa and Mansfield 1993).

If a disputant is motivated more by the desire to avoid major losses than to increase its expected utility, then my arguments about pre-trial settlement don't necessarily hold. If a state is risk averse and faces high uncertainty, then it should place a premium on settlement because settlement allows the state to avoid an uncertain legal outcome. So more uncertainty would create stronger incentives to settle, rather than litigate. Increasing precision would reduce uncertainty about trial outcomes, which could make the state more likely to litigate. If states are extremely risk-averse, then Proposition 3 would no longer be true; precision might increase, rather than reduce, litigation. So my theory is most compelling for situations in which states are less likely to be risk averse.

Precedent

Judicial precedent is also not included in the model. My arguments above about pre-trial settlement apply to how states behave in a single dispute, given their initial beliefs about how judges will behave. If we assume that states interact repeatedly over time, then a court ruling today might create precedent that is applied by the court in future lawsuits. In such a dynamic framework, litigation might enhance precision over time. So higher levels of delegation and obligation, which increase litigation in the short-term, might mitigate their own costs if they enhance precision, which reduces litigation in the future. This certainly appears to be one of the unanticipated effects of the shift from the GATT to the WTO in 1995. After members increased delegation and obligation to the regime's dispute settlement system, panelists engaged in more judicial lawmaking.[23] The articulation of more precise laws can provide public benefits (Fiss 1984; Lauterpacht 1958). However, excessive judicial lawmaking can also lead to jurisprudence that differs significantly from the intent of state members. This can lead to instability as members who lose from the new interpretations have less incentive to remain within the legal regime. Precedent can thus have a mixed impact on international cooperation.

Even if we assume that litigation today increases precision in the future, we should bear in mind three important points. First, precedent plays a murky role in international courts (Guillaume 2011; Lupu and Voeten 2012). Most multilateral courts are created by states that vary in their domestic legal systems. Common law systems place immense importance on precedent in shaping judicial interpretation, while civil law systems do not. The design of international courts is thus a compromise between dramatically different legal practices. For example, the WTO dispute settlement system has not adopted the common law principle of *stare decisis*. Prior WTO rulings are not sources of law; panels and the Appellate Body can only decide cases on the basis of WTO rules. However, most trade law experts acknowledge that the current dispute settlement system operates under *de facto stare decisis* (Bhala 1998-1999; Pelc forthcoming). Panels and the Appellate Body regularly cite prior rulings and strive to maintain a consistent interpretation of WTO law. Similarly, the ICJ does not officially use precedent. Article 59 of the Statute of the ICJ states that: "The decision of the Court has no binding force except between the parties and in respect of that particular case." Article 38 of the Statute states that when deciding legal questions, the Court "shall apply" international treaties, custom, and general principles of law. As a last recourse, jurists can use previous judicial decisions as a "subsidiary means for the determination of rules of law," but only "subject to the provisions of Article 59." In practice, the ICJ regularly invokes its own prior rulings as well as rulings by the Permanent Court of International Justice and arbitral tribunals. When it does so, the Court is careful to note that prior decisions articulate legal reasoning that carries across cases, but these decisions do not constrain the Court's current ruling.

Second, current jurisprudence can only create precedent if an international court is ruling on the same types of issues and actors over time. If states repeatedly have disputes on similar issues, then an individual court ruling can enhance precision in the future. For example, a ruling by the WTO dispute settlement system or the European Court of Justice can have a long-term effect because the constant flow of goods, services, and people across borders creates many opportunities for treaty violations. In contrast, many of the issues that are adjudicated by the ICJ are relatively isolated and rare events, such as the 1988 Lockerbie bombing and the Iran hostage crisis of 1979–1981. ICJ rulings have established a body of jurisprudence for land and maritime border delimitations. However, almost all border disputes have been resolved at this point, thanks in part to the success of the ICJ. There are simply fewer opportunities to apply ICJ law than WTO or ECJ law. We should thus expect that precedent will be more important for courts like the ECJ and WTO dispute settlement system than for courts like the ICJ.

Finally, the overall impact of precedent on pre-trial settlement is not clear: precedent might exacerbate bargaining failure in any given dispute and increase short-term litigation. In the model above, both delegation and obligation increase the importance of beliefs about how the court will rule. When courts grow stronger, uncertainty plays a larger role in pre-trial negotiations and states are less likely to reach an early settlement. Precedent can have a similar impact. If rulings today affect precision tomorrow, then the stakes of litigation grow larger because a short-term legal victory or loss affects not only immediate political outcomes, but also future disputes. Raising the stakes of a given dispute increases the importance of uncertainty about how the court will rule. Allowing a court to create precedent could thus further exacerbate the difficulty of negotiating a pre-trial settlement in any given case. Other bargaining models have identified similar effects. Fearon (1998) shows that as states care more about the future, negotiations becomes more difficult because states have more incentive to lock-in good deals. Similarly, Maggi and Staiger (2011, 479) contains a two-period model of trade litigation in which precedent creates a trade-off between first- and second-period disputes. They find that "precedent reduces the probability of second-period disputes by removing uncertainty about the rights and obligations that will apply should the same state of the world occur again ... [but] precedent increases the frequency of first-period disputes." Precedent can thus exacerbate the difficultly of settling a dispute via diplomatic negotiations.

Strategic Judges and Nonlitigants

Another important factor that could affect the model findings is whether strategic judges and/or nonlitigant states alter their behavior because they can infer that a given ruling can shape subsequent settlement, compliance, and stability. Many factors can influence judicial rulings and the willingness of nonlitigant states to uphold them. International judges consider the content of legal claims, but they can also be influenced by the domestic legal system of their home country, military alliances, and the economic power of the litigants (Mitchell and Powell 2011; Posner and de Figueiredo 2005). International judges are also sometimes motivated by their own policy preferences (Voeten 2008). Finally, international judges may want to uphold the authority of their court by issuing rulings that states implement (Carrubba 2005; Carrubba and Gabel 2013).

In the conflict game, I do not explicitly model how judges make decisions. I assume that both players are uncertain about how the court will behave and that the plaintiff has some private information about how the court will rule if it hears the case on the merits. However, many different political and economic factors can affect judges in my model without changing my theoretical mechanisms. Judicial rulings may depend in part on the identity of the disputants because judges may be more likely to rule in favor of powerful states or their appointing-state. Judges may also be predisposed to certain values or principles, such as trade liberalization or regional integration. All of these accounts are consistent with my argument above. One limitation of my argument, though, is that I do not allow judges to alter their rulings to promote compliance and stability.

The cooperation model shows that as the cost of dispute settlement increases, states are more likely to comply when cooperation is easy and exit when cooperation is difficult. One way to increase both compliance and stability is to impose a high dispute settlement cost on players that find it relatively easy to cooperate, but a low dispute settlement cost on players that temporarily can't comply because of political or economic pressure. Under this scenario, the consequences of a legal violation would vary in response to the difficulty of cooperation. States facing tough times at home would have flexibility to temporarily violate their commitments if they return to cooperation after the tough times pass.

For example, Carrubba and Gabel (2013) construct a theoretical model in which nonlitigant states decide whether to enforce court rulings.[24] In this model, nonlitigants punish the defendant if it refuses to implement an adverse court ruling when the cost of cooperation is low, but allow the defendant to ignore adverse rulings when the cost of cooperation is high. If nonlitigants can correctly infer a defendant's true cost of cooperation, then the expected cost of dispute settlement can be lower when a state is under intense political or economic pressure to violate its commitments. Strategic judges could generate similar outcomes if they condition their rulings on the ability of a defendant to comply. Under either scenario, the court could simultaneously promote both compliance and stability.

The logic behind these arguments is compelling, yet strategic non-litigants and judges can only ensure stability if they can correctly infer a defendant's true cooperation cost. If nonlitigants are uncertain about the cost of cooperation, then they will sometimes mistakenly punish defendants who lack the ability to comply, thereby generating instability. This difficulty is exacerbated by the fact that when punishments and rulings are conditioned on the cost of cooperation, a defendant has incentives to misrepresent its true cost. If states that face high cooperation costs are allowed to violate their commitments with impunity, then all states will have incentive to pretend as though face high costs, even when they find cooperation cheap. As long as judges and nonlitigants are uncertain about a defendant's true cost of cooperation, my theoretical arguments will continue to hold.[25]

Alternative Punishment Schemes and Non-State Actors

One final factor that we should consider is the plausibility of the punishment scheme. In the cooperation model, I assume that if a state decides to exit the treaty regime, the other state imposes a grim trigger punishment: a treaty violator is excluded from the treaty benefits and commitments for all future periods. This grim trigger punishment is commonly used to solve infinitely repeated games because it is the strongest punishment that can be imposed within the game, thereby yielding the highest amount of cooperation. Yet many scholars question the plausibility of grim trigger punishments. Why would two states revert to anarchy forever if they can negotiate a new agreement? Similarly, why can't violators be punished using policy tools outside of the treaty regime? Perhaps a victim state will impose sanctions on a violator or refuse to cooperate with it in other policy-areas. These are reasonable questions, but they do not affect my argument because all of my results are robust to a broad class of punishment schemes. My results hold as long as the punishment is not a function of the size of a violation or the three design attributes (delegation, obligation, and precision). This means that my arguments continue to hold even if we allow violators to negotiate re-entry into the cooperative regime over time.

This robustness is particularly important for scholars who are interested in agreements that involve non-state actors, such as a firms or individuals. For example, a state may pledge to protect human rights within its own borders and yet sometimes be tempted to violate its pledge, especially during a political or economic crisis.[26] If a treaty member cares about individuals in other states, then it benefits from other states' human rights efforts, but is nevertheless sometimes tempted to violate its own commitments. Similarly, a state that is member of a bilateral investment treaty wants for its own citizens to be protected when they invest in foreign countries, yet this state may still be tempted to violate the rights of foreigners who invest in its own economy.

Agreements that involve non-state actors can thus have incentives that match those in the model above, but the grim trigger punishment is not substantively plausible for many of these agreements. For example, suppose that state A violates a human rights treaty by torturing its citizens. How will the other treaty member, state B, respond? A grim trigger strategy would require that state B commit its own violations in future periods. Yet it is completely perverse to believe or require that state B will torture its own citizens in order to punish state A. State B will need other ways to punish state A outside of the treaty regime. Because my model is robust to alternative punishment scheme, my arguments apply to a broad range of agreements that affect non-state actors, including human rights treaties and bilateral investment treaties.

3.5 Institutional Design

The analytical results above demonstrate how changes in delegation, obligation, and precision affect state behavior. These results do not rely upon any assumptions about how or why the design of a legal regime might change over time. As discussed in Chapter 2, courts can be changed in many different ways. Sometimes the design of a legal regime changes because a random or unexpected event changes beliefs about how the court will operate in the future. For example, Chapter 4 examines the *South West Africa* case, which was heard by the International Court of Justice. The Court indicated in 1960 that it would intervene in a lawsuit brought by Ethiopia and Liberia against the Union of South Africa. However, small changes in the composition of the bench resulted in a dramatic reversal of jurisprudence in 1966. The Court dismissed the case using legal reasoning that effectively forestalled future litigation over decolonization. By imposing this self-inflicted wound, the ICJ changed state beliefs about its willingness to rule in future related disputes. The Court constrained its own ability to hear future cases so that it could avoid a substantive ruling in the current and highly politicized case. This example illustrates how actors within an institution—such as judges and bureaucrats—can sometimes change beliefs about how the institution works. The judges did not consider the optimal level of delegation to the ICJ. Rather, a small change in the composition of the bench shifted power to a group of judges that wanted to dispose of a political hot potato.

In contrast, sometimes institutions are created and changed through deliberative and reasoned processes. These processes allow policymakers to consider the impact of possible design choices and rationally calculate how they can best promote cooperation on an issue-area.[27] As detailed below in Chapter 5, members of the GATT grew increasingly frustrated over time at the weaknesses in the GATT dispute settlement system. In the 1980s and early 1990s, GATT members conducted elaborate and prolonged negotiations over how to redesign the multilateral trade regime in order to promote trade liberalization. These negotiations focused on the long-term impact of the institution, rather than the short-term need to dispense with a particular case. External actors—diplomats, economists, and lawyers—recalibrated both the strength of the dispute settlement system and the precision of trade laws.

We cannot expect that all institutions are always optimal for the problems that they are trying to solve. Sometimes institutional designers can make mistakes and create institutions that have unexpected effects. For example, many courts have been created by mimicking the design of earlier institutions, even if those designs are not appropriate for the problem at hand (Alter 2012, 2014). Institutional design may also reflect the preferences of powerful states, rather than the interests of the international community as a whole. Finally, the ever-changing nature of politics and economics means that sometimes institutions grow less effective at solving the problems for which they were initially created. Barton, Goldstein, Josling and Steinberg (2006) provides a compelling account of how changes in the global economy ensured that GATT rules, which were effective under the political constraints of 1947, became less effective over time. Institutions that rely upon external change are unlikely to keep pace with political and economic conditions simply because it is so costly for a group of states to negotiate new rules and dispute settlement procedures. Nevertheless, we can use the insights from my model to answer a normative question: how should courts be designed?

When a rational institutional designer seeks to increase delegation or obligation to an international court, she has already decided that the benefits of legalization outweigh its costs. She will accept less settlement and stability in exchange for more compliance. An institutional designer can offset some of the costs of delegation and obligation if she writes more precise laws because precision enhances the early settlement of disputes. This leads to the first major implication of my model.

Implication 8. *If rational actors want to promote international cooperation by strengthening an international court, they should also make its laws more precise.*

Any change in institutional design comes with contracting costs. When GATT members decided to increase delegation and obligation to the dispute settlement system, they simultaneously enhanced the precision of many important areas of trade law through multilateral negotiations. These negotiations were immensely difficult, requiring states to agree on hundreds of pages of new rules. For example, the 1947 GATT rules on antidumping and countervailing duties consisted of a few modest and general paragraphs. The corresponding WTO rules now fill over sixty extremely dense and detailed pages of treaty texts (WTO 1999). Additionally, the WTO has issued many official publications to further explain and develop the intricacies of these areas of law. One recent official WTO handbook on antidumping investigations, which are only one step in the complex process for imposing antidumping duties, runs over 500 pages (Czako, Human and Miranda 2003). Precise rules must reduce uncertainty about what is appropriate behavior for many different circumstances and contingencies. Precise rules are rarely simple rules—they are usually detailed, complex, and extremely difficult to write.

Delegation, obligation, and precision all increase legalization, yet they come with dramatically different contracting costs. Generally speaking, it is much more difficult to increase the precision of rules than it is to increase delegation or obligation to a court. Nevertheless, precise laws facilitate settlement. Institutional designers that want to promote cooperation should use a combination of delegation, obligation, and precision when they legalize treaty regimes. Delegation and obligation can be used to boost legalization, and then precision can help to ameliorate some of the negative consequences of a strong court.

In addition to increasing precision, an institutional designer can offset the negative impact of a strong court on stability if she is able to raise the cost of exit. This leads to the second major implication of my model.

Implication 9. *If rational actors want to promote international cooperation by strengthening an international court, they should also raise the cost of exit.*

This can sometimes be achieved by changing the court's institutional context. In the model above, the court functioned under anarchy. When a state violated its obligations and refused to participate in dispute settlement, the most severe punishment that its partner could impose was to exclude it from the treaty regime in future periods. However, in the real world, defection can be even more costly if a court is linked to an important political institution. If remaining a member of the court is necessary to participate in the linked political institution, then exit becomes more costly and the legal regime becomes more stable. A strong court still comes with a hidden cost since it will make pretrial settlement less likely, but a strong court should be better able to promote cooperation when it is nested in a political environment that makes exit more costly.

For example, the European Court of Justice (ECJ) is the judicial institution of the European Union, so a EU member cannot exit from ECJ jurisdiction without also exiting the EU. When a violator decides whether to participate in dispute settlement at the ECJ, it is implicitly choosing whether to remain a member of the EU as a whole. This close connection between the court and the EU as a whole suggests that exit is probably an infeasible option.

However, most courts do not operate in such a context. The International Court of Justice is the judicial organ of the United Nations and all UN members must accept the Statute of the ICJ. But this statute does not establish jurisdiction of the court. As detailed in the next chapter, states must take additional action to accept jurisdiction of the ICJ. This means that leaving the jurisdiction of the ICJ or renouncing a treaty that it oversees has no impact on a state's membership in the UN. When there is a relatively low cost for exit, stability will be a more important concern. In such situations, the costs of a strong court will likely outweigh the benefits.

3.6 Conclusion

One hidden cost of strong courts is that they make the pre-trial settlement of disputes more difficult. By increasing the likelihood that the court will rule on the merits or the political impact of a legal ruling, strong courts increase the importance of uncertainty about how the court will behave. This uncertainty in turn makes it more difficult for states to resolve their disputes without resorting to litigation. Of course, litigation can sometimes create public benefits by establishing precedent that may reduce uncertainty in the long-term (Fiss 1984; Lauterpacht 1958). However, litigation generates costs for the disputants in the short-term, so disputants prefer settlement to trial in any given dispute.

This view of international courts stands in stark contrast to previous theories of international institutions. Most scholars argue that international institutions promote cooperation by reducing transaction costs and facilitating the exchange of information (Keohane 1982, 1984). If we compare state behavior under only two possible worlds—one with an institution and one without—then institutions can facilitate cooperation by monitoring and providing information about state behavior (Milgrom, North and Weingast 1990). However, what these earlier theories do not consider is that the existence of an international institution creates a new source of uncertainty: uncertainty about how the institution will behave.

Courts, which are relatively complex institutions, are given the authority to conduct a broad range of tasks, such as interpreting laws and filling holes in incomplete contracts. When we make courts stronger, we may be increasing the likelihood that states comply with legal rules, but we are also increasing the importance of uncertainty about how the institution will behave. Institutions can thus create new informational problems. These informational problems can make it more difficult for states to amicably resolve their disputes without going to the court. So strong courts increase transaction costs by making it more likely that states will litigate, rather than negotiate. These effects do not reduce the value of institutions in facilitating cooperation relative to anarchy. A world with excessive litigation is probably preferable to one with no cooperation whatsoever. But this analysis shows that institutions can create new informational problems and transaction costs. It is not always true that granting institutions more authority will lead to better outcomes.

The conventional wisdom among scholars has been that more enforcement generates more cooperation in the international system (Downs, Rocke and Barsoom 1996). Under this logic, an institution is most effective when it is rigid by imposing high costs for noncompliance. Recent scholars have challenged this view. They argue that while large costs enhance compliance, they also reduce stability. Governments must sometimes violate their legal commitments, and rigid international agreements make these governments less likely to remain treaty members (Downs and Rocke 1995; Rosendorff 2005; Rosendorff and Milner 2001). Scholars who adopt this view argue that treaties can be more effective if they are flexible by allowing states to break their commitments at a low cost. Such flexibility makes states less likely to comply, but more likely to remain treaty members during tough times. Additionally, flexibility allows states to make deeper commitments to cooperation (Johns 2014). When most scholars think of flexibility, they think about substantive rules, such as derogation clauses in human rights treaties or antidumping rules in the WTO (Hafner-Burton, Helfer and Fariss 2011; Kucik and Reinhardt 2008). This research has not yet considered how flexibility can be built into a court's design.

My models show that delegation and obligation create rigidity in a legal regime. Both design attributes mimic the effects of rigid rules: they promote compliance with a treaty, but reduce its stability. Just as many scholars now argue in favor of more flexible rules, one of the major conclusions of this book is that there are often good reasons to design legal regimes with weak courts.

Since legalization has mixed effects, a rational actor must balance these trade-offs when she designs institutions. My analytical model has two major implications for strengthening international courts. First, if a rational actor wants to make a court stronger to promote international cooperation—by increasing delegation or obligation—she should also increase the precision of the law. Both delegation and obligation exacerbate the difficulty of pre-trial negotiations, but an institutional designer can offset this negative effect if she increases precision of the law. Second, she should try to increase the cost of exit, if possible, to ameliorate the effect of a strong court on stability. One way to do this is to nest a strong court in a political context that makes exit difficult, such as the European Union or the World Trade Organization.

The next two chapters use case studies of the International Court of Justice and the WTO's dispute settlement system to both illustrate and assess my theoretical arguments. These case studies differ from each other dramatically because they examine two different types of institutional change. The Statute of the ICJ has not changed since its creation in 1946. However, there have been a few unexpected judicial rulings that served as turning-points in the Court's interpretation of its own authority. We can therefore examine how changes in delegation and obligation via judicial rulings affected the behavior of ICJ members, and consider the plausibility of Propositions 2, 6, and 7. In contrast, the creation of the WTO in 1995 gives us a case in which regime members rationally calculated how they could best promote cooperation on an issue-area. We cannot properly assess the validity of the relationships in Table 3.1 in the WTO because all three design elements changed at the same time and because precision has an effect that should offset the impact of changes to delegation and obligation. However, the transition from the GATT to the WTO allows us to consider the validity of Implication 8: increases delegation or obligation by rational actors should be accompanied by enhanced precision of law.

4

Strengthening the International Court of Justice

4.1 Introduction

The International Court of Justice (ICJ)—often called the "World Court"—is the oldest international court that still exists, and its jurisprudence is the bedrock of public international law. Many other courts, such as the European Court of Justice and the GATT/WTO dispute settlement system, have developed jurisprudence for specialized areas of law, but the ICJ has historically been the most important arbiter of general questions of international law.[1] Any general theory of international courts must, at a minimum, enhance our understanding of the ICJ. I thus use ICJ cases in this chapter to both illustrate and assess my theoretical arguments.

Despite its long history, the ICJ is one of the weakest international courts. As described below, both delegation and obligation to the Court are very weak. Most respondents attempt to have cases dismissed by arguing that either the ICJ lacks jurisdiction or the case is inadmissible. ICJ members often provide reciprocal informal enforcement of Court rulings, as described in the account of the *Bakassi* case in Chapter 2, but it is nearly impossible for a litigant to secure formal enforcement of Court rulings.

This weakness makes the ICJ a problematic case for advocates of legalization. Many criticize the ICJ as ineffective, monolithic, old-fashioned, and irrelevant while others simply ignore the Court altogether and focus exclusively on strong institutions, like the European Court of Justice (Alter 2006). The ICJ is therefore a difficult case for legalization advocates precisely because it remains weak and thus does not conform to normative accounts of the development of transnational justice (Slaughter 1992, 2003). However, to understand institutions, we must learn from both the weak and the strong. If we only examine strong institutions that have the uncontested authority to issue rulings that are respected and upheld by court members, then we are only seeing part of the broad diversity of international legal bodies.

The Court is also a challenging case because it has not experienced any external change since its creation in 1946. We cannot ask, for example, how changes in the ICJ Statute changed state behavior. However, the history of the ICJ provides several examples of internal change. The ICJ has issued key judgments that changed state beliefs about delegation and obligation to the Court and allow us to examine the impact of changes in the design of a legal regime on state behavior.

The ICJ's lack of external change might initially appear to be a liability that makes the ICJ a difficult case for theories of institutional design. However, the absence of external change is actually useful for both illustrating and assessing the impact of legal design. When states impose external changes, they can manipulate many different institutional attributes to offset the impact of any individual change. I argue in the next chapter that this occurred in the transition from the GATT to the WTO: when members increased the strength of the dispute settlement system, they simultaneously increased the precision of trade law. In contrast, we have a methodological advantage if we study the effect of an individual ICJ ruling. Each ruling changed jurisprudence on a particular question, but all other elements of the legal and political environment remained constant. We can leverage the lack of external change to more precisely identify the effects of internal changes on state behavior. Under my theory, changes in delegation or obligation to the ICJ should have observable impacts on pre-trial settlement, compliance with treaty commitments, and the stability of the legal regime. For the reasons detailed below, I examine two ICJ turning-points: the *South West Africa* case of 1960–1966 and the consular relations cases of 1998–2004.

In the *South West Africa* case, Ethiopia and Liberia sued the Union of South Africa—a country governed by white-minority rule—over its colonial administration of South West Africa.[2] Ethiopia and Liberia wanted to promote self-determination for the black natives of South West Africa and to eradicate the Union's apartheid policies. In 1962, the Court ruled that Ethiopia and Liberia had a legal interest in the case. However, the Court unexpectedly reversed itself and dismissed the case in 1966. The international community was shocked and interpreted the reversal as a sign that the ICJ was unlikely to rule on other decolonization cases. By limiting its ability to rule on future cases, the Court reduced its own delegation. Under my theoretical arguments, this weakening of the court should increase pre-trial settlement, reduce compliance, and enhance stability.

In the consular relations cases, Paraguay, Germany, and Mexico sued the United States because it had arrested, convicted, and sentenced foreign nationals to death without adhering to proper procedure. These countries alleged that the United States violated the Vienna Convention on Consular Relations because it had not notified them of the arrests, preventing them from assisting their nationals. The Court issued two major rulings against the United States that progressively increased the Court's strength. My theory would expect that this strengthening of the court would have lead to more litigation, more compliance, and less stability.

I begin by providing a brief overview of the ICJ and then discuss my theoretical hypotheses and case selection. I next examine the *South West Africa* case, followed by the consular relations cases. For each of these examples, I provide background information and summarize the legal rulings. Then I examine state behavior before and after the ICJ judgment to see if each example is consistent with my theoretical arguments.

4.2 Overview of the ICJ

Cases, Rulings, and Sources of Law

The International Court of Justice was created in 1946 as part of the United Nations system and it has ruled in many important international disputes over the past 60 years.[3] As shown in Figure 4.1, states filed many cases early on, but the Cold War stalemate between the United States and the USSR reduced the number of filings. A dramatic resurgence in ICJ cases occurred at the end of the Cold War. In recent years, the ICJ has set new records for the number of cases hears, although some scholars argue that this increase is due to an increase in the number of states in the international system (Posner 2006).

The ICJ has no subject-matter restrictions. Nevertheless, most ICJ disputes are about the distribution of resources or liability for past actions. Most ICJ cases are land or maritime border disputes, often involving oil or fishing rights.[4] As shown in Table 4.1, five other types of ICJ disputes are also common. First, many ICJ cases involve the use of force, such as recent conflicts in the Democratic Republic of the Congo and Yugoslavia.[5] Second, many ICJ cases involve property rights, such as property seizures and the regulation of foreign-owned companies.[6] Third, the ICJ often adjudicates aerial incidents, such

Figure 4.1: ICJ Docket over Time

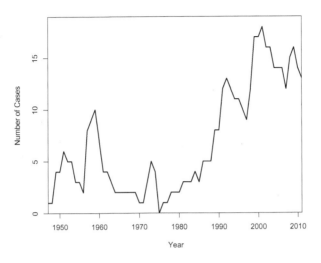

Note: The 1999 cases filed by Yugoslavia against NATO members are excluded.

as the 1988 bombing of Pan Am flight 103 over Lockerbie, Scotland. Fourth, the ICJ has heard many disputes over diplomatic and consular relations, including a case between the United States and Iran over the Iranian hostage crisis of 1979–1981. Finally, a few ICJ cases involved UN trusteeship agreements and decolonization, including the *South West Africa* case discussed below.

Most ICJ rulings involve provisional measures, preliminary objections, or the merits of a case.[7] The Court may order provisional measures that preserve the political and economic status quo until it can rule on substantive matters. In the consular relations cases, the Court ordered the United States to stay executions pending the outcome of international litigation. Preliminary objections usually consist of challenges to jurisdiction and admissibility. Finally, rulings on the merits involve findings of facts and legal interpretation.[8]

The International Court of Justice rules on an unwieldy and imprecise body of law.[9] One source of ICJ law is written international agreements. States often disagree about how to interpret these texts. Another is customary international law, which is established by a combination of state practice and a legal finding of *opinio juris sive necessitatis*—"the belief by a state that behaved in a certain way that

Table 4.1: Types of Interstate Disputes Adjudicated by the ICJ

Dispute Type	Number	Example
Border Dispute	26	*Bakassi* (1994–2002): Cameroon sues Nigeria over the oil-rich Bakassi peninsula.
Use of Force	21	*Oil Platforms* (1992–2003): Iran sues United States for destroying three offshore oil platforms.
Property Rights	14	*Interhandel* (1957–1959): Switzerland sues United States over assets seized during World War II.
Aerial Incident	8	*Lockerbie* (1992–2003): UK and United States sue Libya for the bombing of a civilian airplane in 1988.
Diplomatic and Consular Relations	10	*Avena* (2003–2004): Mexico sues United States for imposing the death penalty on foreign nationals without informing them of their right to consular assistance.
Trusteeship and Decolonization	4	*Phosphate Lands* (1989–1993): Nauru sues Australia for maladministration of phosphate reserves under colonial rule.

Note: This reflects closed cases only. "Border disputes" includes land and/or maritime delimitations. A single case can be included in multiple dispute type categories.

it is under a legal obligation to act that way" (Shaw 2008, 75). The Court can also rule on the basis of general principles of law, judicial decisions, and even scholarly writings. Overall, states and judges can make legal arguments based on a variety of sources. The Vienna Convention on the Law of Treaties establishes general principles of treaty interpretation. The ICJ usually gives the most deference to plain text readings of written treaties. Under this mode of treaty interpretation, judges consider only the natural language meaning of the treaty text. If the plain text does not yield a clear interpretation, then states can appeal to a broad range of other sources to establish either the intentions of the original members or the object and purpose of the treaty. These sources include: private diplomatic exchanges, public statements, documents from treaty negotiations (called *travaux preparatoires*), resolutions adopted by international organizations, the history of state practice, and even general principles of law such as equity and good faith. ICJ judges are not formally bound by precedent. Nevertheless, the court strives "to maintain judicial consistency," and its prior decisions are themselves a source of ICJ law (Brownlie 2008, 21; Guillaume 2011).

Delegation

Delegation to the Court is very limited and states are often uncertain about whether the Court will issue a substantive ruling.[10] The Court operates on the principle of consent, so states must accept ICJ jurisdiction before the Court can hear a case. There are four primary ways they can do so.[11] First, a state can make a unilateral declaration that it accepts ICJ jurisdiction, as occurs in over 40 percent of ICJ cases.[12] Second, ICJ jurisdiction can be established by a compromissory clause in a treaty, which specifies that the ICJ can hear disputes about the treaty's interpretation or application. About 65 percent of ICJ cases involved a compromissory clause, including the consular relations cases. Third, states can agree specifically to ICJ jurisdiction for a particular dispute.[13] About 17 percent of ICJ cases have used special agreements, and this practice has become common in territorial disputes. Finally, a state can submit a case and invite its legal opponent to accept jurisdiction.[14] However, the ICJ will not consider such a case unless the respondent accepts the invitation.[15]

The principle of consent is very murky in practice. States regularly disagree about whether the ICJ has jurisdiction, particularly for cases filed under unilateral declarations or compromissory clauses. Additionally, as mentioned in Chapter 2, states often include reservations when they accept ICJ jurisdiction, which lead to more arguments about whether jurisdiction exists for a given dispute. In over two-thirds of ICJ cases, a state argues that the Court lacks jurisdiction to hear the case.[16] The Court itself makes the final decision about whether it has jurisdiction to hear the case.

For example, when Nicaragua sued the United States in 1984, it argued that each state had previously accepted ICJ jurisdiction via a unilateral declaration.[17] In 1929, Nicaragua signed the Statute of the Permanent Court of International Justice (PCIJ) and wrote an informal one-sentence declaration that it accepted jurisdiction of the PCIJ. But under the PCIJ Statute, a state could only accept jurisdiction if it secured domestic ratification of its declaration and then sent the official ratification instrument to the League of Nations Secretary-General in Geneva. The Nicaraguan government ratified the declaration in 1935, but the League of Nations never received the official instrument.[18] So under League rules, Nicaragua never officially accepted jurisdiction of the PCIJ.

When the United Nations was created, states that were under the jurisdiction of the PCIJ automatically fell under the jurisdiction of the new ICJ. Article 36(5) of the ICJ Statute specifies that:

> **Declarations** made under Article 36 of the Statute of the
> Permanent International Court of Justice and which are
> **still in force** shall be deemed ... to be acceptances of
> the compulsory jurisdiction of the International Court of
> Justice.[19]

Nicaragua argued that its informal 1929 declaration met the Article
36(5) criteria, so Nicaragua was subject to the jurisdiction of the ICJ.
However, the United States argued that the 1929 declaration was never
"in force" because it was an informal declaration, rather than a ratified
instrument on file with the League of Nations. If Nicaragua never
officially accepted jurisdiction of the PCIJ, the United States argued,
then Nicaragua did not meet the Article 36(5) criteria and the ICJ did
not have jurisdiction over Nicaragua.

The Court ultimately ruled in favor of Nicaragua and heard the
case on the merits. However, this example shows that states often
disagree about whether the ICJ has jurisdiction to hear a particular
case. States usually go to great lengths to try to argue that the Court
lacks authority to hear a case. This stands in stark contrast to other
international courts, like the GATT/WTO dispute settlement system
or the European Court of Justice, in which jurisdiction is automatic if
a state is a member of the organization.

Even if the Court finds that it has jurisdiction to hear a case, it
may still refuse to rule if it finds that the case is inadmissible. As
explained by Shaw (2008, 1071–1072):

> Admissibility refers to the application of relevant general
> rules of international law ... Objections to admissibility
> normally take the form of an assertion that, even if the
> Court has jurisdiction and the facts stated by the applicant
> state are assumed to be correct, nonetheless there are rea-
> sons why the Court should not proceed to an examination
> of the merits.

For example, cases can be ruled inadmissible if a party has not exhausted local remedies (such as engaging in litigation at the domestic
level) or if there was excessive delay in the filing of a case.[20]

Obligation

Obligation to the Court's rulings is relatively weak. If a state does
not follow an ICJ ruling, its opponent can refer the dispute to the UN
Security Council (UNSC), which can impose multilateral sanctions or

authorize the use of force.[21] However, the permanent members of the Security Council can veto such actions, and the UNSC has never acted to enforce a ruling (Gill 2003, 33–34). The ICJ lacks an effective formal mechanism for enforcing its rulings.

However, as discussed in Chapter 2, states often provide informal enforcement of Court rulings. ICJ disputants may abide by a court ruling because of reputational concerns (Keohane 1986). These concerns are probably weaker in the ICJ than in other international courts—like the European Court of Justice and the WTO—because the ICJ hears far fewer cases and states thus have fewer opportunities to engage in reciprocity. Nonetheless, if defiance results in exclusion from future cooperation, then an ICJ disputant may be willing to bear the short-term cost of implementing a ruling in exchange for the long-term benefits of cooperation. Additionally, ICJ rulings often open the door to third party involvement in disputes (Fang 2010; Johns 2012; Paulson 2004). States that previously were not involved in the dispute are often willing to facilitate a peaceful settlement after the Court has intervened, as illustrated by the *Bakassi* case in chapter 2. Finally, domestic political pressure can also sometimes prompt a state to abide by international law (Dai 2005; Simmons 2009).

4.3 Settlement, Compliance, and Stability: Theory and Hypotheses

When states negotiate in the shadow of an international court, they often have different beliefs about how the court will behave if it rules on the merits. This uncertainty can lead to bargaining failure. If a court becomes more likely to rule on a case or if its rulings have a larger political impact, then uncertainty about how the court will rule becomes more important and states are less likely to reach a negotiated settlement. Stronger courts increase the probability of litigation.

In my theory, each state has three options. First, it can comply with the rules of the legal regime, which ensures that it cannot be sued by other states. Second, it can violate the rules but then participate in dispute settlement at a court like the ICJ. This ensures that it can remain a member of the regime in the future. Third, it can violate the rules and then exit the regime altogether. When a court grows stronger, the cost of dispute settlement increases for a treaty violator. If the cost of cooperation is low, a stronger court makes compliance more likely. However, if the cost of cooperation is high, compliance may not be feasible and a stronger court makes exit more likely. Strong courts thus promote compliance, but reduce stability.

In this chapter, I use ICJ rulings to illustrate and examine the plausibility of Propositions 2, 6, and 7 from Chapter 3. Any attempt to assess a theory using individual cases must be able to answer an important question: Why were these particular cases chosen (King, Keohane and Verba 1994)? I focus on the *South West Africa* and consular relations cases for multiple reasons.

First, both cases are difficult for accounts of adjudication because they involved high power politics. Powerful states should be the least likely to be affected by adjudication so any behavior that we can observe is likely to extend to cases involving weaker states. Decolonization was one of the most important political issues in the mid-twentieth-century, and the *South West Africa* case embodied complex North-South tensions. Developing nations viewed this case as a touchstone in how major international organizations, which were created by developed Western nations, would handle their rising political power. Additionally, the Union of South Africa served as a proxy for those European countries that still oversaw colonial territories, including the United Kingdom and Portugal. The consular relations cases involve the United States, which has been relatively uninvolved in the ICJ since the 1980s, and the use of the death penalty by state courts. All of the key ICJ rulings in these cases occurred during the presidency of George W. Bush, a supporter of both states' rights and the death penalty who had a well-known antipathy to international law and courts. All of these factors—a powerful state, an important policy issue, and a domestic government ideologically opposed to implementing the ICJ rulings—stack the deck against seeing any impact whatsoever of the ICJ rulings on state behavior. If the ICJ can compel a conservative United States administration to follow rulings that challenge states' rights and the use of the death penalty, then court rulings should have an even larger impact on weaker states and/or less important issues. The political importance of these cases ensured that they were closely watched, commented upon, and documented by secondary sources in English. Sources other than ICJ records exist that show political reactions to the legal rulings and both cases provoked the attention of both the media and legal scholars. I hope that this attention will make these cases accessible to readers with some background in international law. After all, many ICJ experts would be hard pressed to give an opinion on the Court's ruling in the *Kasikili/Sedudu Island* case, a recent border dispute between Botswana and Namibia. However, almost all ICJ experts have a strong opinion about the consular relations and *South West Africa* rulings, even though it has been over 45 years since the latter.

Second, since we want to observe the effect of internal change, it is important to examine cases in which the ICJ judgment dramatically changed beliefs about how the Court would behave in the future. If a Court rules exactly as the players expected, nothing fundamental about the institution has changed and we should not expect to observe significant changes in state behavior. Similarly, it is possible for a Court to slowly build up jurisprudence over time in a way that alters beliefs about its authority (Carrubba 2009). However, we are unlikely to observe dramatic changes in state behavior under such circumstances because a slowly evolving court should lead to slowly changing state behavior. From a research design standpoint, it is important that we examine unexpected and decisive changes in jurisprudence. This allows us to examine state behavior immediately before and after the ruling, while the broader political context is held constant.

For each case, I begin by providing background on the cases and describing the ICJ rulings. I then explain why states interpreted these rulings as changes in delegation and obligation to the Court. Finally, I describe the impact of these changes on my three dependent variables: settlement, compliance, and stability. When I describe the impact on settlement, I ask: how did the ICJ ruling affect the willingness of states to litigate on similar legal disputes? For compliance, I ask: did the respondent change its behavior after the ICJ ruling? For stability, I ask: how did the ICJ ruling affect consent to ICJ jurisdiction?

This research design comes with a cost: the impact of isolated ICJ rulings will be much more limited than the impact of grand external change. Modest changes in jurisprudence may only affect a few states or a single issue-area. For example, a change in ICJ jurisprudence on consular relations should not affect state behavior for cases about the use of force. I argue below that the 1966 *South West Africa* ruling severely limited the ability of newly independent states to challenge colonial administration. However, it did not impact all ICJ members or all legal issues, such as territorial disputes. Similarly, the consular relations rulings increased the ability of states to use international law to challenge the death penalty. However, these rulings did not affect United States behavior on other dimensions, such as the use of force.

4.4 *South West Africa* Case

In the early 1960s, African states under black-majority rule, known collectively as the African bloc, were optimistic that the ICJ would adjudicate decolonization disputes.[22] Members of the African bloc wanted to use the ICJ to challenge past colonial injustices and prompt further decolonization. Their primary target was the Union of South Africa (the "Union"), a state that was under white-minority rule and had colonial authority over South West Africa.[23] With the support of the African bloc, Ethiopia and Liberia filed ICJ lawsuits alleging that the Union's administration of South West Africa violated its legal obligations. The ICJ treated these suits as a single proceeding called the *South West Africa* case.[24]

The Court initially decided to hear the case. However, in 1966 it unexpectedly reversed itself and found that Ethiopia and Liberia lacked standing to sue. Below I argue that the 1966 ruling unexpectedly weakened the Court by constraining its ability to adjudicate future colonial disputes. My theory suggests that this change should have had three effects: litigation should have been less likely in future disputes; the Union of South Africa should have complied less with its legal commitments; and the cooperative regime should have been more stable. I ask three empirical questions. First, did the 1966 judgment change the willingness of African states to sue former colonial powers? Second, did the 1966 judgment affect the Union of South Africa's compliance with its legal commitments? Finally, did the 1966 ruling affect the ICJ's jurisdiction over affected states? After assessing the impact of the judgment, I discuss a possible alternative explanation: that state behavior was driven by power politics rather than changes in legal design.

Background on the Case

World War I created a power vacuum in much of the world. Germany and Turkey surrendered their colonies, and victorious states scrambled to gain control over them. Woodrow Wilson, a vocal opponent of colonialism, refused to support the Treaty of Versailles unless colonial powers became subject to international supervision. The final compromise between supporters and opponents of colonialism was reflected in the design of the League of Nations.

The League of Nations Covenant stated that its members had a "sacred trust" to promote "the well-being and development" of colonial territories.[25] To achieve this goal, the World War I victors created the League's mandate system.[26] Each dependent territory was assigned a colonial power known as its mandatory. A corresponding written treaty, known as a mandate, established the mandatory's rights and responsibilities to its dependent territory. Each mandatory was required to submit annual reports about conditions in its territories. The League could not punish mandate violations, but it could investigate complaints and issue public reports.

The Union of South Africa gained control over South West Africa (SWA) in 1920. Its mandate gave the Union "full power of administration and legislation over the territory," but it also placed some constraints on the Union. For example, it specified that "no military or naval bases shall be established" in SWA and required the free movement of missionaries. Additionally, the mandate required the Union to promote the "well-being and the social progress of the inhabitants" of SWA.[27]

The collapse of the League of Nations left the mandate system in limbo, and the defeat of the Axis powers in World War II left new territories without an administering authority. Once again, the victors reallocated these territories and then created the UN trusteeship system. Its primary objective was "to promote ... progressive development towards self-government or independence."[28] Each mandatory was allowed to negotiate a new trusteeship agreement that granted supervisory powers to the UN Trusteeship Council.

In 1947, the Union informed the UN that it refused to write a trusteeship agreement, and two years later it announced that it did not recognize the UN's authority to oversee the Union's mandate.[29] Many UN members believed that the Union intended to annex South West Africa rather than help it achieve independence. They also argued that the Union had violated its 1920 mandate by building military bases in SWA and imposing apartheid policies. These countries pressured the Union to submit itself to the authority of the Trusteeship Council. When their efforts failed, the General Assembly asked the ICJ for an advisory opinion on the legal status of South West Africa.

The Court's 1950 advisory opinion held that the 1920 mandate was still in effect. The Union had legal authority over South West Africa, but it also had legal responsibilities to the UN. For example, the Union could not annex the SWA absent UN consent. The ICJ also ruled that while the Union could create a trusteeship agreement for SWA, it was not required to do so. Since the Union could not be forced into the UN Trusteeship System, UN members began to examine how they could compel the Union to comply with its existing mandate.

After years of tortuous negotiations, the UN General Assembly created the Committee on South West Africa in late 1953 to document the Union's maladministration of SWA. Four years later, the General Assembly asked the Committee to study whether litigation could be initiated against the Union at the ICJ. The Committee concluded that former members of the League of Nations could sue the Union of South Africa at the ICJ.[30] The Committee had no legal authority to create ICJ jurisdiction or standing, but its conclusion demonstrates that the legal consensus in the late 1950s was that League members could sue the Union. Ethiopia and Liberia filed suit against the Union in 1960.[31]

Ethiopia and Liberia had two objectives. First, they wanted the Court to reiterate its 1950 rulings. ICJ advisory opinions are not legally binding; as their name suggests, they are merely advisory. Ethiopia and Liberia wanted the earlier rulings to be restated in a legally binding judgment. Second, they asked the Court to find that the Union had violated the mandate. Namely, they argued that the Union "failed to promote ... the material and moral well-being and social progress of [South West Africa's] inhabitants." They argued that the Union's apartheid policy violated the 1920 mandate and that the Union was "suppress[ing] the rights and liberties of [SWA] inhabitants."[32]

Legal Rulings

When the *South West Africa* cases began, the ICJ first had to determine whether it could hear the case. The Union's key objective at this point was to convince the Court that either the Court lacked the jurisdiction to hear the case, or that the case was inadmissible. The 1920 mandate included a compromissory clause that granted jurisdiction to the Permanent Court of International Justice (PCIJ), the judicial body of the League of Nations. The Union argued that the collapse of both the League and the PCIJ meant that the 1920 mandate was not a valid legal agreement, and therefore the Court lacked jurisdiction to hear the case. In 1962, the Court reiterated its earlier ruling that the mandate remained in force, which ensured that the ICJ, as the successor to the PCIJ, had jurisdiction to hear the case.

The Court then turned to the issue of standing. It ruled that Ethiopia and Liberia—in their capacity as former member-states of the League of Nations—could sue South Africa. The Court reasoned:

> Those States who were Members of the League at the time of its dissolution continue to have the right to invoke the compulsory jurisdiction of the Court ... That right continues to exist for as long as the Respondent holds on to the right to administer the territory under the Mandate.[33]

A key element of the Court's reasoning was the fact that only states could file contentious cases in both the PCIJ and the ICJ:

> [N]either the Council nor the League was entitled to appear before the [PCIJ]. The only effective recourse for protection of the sacred trust would be for a Member or Members of the League to ... bring the dispute as also one between them and the Mandatory to the [PCIJ] for adjudication.[34]

Finally, the Court made a ruling that would later come to haunt it. The Union argued in its preliminary objections that no legal dispute existed between the states since the disagreement "does not affect any material interests of the Applicant States or their nationals."[35] The ICJ rejected this argument, ruling that:

> the manifest scope and purport of [the Mandate] indicate that the Members of the League were understood to have a legal right or interest in the observance by the Mandatory of its obligations both toward the inhabitants of the Mandated Territory, and toward the League of Nations and its Members.[36]

However, the 1962 finding that Ethiopia and Liberia had a "legal right or interest" would soon be overthrown by the Court.

In the second round of legal proceedings, litigants focused on the merits of the dispute—rather than jurisdiction or admissibility—and argued about whether the Union had violated its 1920 mandate for South West Africa. In its final submissions, the Union did not even argue that Ethiopia and Liberia lacked a legal right or interest in the dispute.[37] However, the Court's 1966 judgment unexpectedly returned to the question of whether Ethiopia and Liberia could sue the Union. This question created a 7–7 tie among the judges that heard the case. ICJ procedure dictates that when a tie occurs, the President of the Court gets an extra vote that determines the final outcome. The President ruled in favor of the Union.

The 1966 written judgment reexamined whether Ethiopia and Liberia had a "legal right or interest in the subject-matter of their claim."[38] The Court began by creating a new taxonomy of legal provisions. It argued that the 1920 mandate contained two different types of provisions: conduct provisions and special interests provisions. The Court stated that conduct provisions regulated administration of the territory, such as the requirement that the Union promote the "well-being and social progress" of SWA inhabitants. In contrast, special interest provisions granted privileges to non-mandatory states, such the free movement of missionaries. Ethiopia and Liberia were challenging the conduct of the Union. They did not allege that the Union refused to give them special privileges.

Next, the Court argued that individual League members could not sue on the basis of conduct provisions. The majority opinion noted that "[t]he mandatories were to be the agents of, or trustees for the League—and not of, or for, each and every member of it individually." The Court reasoned:

> [E]ven in the time of the League, even as members of the League when that organization still existed, the Applicants did not, in their individual capacity as States, possess any separate self-contained right which they could assert, independently of, or additionally to, the right of the League, in the pursuit of its collective, institutional activity, to require the due performance of the Mandate in discharge of the "sacred trust."[39]

This reasoning stood in stark contrast to the earlier 1962 ruling that "the Members of the League were understood to have a legal right or interest in the observance by the Mandatory."[40]

These arguments shocked the seven dissenting judges. Judge Koretsky voiced their opinion when he wrote that "the question of [Ethiopa and Liberia's] 'legal right or interest' ... was decided already in 1962." Judge Padilla Nervo added: "I am convinced that it has been established beyond any doubt, that [Ethiopia and Liberia] have a substantive right and a legal interest in the subject-matter of their claim." Judge Jessup went so far as to describe the majority judgment as "completely unfounded in law."[41]

The *South West Africa* cases were over. The ICJ evaded controversial political questions, and limited the ability of states to sue current or former colonial powers for maladministration.

Assessing the Theory

The 1966 judgment created a negative perception of the ICJ among developing states. The African bloc believed that the Court was too conservative to support black-majority rule. Even optimists, who hoped that changes in the bench might yield more progressive rulings, admitted that the case "generated widespread hostility to the ICJ" and "damaged the cause of international law in general" (Falk 1967, 1). My theory suggests that when a court grows weaker, states will be less likely to litigate disputes, less likely to comply with agreements, and less likely to exit the Court's jurisdiction. I first examine political reactions to the ruling and show that the international community perceived the 1966 ruling as an abrupt and unexpected decrease in delegation. I then examine whether the ruling affected settlement, stability, and compliance.

Weakening the ICJ

Why did the ICJ so dramatically reverse its prior ruling? Both political and legal arguments can be made to explain the ICJ's action. With the benefit of hindsight, court documents, and other historical records we can now see that political maneuvering within the ICJ judiciary changed the balance of power within the Court. Under normal circumstances, the Court has 15 sitting members and each side of a case may appoint an *ad hoc* judge, resulting in a total of 17 judges. As shown in Table 4.2, two sitting judges (Tanaka and Cordova) were not able to participate in the 1962 ruling for medical reasons. The 1962 ruling passed by an 8–7 vote against the Union, but if Tanaka and Cordova had been able to participate, the likely vote would have been 10–7 against the Union.[42] The 1962 official vote thus underrepresented the ICJ's opposition to the Union.

Under the UN system, ICJ judges are chosen by staggered elections every three years. Because of extremely complex voting procedures, the permanent members of the UN Security Council have *de facto* permanent seats at the ICJ. The other seats are allocated to ensure regional representation. In 1964, between the two rulings, there was a UN election in which 5 of the 15 seats were up for reelection. As shown in Table 4.2, the pro-Union bloc had the good fortune of experiencing little disruption. The only change within this coalition was a change in the French judge (from Basdevant to Gros). This stability ensured that by 1966 the pro-Union judges had an average of over eight years of experience at the ICJ.

In contrast, the anti-Union bloc had the misfortune of electoral upheaval between 1962 and 1966. Some anti-Union judges lost their seats at the Court. While the partisan composition of the bench did not change—a 10–7 split remained because the replacement judges also opposed the Union—the upheaval ensured that the anti-Union bloc had much less ICJ experience than the pro-Union bloc. Additionally, the anti-Union bloc once again lost two votes to illness and death.[43] Bustamante of Peru, who opposed the Union in 1962, was so ill in 1966 that he was unable to vote. Additionally, Badawi of Egypt died between the 1962 and 1966 rulings and his replacement (Ammoun of Lebanon) was not able to transition into office quickly enough to participate in the 1966 ruling. These absences ensured another 8–7 split against the Union.

Table 4.2: Judicial Behavior and Experience in 1962 and 1966

Pro-Union Judges

1962 Ruling		1966 Ruling	
Country (Judge)	Years	Country (Judge)	Years
Australia (Spender)	4	Australia (Spender)	8
France (Basdevant)	16	France (Gros)	2
Greece (Spiropoulos)	4	Greece (Spiropoulos)	8
Italy (Morelli)	1	Italy (Morelli)	5
Poland (Winiarski)	16	Poland (Winiarski)	20
South Africa (van Wyk)*	–	South Africa (van Wyk)*	–
UK (Fitzmaurice)	2	UK (Fitzmaurice)	6
Average:	7.2	Average:	8.2

Anti-Union Judges

1962 Ruling		1966 Ruling	
Country (Judge)	Years	Country (Judge)	Years
Argentina (Quintana)	7		
China (Koo)	5	China (Koo)	9
Egypt (Badawi)	16		
Nigeria (Mbafeno)*	–	Nigeria (Mbafeno)*	–
Panama (Alfaro)	3		
Peru (Bustamante)	1		
US (Jessup)	1	US (Jessup)	5
USSR (Koretsky)	1	USSR (Koretsky)	5
		Japan (Tanaka)	5
		Mexico (Padilla Nervo)	2
		Senegal (Forster)	2
Average:	4.9	Average:	4.7

Missing Judges

1962 Ruling		1966 Ruling	
Country (Judge)	Vote?	Country (Judge)	Vote?
Japan (Tanaka)	Anti	Lebanon (Ammoun)	Anti
Mexico (Cordova)	Anti	Pakistan (Zafrullah Khan)	Anti
		Peru (Bustamante)	Anti

* denotes an *ad hoc* judge, which hears only a single case

President Percy Spender of Australia—a Union supporter—saw an opportunity. One of the new anti-Union judges was Muhammad Zafrullah Khan of Pakistan, who had previously served as Pakistan's representative to the UN and President of the UN General Assembly.[44] Spender—who could have easily anticipated an 8–7 vote—put intense private pressure on Zafrullah Khan to recuse himself from the bench. Spender argued that Zafrullah Khan should not be allowed to hear the case because he had voted in favor of General Assembly resolutions that condemned the Union.

This pressure on Zafrullah Khan to resign was unprecedented. The ICJ Statute contains rules under which the President can attempt to have a judge removed from a case for a "special reason," but provides no examples of what constitutes such a reason.[45] Additionally, in the mid-1960s, most ICJ judges had previously held political positions in which they voted on UN resolutions. From 1957–1966, over 64 percent of newly appointed judges had previously served as a representative to the UN General Assembly, and 35 percent had served as a representative to the UN Security Council.[46] While most current ICJ judges have backgrounds as academics, government legal advisors, or domestic judges, it was not uncommon in the 1950s and 1960s for the UN to elect politicians to the ICJ. From 1957–1966, almost 30 percent of newly appointed judges had held elected office. Nonetheless, Zafrullah Khan bowed to Spender's pressure and agreed to recuse himself. By removing Zafrullah Khan—an anti-Union vote—Spender ensured that the bench was evenly split 7–7. As President of the Court, Spender's vote in favor of the Union became decisive.

From a political perspective, the pro-Union judges got what they wanted: they kept the ICJ from making a substantive ruling on the *South West Africa* case. This ruling had the added benefit, from their perspective, of limiting the Court's ability to intervene in future North-South disputes over decolonization. Political scientists often argue that judges are motivated, at least in part, by the desire to enhance the authority and influence of their court. But this case shows that sometimes judges want the opposite: they want to keep their court out of political disputes. The pro-Union judges wanted the ICJ to be weak.

From a legal perspective, the Court was careful in its 1966 ruling to construct an elaborate logic about when a League of Nations member could and could not have a legal interest in a mandate. Strictly speaking, the 1966 ruling did not completely contradict the 1962 ruling. While dismissing the case in 1966, the ICJ noted that there were some circumstances in which a League of Nations member could sue the Union. Namely, the ICJ ruled that a member could sue a mandatory if it violated a "special interest provision" that granted privileges to the member, such as trading rights and the free movement of missionaries. However, a League member could not sue on the basis of a "conduct provision" that regulated the administration of the territory. Pro-Union jurists could thus claim that they had not contradicted the earlier 1962 ruling: Ethiopia and Liberia still had a legal interest and right in the 1920 mandate, but not in the specific claims that they made in the

South West Africa case. Some individuals may thus believe that the 1966 ruling was made purely on the basis of legal principles and not on politics.[47]

Nearly fifty years later, voting patterns, memoirs, and historical accounts can help us to understand the Court's reversals *ex post*. But *ex ante*, disputants did not expect or contemplate that the Court would refuse to hear the case after the 1962 ruling; they believed that the Court would rule on the merits. This is apparent from contemporary news coverage, legal scholarship, and state behavior. In my own reading of contemporary United States news coverage, I did not find any article that suggested that the Court would revisit the question of whether it could rule on the merits. All press coverage focused on the merits of the case, particularly on the issue of apartheid.[48] I also did not find any article that reported the vote distribution for the 1962 ruling. Contemporary press coverage portrayed the Court as an unitary actor and ignored the internal judicial politics that are now apparent *ex post*.

Legal scholars also expected the Court to rule on the merits of the SWA dispute. The Court's 1950 advisory opinion clearly indicated that it was willing to adjudicate decolonization cases, and its 1962 judgment on preliminary objections indicated that it could rule on the merits because members of the League of Nations had a "legal right or interest" in the Union's mandate. To contemporary legal experts, the 1962 ruling firmly settled all issues of jurisdiction and admissibility. As legal scholar Ronald B. Ballinger wrote in 1964:

> The broad, clear, and precise language made it obvious that Members of the League had been understood to have a legal interest in the observance of its obligations towards the inhabitants of South West Africa by the Mandatory.[49]

Shortly after the ruling, prominent legal scholar Richard Falk (1967, 6) reflected that: "[a]fter the 1962 judgment there was no evidence of any further doubt ... that the Court would in 1966 answer [the] substantive questions [on the merits] one way or the other." This has also been the consensus view of later scholars. Dugard (1973, 332) noted that the 1966 ruling "has provoked academic criticism unparalleled in the history of the [ICJ]." Later scholars described the 1966 ruling as an unexpected "*volte-face*" that shocked the international community (Janis 1987, 144; Pomerance 1999).

Finally, the key actors in the case acted as though the issues of jurisdiction and admissibility had been firmly settled. Oral arguments between the 1962 and 1966 rulings addressed the merits of the case. Litigants argued exclusively about how the Court should rule, not about whether it should rule. Not only was the Court expected to rule on the merits, but it was expected to rule against the Union of South Africa. The *New York Times* reported that the ICJ "is expected by officials [in Washington] to grant the United Nations at least some supervisory rights over the former German colony, thus giving impatient African nations a direct chance to challenge South Africa's policy of apartheid, or racial separation."[50] British leaders feared that the ruling would force them to participate in international action against South Africa, which was a costly prospect because of the UK's perilous domestic economy and its ongoing difficulties over Southern Rhodesia.[51] The belief that the Court would rule against the Union was so strong that the United States State Department could not issue a public response to the ruling; all of the State Department's prepared documents and statements assumed that the Union would lose the case.[52]

Regardless of why the Court dismissed the case in 1966, the key factor for assessing my theory is whether the 1966 ruling dramatically and unexpectedly changed the beliefs of political actors about how the Court would rule in the future. Since states make decisions about settlement, compliance, and stability based on their beliefs about how the Court will behave, institutional change occurs when those beliefs change (North 1990). While it is interesting to contemplate why the ICJ behaved as it did, the important factor for my purposes is to establish that the rulings changed beliefs about the ICJ's future behavior.

The 1966 judgment substantially weakened delegation because it reduced the likelihood that the ICJ would adjudicate future decolonization disputes. The reasoning in the *South West Africa* case implied that independent states could not sue colonial powers over their current behavior unless they could demonstrate a special interest. Colonial territories, which clearly had a legal interest in how they were administered, lacked standing to sue on their own behalf because they were not independent states and hence could not be members of the ICJ. The United Nations cannot obtain a binding ICJ ruling, and individuals lack standing before the Court.[53] Finally, the Court also heard the *Northern Cameroons* case in the early 1960s in which a newly independent state sued its former colonizer for previous maladministration. As described in chapter 2, the ICJ refused to rule and argued that any ruling would lack "object or purpose" because colonial administration had ended.[54] Of course, no two cases are ever exactly alike. African states could have filed more lawsuits after 1966 in the hope that the Court would reverse or carve out exceptions to its previous rulings, as it did in the 1966 *South West Africa* ruling. Nonetheless, by 1966, African states believed, quite reasonably, that the ICJ was unlikely to

Figure 4.2: Colonial Southern Africa in 1963

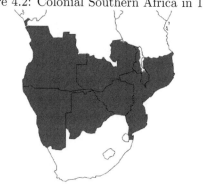

Note: Shaded regions show African territories that lacked independence in 1963.

rule on future cases involving white-minority rule.

Settlement, Stability, and Compliance

The 1966 ruling provoked dramatic responses from both sides. The African bloc proclaimed that the ruling would "diminish [the ICJ's] prestige and create doubts regarding its integrity."[55] Power within the African bloc shifted away from moderate leaders, who promoted litigation, and towards more extreme leaders, who advocated violence.

The Union of South Africa's reaction to the 1966 judgment was triumphant. South African leaders interpreted the verdict as confirmation that the United Nations lacked supervisory authority over South West Africa.[56] In a notorious incident shortly after the ruling, Harald Taswell, the South African ambassador to the United States, informed the State Department that his superiors believed that the Court's judgment "strongly suggest[s] there no longer exists any obligation on South Africa's part to report and account to any entity or body."[57] These reactions affected future litigation, ICJ membership, and compliance with the 1920 mandate.

Settlement

When members of the African bloc decided to pursue the *South West Africa* case, they anticipated that the case would set a precedent. While much of Africa was governed under black-majority rule by this point, a large portion of the south was still governed under white-minority rule, as shown in Figure 4.2. A major priority of the African bloc was to secure independence for Southern Rhodesia and the remaining Portuguese colonies in Africa, including Angola and Mozambique. In the language of my model, these were all preexisting disputes in the early 1960s.

My theory suggests that when a court grows weaker, states should be more likely to settle their disputes and less likely to engage in litigation. However, it is important to remember that a settlement does not necessarily make both sides happy. My theory does not require that colonial powers should have made concessions to the African bloc after the 1966 ruling. But it does imply that there should have been less litigation of preexisting disputes. So we need to ask: did the 1966 judgment deter members of the African bloc from filing other complaints against colonial powers? Assessing the counterfactual—how states would have behaved if the Court had ruled differently—is difficult. Yet some key aspects of future behavior bolster my first hypothesis.

First, the members of the African bloc did not file any future lawsuits about territories under white-minority rule.[58] Southern Rhodesia, Angola, Mozambique, and other Portuguese colonies in Africa were major sources of conflict in the UN at the time. The bloc abandoned litigation as a tool for decolonization. Second, there were no cases between African nations whatsoever for the twelve years following the *South West Africa* cases. The dashed line in Figure 4.3 shows that the number of independent African states exploded in the early 1960s. This suggests that the number of potential African lawsuits also increased because these states were now legal entities with ICJ standing. However, the bold line in Figure 4.3 shows that African countries did not use the ICJ at all in the late 1960s and early 1970s. When African states began to use the ICJ in the late 1970s, their cases focused on border disputes, an area in which the ICJ had abundantly demonstrated its willingness to adjudicate. It took the ICJ over twenty years to hear any other cases involving colonialism in any part of the world.[59]

Both patterns suggest that the ICJ's 1966 judgment deterred future litigation. Of course, changes in jurisprudence should only affect those states and issue-areas that are affected by the jurisprudence. It would be unrealistic to expect that the 1966 judgment would change the behavior of all developing nations. Similarly, it is not troubling from a theoretical perspective that African states later used the ICJ for territorial disputes because the 1966 *South West Africa* judgment pertained to colonial administration. Nothing in the ruling constrained African states from using the Court to adjudicate other types of disputes.

Figure 4.3: African Participation in the ICJ Docket over Time

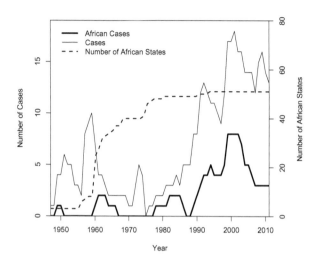

Note: The 1999 cases filed by Yugoslavia against NATO members are excluded.

Stability

The second claim of my theory is that weak institutions will be more stable than strong institutions because states will be less likely to exit the institution when they are under intense pressure to violate a treaty. In the context of the ICJ, states are members of the cooperative regime if they accept ICJ jurisdiction, and states are non-members if they refuse jurisdiction. So a decrease in ICJ strength should make it less likely that members will renounce ICJ jurisdiction. Recall that there are many different ways that a state can accept jurisdiction of the Court, which makes it exceptionally difficult to track jurisdiction over time. A state's membership in the legal regime can be established and revoked in many different ways, and hundreds of treaties contain a compromissory clause.[60] However, we can examine Court records and ask: were there any states that revoked their unilateral declarations—thereby exiting, at least partially, from the ICJ's jurisdiction—in response to the 1966 ruling?

The UK and Portugal were the colonial powers that were under the threat of litigation. The UK has been continuously under ICJ jurisdiction via a unilateral declaration since the Court's founding. Similarly, Portugal issued a unilateral declaration in 1955 and never

Table 4.3: Unilateral Declarations by Majority-Rule African States

Majority-Rule African State	Date of Majority-Rule	Date of ICJ Unilateral Declaration
Liberia	pre-1946	1952
Ethiopia	pre-1946	–
Libya	1951	–
Egypt	1952	1957
Sudan	1956	1958
Morocco	1956	–
Tunisia	1956	–
Ghana	1957	–
Guinea	1958	1998
Cameroon	1960	1994
Togo	1960	1979
Mali	1960	–
Senegal	1960	1985
Madagascar	1960	1992
Congo (Kinshasa)	1960	1989
Somalia	1960	1963
Benin	1960	–
Côte d'Ivoire	1960	2001
Chad	1960	–
Central African Republic	1960	–
Congo (Brazzaville)	1960	–
Gabon	1960	–
Nigeria	1960	1998
Mauritania	1960	–
Sierra Leone	1961	–
Tanzania	1961	–
Burundi	1962	–
Rwanda	1962	–
Algeria	1962	–
Uganda	1962	1963
Kenya	1963	1965
Malawi	1964	December 1966
Zambia	1964	–
Gambia	1965	June 1966

revoked it. Clearly colonial powers felt no need to exit the legal regime in 1966.

There were 34 African states under black-majority rule when the ICJ issued its judgment in July 1966. These states are shown in Table 4.3. Seven of these states had accepted ICJ jurisdiction via a unilateral declaration prior to the Court ruling.[61] None of these states withdrew from their declarations after the July 1966 ruling. Clearly the ICJ ruling did not harm the stability of the Court with regard to its pre-existing members.

My theoretical model begins with the assumption that states are members of a cooperative regime and then examines their willingness to leave the regime. However, if a strong court decreases stability, it is natural to believe that a weak court will increase stability and hence expand in membership. This intuition is not supported by the evidence in this case. About half of these African states—18 out of 34—never issued a unilateral declaration. They limited their participation in the Court both before and after the 1966 judgment. Only nine African states made unilateral declarations after the July 1966 ruling. Overall, this case does not contradict my theory's stability hypothesis. The behavior of ICJ members in 1966 is consistent with my theoretical arguments, but the behavior of non-members is less encouraging. This suggests that one possible avenue for future research is to examine how the design of a legal regime affects a state's initial decision about whether to join a cooperative regime.

Compliance

The final claim of my theory is that weak courts will reduce compliance with treaty obligations. As a court grows weaker, the cost of dispute settlement grows smaller. This in turn reduces the cost of noncompliance. So we must ask: what impact did the 1966 judgment have on compliance with the relevant agreement?

The ICJ's early rulings all suggested that the Court would adjudicate the *South West Africa* case, and most observers believed that the Union would lose on the merits. After the 1962 ruling, Union leaders tried to craft a new governance plan for SWA that would both be palatable to the ICJ with respect to the "social progress" criterion, and allow the Union to retain its political control and apartheid policies. The result was the 1964 Odendaal Plan. This government proposal divided South West Africa into ten ethnic homelands segregated by race. These homelands would be given limited local self-government and development funds, provided that they retained the Union's apartheid policies.

After the 1964 plan was announced, the African bloc—who were confident in the ICJ's support for their cause—threatened to seek an immediate injunction from the Court. As reported by the *New York Times*, "A sizable segment of the diplomatic community in Pretoria [the capital of South Africa] feels that an injunction could be a far greater threat to South Africa than recent United Nations resolutions on apartheid."[62] Union leaders quickly backed down and shelved the Odendaal Plan.

However, the Union became more defiant after the ICJ weakened its delegation in the 1966 judgment. At the international level, the Union continued to ignore General Assembly resolutions that called for SWA independence, and dismissed threats of military action by the Organization of African Unity.[63] At the domestic level, the Union tightened its reign over SWA using two major pieces of legislation.

First, the Union passed the Terrorism Act of 1967, which drastically increased the power of Union law enforcement officials to suppress dissent from black natives in SWA. The legislation gave police the authority to detain suspected dissidents indefinitely without trial, and allowed the domestic courts to impose retroactive punishments. After the Act was enacted, the government arrested and convicted dozens of political dissidents for crimes against the state. We do not know how many additional dissidents were arrested and held without trial.

Second, the Union revived the 1964 Odendaal Plan. This plan was implemented by legislation called the Self-Government for the Native Nations of South West Africa Act of 1968. Under this legislation, the government reorganized SWA administration along ethnic lines. The government also increased the power and wealth of the white minority by reallocating SWA property rights on the basis of race. White settlers—who were only 16 percent of the SWA population—were given full control over more than half the territory, including valuable farms and mines, while the black natives were assigned to the remaining barren pieces of land.[64] The Court's 1966 ruling clearly emboldened South Africa to violate its duties as a mandatory.

Alternative Explanation

One possible alternative explanation is that perhaps state behavior was driven by power politics, and not by legal design. Perhaps the 1966 ruling signaled to independent African states that powerful Northern states were not going to support the cause of decolonization. Such a signal could lead newly independent Southern states to refrain from using the Court and the Union to increase its defiance. Power politics could thus explain the settlement and compliance behavior.[65]

However, many aspects of the rulings defy the logic of power politics. First, the change in jurisprudence was not caused by a shift in political preferences. In both 1962 and 1966, ten judges opposed the Union and seven supported it. The change in the judicial outcome was driven by random and unexpected events, including death, illness, and which seats happened to be up for reelection in 1964. Additionally, as shown in Table 4.2, many powerful states supported Ethiopia and Liberia at the ICJ in both rulings, including the United States, USSR, and China. While the UK and France supported the Union, the 1966 ruling did not arise from a clear divide between developed and developing states.

Events after the 1966 ruling also contradict a power politics explanation. If the 1966 ruling signaled that powerful developed states opposed decolonization, then the African states should have believed that they couldn't achieve their objectives through other international organizations that were driven by power politics. The opposite in fact occurred. Shortly after the ICJ ruling, the UN General Assembly (UNGA), which was shocked by the ruling, passed a resolution that terminated the Union's mandate over South West Africa.[66] Because UNGA resolutions are not a source of binding law, the African states then appealed to the UN Security Council (UNSC), whose resolutions are legally binding. In January 1968, the UNSC voted to uphold the earlier UNGA resolution and then passed a flurry of additional resolutions against the Union in subsequent years.[67] These UNSC resolutions are particularly important because they could have been easily blocked by France or the United Kingdom, both of which supported the Union at the ICJ.

While the 1966 ruling kept African states from filing future contentious cases, it did not limit the ability of the UN Security Council to seek an advisory opinion. In 1970, the UNSC referred the matter back to the Court. One year later, on June 21, 1971, the ICJ issued yet another dramatic ruling. As shown in Table 4.4, the tide had turned once more. Both France and the United Kingdom continued to support the Union's control over South West Africa. However, two rounds of ICJ elections—in 1967 and 1970—had whittled away all of the Union's other supporters. In its 1971 advisory opinion, the Court ruled by a dramatic vote of 13–2 that "the continued presence of South Africa in Namibia being illegal, South Africa is under obligation to withdraw its administration from Namibia immediately and thus put an end to its occupation of the [South West Africa] Territory."[68] This 1971 ruling clearly demonstrates that the ICJ's 1966 ruling that Ethiopia and Liberia lacked the standing to file the case did not imply that their legal claims were without merit. Judicial decisions about whether states can sue affect whether states can secure remedy for a legal violation, but they do not provide precision about substantive legal claims.

The 1971 advisory opinion clearly showed that the ICJ supported substantive claims against colonialism. If anything, power politics in the early 1970s should have encouraged African states to file even more lawsuits. Yet African states did not return to the Court. The con-

Table 4.4: Judicial Behavior and Experience in 1971

Pro-Union Judges

Country (Judge)	Years
France (Gros)	7
UK (Fitzmaurice)	11
Average:	9

Anti-Union Judges

Country (Judge)	Years
Benin (Ignacio-Pinto)	1
Lebanon (Ammoun)	6
Mexico (Padilla Nervo)	7
Nigeria (Onyeama)	4
Pakistan (Zafrullah Khan)	14
Philippines (Bengzon)	4
Poland (Lachs)	4
Senegal (Forster)	7
Spain (de Castro)	1
Sweden (Petren)	4
Uruguay (Jimenez de Arechaga)	1
US (Dillard)	1
USSR (Morozov)	1
Average:	4.2

straints that the Court imposed upon itself in 1966, when it refused to grant Ethiopia and Liberia standing to sue a colonial power, continued to hold. State behavior was therefore clearly affected by beliefs about the Court's willingness to rule, and not simply by power politics.

***

The *South West Africa* case had long-term effects on perceptions of the ICJ. When speaking before the American Society of International Law in 1970, United States Secretary of State William Rogers said: "we should recognize that the Court is at least partly to blame for its state of neglect. There is no doubt that its reputation was damaged by its decision in the South-West Africa case."[69] The 1966 judgment is now arguably the most notorious in the ICJ's history and is often described as a self-inflicted wound.

Decolonization conflicts continued long after the *South West Africa* case ended. South West Africa did not gain independence as the state of Namibia until 1989, over twenty years after the Court's controversial ruling. Similarly, Portugal did not surrender control of Angola and

Mozambique until 1975, and Southern Rhodesia was governed under white-minority rule until 1980. Of course, it is possible that the ICJ ruling had no impact on these transitions. Perhaps these were simply the tough cases that would have taken many years to resolve, regardless of what the Court had ruled.

Nevertheless, the *South West Africa* case yields support for my theoretical arguments. First, the 1966 judgment forestalled other decolonization lawsuits. Opponents of colonization shifted from the legal to the political realm. Second, ICJ membership remained stable after 1966. The UK and Portugal, which controlled African territories, retained their ICJ memberships. Amongst the African states under black-majority rule, nonmembers did not rush to accept ICJ jurisdiction, but neither did they exit it. Finally, when the ICJ refused to rule in 1966, South African compliance with the 1920 mandate decreased. Union leaders interpreted the ruling as an indication that the ICJ would not adjudicate future similar disputes, and as evidence that the UN did not have authority to oversee the Union's administration of SWA. The Union no longer believed that it needed to promote, even half-heartedly, social progress and self-determination.

4.5 Consular Relations Cases

From 1998 to 2009, the United States was sued three times under the Vienna Convention on Consular Relations (VCCR). All of these cases involved foreign nationals who were convicted of crimes and sentenced to the death penalty by state courts. The United States did not inform these foreign nationals that the VCCR grants the right to consular notification and assistance. The three ICJ cases are commonly referred to as *Breard*, *LaGrand*, and *Avena*, the names of three of the affected foreign nationals.[70]

The Court issued two judgments, one in 2001 and the other in 2004, that increased delegation and obligation to the ICJ. So two distinct changes occurred in the Court's strength over time, yet the issue area (consular relations) and the affected state (the United States) remain constant over the eleven years. We thus have two opportunities to examine how changes in the design of a legal regime affected settlement, compliance, and stability. My theory implies that as the ICJ grew progressively stronger, litigation and compliance should have increased while stability decreased. In this section I ask three empirical questions. First, did the rulings lead to more litigation of similar disputes? Second, did the rulings increase United States compliance with the VCCR?

Finally, did the rulings reduce the willingness of the United States to remain under ICJ jurisdiction? I then examine a possible alternative explanation for the observed behavior.

Background on the Cases

Angel Francisco Breard, a citizen of Paraguay, was arrested in Virginia in 1992 for murder and attempted rape. He confessed his guilt and was sentenced to the death penalty in 1993. Virginia officials did not notify the Paraguayan consulate of Breard's arrest, conviction, or sentencing. Breard had no communication with consular officials and received no assistance from Paraguay at the time of his arrest and conviction. Paraguay learned of Breard's conviction and sentencing three years later. What began as a routine criminal conviction turned into an international cause célèbre.

Paraguay believed that the United States had violated international law. Paraguay alleged that actions taken by Virginia and the subsequent rulings of United States federal courts violated the Vienna Convention on Consular Relations of 1963. It demanded that the United States revoke the death penalty sentence or overturn Breard's conviction altogether. Shortly after Virginia set Breard's execution date, Paraguay filed a lawsuit against the United States at the ICJ. Paraguay asked the Court to order the United States to delay Breard's execution until the ICJ case was resolved. The ICJ agreed that such immediate action was necessary and issued an order of provisional measures to stay the execution.[71] However, Virginia authorities ignored the ICJ order and executed Breard five days later.

The 1963 Vienna Convention on Consular Relations (VCCR), which provided the basis of Paraguay's legal claims, codified long-standing practice in consular relations. Consular officials perform a wide range of functions, such as issuing travel documents, promoting "commercial, economic, cultural and scientific relations" between states, and protecting their nationals who are living or traveling in foreign countries.[72] The VCCR protects consular officials and regulates their ability to assist their nationals.[73]

Paraguay based its legal arguments on Article 36 of the VCCR. Key extracts from this text are shown in Table 4.5. Article 36 of the VCCR grants consular officials the right to visit and communicate with a national who is arrested or detained in a foreign country. It also requires the receiving state to notify arrested foreign nationals that the VCCR allows consular communication and visitation. The VCCR also contains an Optional Protocol that creates ICJ jurisdiction for "any

Table 4.5: Key Extracts from the Vienna Convention
on Consular Relations

Section	Relevant Text
Preamble	"[T]he purpose of such privileges and immunities [created by the VCCR] is not to benefit individuals but to ensure the efficient performance of functions by consular posts on behalf of their respective States."
Art. 36, para. 1(a)	"[C]onsular officers shall be free to communicate with nationals of the sending State and to have access to them. Nationals of the sending State shall have the same freedom with respect to communication with and access to consular officers of the Sending state."
Art. 36, para. 1 (b)	"[I]f he so requests, the competent authorities of the receiving State shall, without delay, inform the consular post of the sending State if . . . a national of that State is arrested or . . . detained in any other manner. Any communication addressed to the consular post by the person arrested . . . shall be forwarded by the said authorities without delay. The said authorities shall inform the person concerned without delay of his rights under this subparagraph."
Art. 36, para. 1 (c)	"[C]onsular officers shall have the right to visit a national of the sending State who is in prison, . . . to converse and correspond with him and to arrange for his legal representation."
Art. 36, para. 2	"[T]he laws and regulations of the receiving State . . . must enable full effect to be given to the purposes for which the rights accorded under this article are intended."

dispute arising out of the interpretation or application" of the treaty.[74] This Optional Protocol had been signed and ratified by all litigants in the consular relations cases and it created the ICJ's jurisdiction over these cases.

The consular relations cases involved a legal doctrine known as the procedural default rule. In the United States, an individual who is convicted by state court may appeal to a federal court. However, the procedural default rule limits the arguments that an individual can raise during his federal appeal. Loosely speaking, the rule prohibits an individual from raising arguments that he had not invoked during the state court proceedings.

As the United States clarified in its filings with the ICJ:

> [Procedural default] is a federal rule that, before a state criminal defendant can obtain relief in federal court, the claim must be presented in state court . . . One important purpose of this rule is to ensure that the state courts have an opportunity to address issues going to the validity of

state convictions before the federal courts intervene.[75]

During his initial trials in Virginia state courts, Angel Breard did not argue that his rights under the VCCR had been violated because he was not aware of the VCCR until after state court proceedings had ended. So the procedural default rule barred federal courts, including the United States Supreme Court, from considering an alleged violation of the VCCR when Breard appealed his case.

Even if Breard's claims were not barred by procedural default, it is unlikely that any United States court would have ruled that the VCCR applied to Breard's case. At that time, the United States government's position was that the VCCR created rights only for nation-states, not for individuals. While the treaty text often refers to the rights of consular officials, the traditional interpretation of this body of law had been that a consular official has rights only in her capacity as a representative of her nation-state. For example, the United States sued Iran at the ICJ in 1979 after members of the United States diplomatic and consular staff were taken hostage by Iranian revolutionary groups.[76] The United States argued that Iran had violated multiple diplomatic and consular relations treaties, including the VCCR. However, the United States government sued on its own behalf, and not on behalf of the individuals who were taken hostage. That is, the United States argued that Iran had violated the rights of the United States. It did not argue that Iran violated the rights of individual United States citizens.

Angel Breard was not alone. Many other foreign nationals were in a similar position because they did not raise VCCR claims during state court proceedings. Karl and Walter LaGrand—brothers who were German citizens—were convicted in 1984 in Arizona for murder and attempted armed robbery without consular notification or assistance. They were then sentenced to death. After Karl LaGrand's execution in February 1999, Germany filed suit against the United States to prevent the execution of Walter. As in the *Breard* case, the ICJ ordered the United States to delay the execution, but the authorities in Arizona executed Walter before the ICJ could rule on the merits of Germany's legal claims.[77] Mexico subsequently identified 52 of its own nationals who were appealing death penalty sentences in United States federal courts, but who could not raise VCCR claims because of the procedural default rule. Mexico filed suit against the United States in 2003.[78]

Legal Rulings

The consular relations cases—*Breard, LaGrand,* and *Avena*—revolved around four legal questions.

1. Did the United States violate international law by not following ICJ orders to delay the executions?

2. Does the VCCR create rights for individuals, or just for nation-states?

3. Does the procedural default rule violate the VCCR?

4. What remedies are available for VCCR violations?

ICJ members often violate orders of provisional measures. The ICJ ordered that the United States "should take all measures at its disposal" to ensure that Angel Breard and Walter LaGrand were "not executed pending the final decision" of the ICJ.[79] Nevertheless, both men were executed before the ICJ could rule on the merits of the legal claims of Paraguay and Germany. Many states regard such orders as hortatory rather than legally binding because the ICJ can issue provisional orders even if it has not firmly established that it has jurisdiction to hear a case.[80] Before the consular notification cases, the Court had never ruled on the legal status of its provisional orders (Kingsbury 1998, 684). One of the first legal questions in the consular relations cases was therefore whether the United States had violated international law by not following ICJ orders to delay the executions.

During the *LaGrand* case, Germany detailed many ways in which various United States authorities ignored the ICJ's order. For example, the United States Supreme Court did not intervene in the case and the Governor of Arizona did not stay the execution. The United States argued that the Court's provisional order was not binding. When making this argument, the United States relied primarily on a plain text interpretation of the relevant UN treaty. The English version of this treaty specified that a nation-state "should" implement ICJ orders. However, the French version used the phrase "doivent etre prises," which means that states "must" implement orders. The United States also invoked previous state practice, arguing: "This is not the law, and this is not how States or this Court have acted in practice." Finally, the United States argued that it "did what was called for by the [Court]" when it transmitted the ICJ order to Arizona officials because the executive branch of the federal government cannot stay state-level executions.[81]

The Court ruled in favor of Germany. Since the French and English translations of the UN treaties had contradictory language—the "should" versus "must" distinction—the Court made complicated arguments about the object and purpose of these treaties, concluding that: "orders on provisional measures ... have binding effect."[82] For the first time in its jurisprudence, the Court declared that its provisional orders are binding.

The second question addressed by the ICJ was: Does the VCCR create rights for individuals, or just for nation-states? Both Germany and Mexico argued that a plain text reading of the treaty shows that the VCCR creates individual rights. Consider the Article 36 extracts in Table 4.5. Paragraph 1(a) states that "consular officers shall be free to communicate with nationals of the sending State and to have access to them. Nationals of the sending State shall have the same freedom with respect to communication with and access to consular officers." Paragraph 1(b) states that if a foreign national is arrested or detained, authorities of the receiving state "shall inform the person concerned without delay of **his rights**."[83]

The United States countered this plain text interpretation of Article 36 with two arguments. First, the VCCR preamble clearly states that the treaty creates privileges for nation-states, not individuals themselves: "[T]he purpose of such privileges and immunities [created by the VCCR] is not to benefit individuals but to ensure the efficient performance of functions by consular posts on behalf of their respective States." So a plain text reading of the entire treaty does not yield a consistent interpretation. Second, previous state practice supported the view articulated in the preamble. Throughout the development of consular relations law, individuals received legal protection only in their capacity as representatives of nation-states. However, the ICJ sided with Germany and Mexico, ruling that a plain text reading of Article 36 prevailed over the competing arguments. The Court ruled that the VCCR creates rights for both nation-states and individuals.

The third question that the ICJ encountered was: Does the procedural default rule violate the VCCR? United States lawyers acknowledged that the United States violated the VCCR when it failed to inform Breard, LaGrand, and the Mexican nationals that they could contact their consulate. However, Germany pushed its claims a step further and argued that "the procedural default rule had 'made it impossible for the LaGrand brothers to effectively raise the issue of the lack of consular notification after they had at last learned of their rights.'"[84] Since the procedural default rule barred the LaGrand brothers from raising the VCCR in their federal appeals, Germany argued that the

United States violated Article 36, paragraph 2 of the treaty. This clause requires that: "[T]he laws and regulations of the receiving State ...must enable **full effect** to be given to the purposes for which the rights accorded under this article are intended."[85] Germany argued that by applying the procedural default rule, the United States failed to give "full effect" to the treaty because the LaGrand brothers could not raise VCCR violations in their federal appeals.

The United States responded that Germany's interpretation of the "full effect" clause went far beyond a plain text reading of the treaty, the intentions of states during VCCR negotiations, and the history of state practice. The United States argued that the VCCR does not regulate domestic "rules of criminal law and procedure" and that the VCCR does not create "individual remedies in criminal proceedings" for treaty violations.[86]

The Court's ruling on this question was murky. The Court was sympathetic to Germany's argument that the "full effect" clause requires an individual remedy for a VCCR violation. However, the Court would not adjudicate on the procedural default rule, noting that: "a distinction must be drawn between that rule as such and its specific application in the present case."[87] The Court would not consider the legality of the rule itself, but the Court found that the application of the rule in the LaGrand trials was a violation of international law.

By this point, the Court had ruled that the VCCR creates individual rights and that the United States violated these rights by not informing arrested individuals of VCCR protections, and by using the procedural default rule to bar VCCR claims in federal appeals. The final question that the Court had to answer was: What remedies are available for VCCR violations?

Paraguay, Germany, and Mexico presented a broad array of arguments about appropriate remedies. They asked the Court to find that they were entitled to *restitutio in integrum*, a principle from contract law that requires that a contract violator must return his victim to her pre-violation condition. This remedy could potentially require the United States to overturn the convictions because the VCCR violations occurred prior to all judicial proceedings. Absent such a strong remedy, the applicants asked the Court to order that the United States must review all of the criminal trials and issue an assurance of non-repetition.

During the *LaGrand* case, the United States argued that an official apology to Paraguay, Germany, and Mexico was a sufficient remedy for a VCCR violation. After all, the United States did not believe that the treaty created individual rights, only rights for nation-states. After the *LaGrand* ruling that the VCCR creates individual rights, the United

States State Department began a massive public education campaign to inform law enforcement officers that they must provide consular notification and access to foreign nationals. When Mexico again raised the issue of remedies in the *Avena* case, the United States used two strategies. First, the United States argued that its public education campaign was a sufficient attempt to prevent future violations. Second, the United States argued that state clemency boards, which review criminal convictions for the executive branch of state governments, provided effective review of the criminal cases.

The ICJ did not order the United States to overturn all of the sentences to achieve *restitutio in integrum*. However, the Court was emphatic in the *LaGrand* judgment that an apology was not a sufficient remedy:

> [A]n apology would not suffice in cases where the individuals concerned have been subjected to prolonged detention or convicted and sentenced to severe penalties. In the case of such a conviction and sentence, it would be incumbent upon the United States to allow the review and reconsideration of the conviction and sentence by taking account of the violation of the rights set forth in the [VCCR].[88]

The Court later elaborated in the *Avena* judgment that "review and reconsideration" must be a judicial process. In the Court's view, state-level clemency boards did not provide adequate review because the United States could not guarantee that these clemency boards would consider VCCR violations during their deliberations. The *Avena* judgment ordered the United States to provide judicial review of all of the criminal cases.

Assessing the Theory

The three consular relations cases—*Breard*, *LaGrand*, and *Avena*—yielded two substantive rulings.[89] In these rulings, the Court asserted that its orders of provisional measures were legally binding and that it had the authority to rule on VCCR violations of individual rights. The Court therefore grew stronger because its members could reasonably expect that delegation and obligation to Court orders would be greater in future cases. My theory suggests that increasing either delegation or obligation to a court's ruling magnifies the importance of uncertainty about how a court will rule, which in turn makes pre-trial settlements less likely. If my argument is correct, we should see three patterns in the consular relations cases. First, the rulings should have increased future litigation of disputes, conditional on the United States remaining under ICJ jurisdiction. Second, the United States should have increased its compliance, conditional on remaining under ICJ jurisdiction. Finally, the United States should have grown more willing to exit from ICJ jurisdiction. I first discuss how the rulings increased delegation and obligation to the ICJ. I then examine whether the rulings affected settlement, compliance, and stability.

Strengthening the ICJ

The rulings in the consular relations cases helped the Court to grow stronger by changing the beliefs of the Court's members about how the Court would behave in the future. First, the rulings increased delegation to the ICJ. For the first time ever, the ICJ ruled that the VCCR creates individual rights. Additionally, it found that the United States violated the rights of both the sending country and individual foreign nationals. At the end of the *LaGrand* judgment, the ICJ stated that "the United States of America breached its obligations to the Federal Republic of Germany and **to the LaGrand brothers**."[90]

In the past, the ICJ has operated under a traditional view of international law, in which treaties create obligations between states. Court procedures reflect this view: states can bring a case to the ICJ, but individuals cannot. The ICJ's practices stand in stark contrast to more modern transnational courts, such as the European Court of Human Rights, that allow individuals to sue states.

The consular relations rulings signaled that the ICJ was willing to hear cases that involve individual rights, and to rule that a state had violated individual rights. As always, the Court would only hear a case if it was filed by a state. But the consular relations cases are notable in large part because they indicate a shift in the Court's worldview and open the door to adjudication of individual claims in other issue areas.

Second, the rulings increased obligation to the ICJ. The Court definitively asserted in the *LaGrand* judgment that its orders for provisional measures are legally binding. This ruling will likely increase the impact of future Court orders on political outcomes through two different channels.

At the international level, the Court cannot formally enforce its orders. However, the international community often pressures litigants to implement Court judgments. An ICJ ruling opens the door to coordinated third party enforcement (Johns 2012). In the past, litigants have been under little pressure to follow provisional orders because many states believed that these orders lacked the legal force of a final judgment. The Court's *LaGrand* ruling should increase international pressure on states to abide by these orders.

At the domestic level, the Court's ruling ensures that many domestic legal systems can now enforce an ICJ provisional order. Domestic legal systems differ substantially in their treatment of international law. At one extreme are countries like the United States with dualist legal systems, in which international legal commitments do not necessarily translate into domestic legal commitments. However, for countries like Germany with monist legal systems, international legal commitments are automatically a part of domestic law.[91] In such countries, binding ICJ rulings are directly enforceable in domestic courts. Now that the ICJ has ruled that its provisional orders are legally binding, future litigants can use domestic courts to enforce ICJ orders.

Settlement, Compliance, and Stability

The consular relations cases are unique in that multiple states successively sued the United States. There are a few previous ICJ cases in which multiple states sued a single state at the same time, such as the *South West Africa* case. Similarly, there are a handful of cases in which a litigant asked the Court to reinterpret an unclear ruling, or reconsider a previous ruling in light of new evidence.[92] However, the consular relations cases are the only example in which multiple states successively sued the same state on the same issue. This gives us more opportunities to examine how shifts in Court jurisprudence changed the behavior of the United States.

Settlement

The consular relations cases are a clear example of how strengthening a court can make states less likely to settle their disputes and more likely to litigate them. Paraguay filed the first case against the United States in 1998. At the time, Paraguay's tactic was unusual. The ICJ had previously heard VCCR cases, but all of these cases involved the treatment of consular officials. No country had ever used the VCCR to sue on behalf of an individual who was not a consular official. Paraguay's arguments were a major legal innovation. But given the novelty of these arguments, Paraguay had little reason to believe that the ICJ would hear the case and rule favorably. After the execution of Breard, Paraguay reached a settlement with the United States and withdrew its case.

Germany filed the second consular relations case a year later. The ICJ once again issued an order to stay an execution, and the United States once again violated it. However, unlike Paraguay, Germany continued its case even though both Karl and Walter LaGrand were dead. Anti-death penalty groups pressured the German government to file and then continue the lawsuits. Additionally, while the legal arguments in *Breard* and *LaGrand* were still innovative, the ICJ had at this point issued two separate orders of provisional measures, which indicated that the Court might be amenable to using the VCCR to challenge the death penalty. This case ultimately led to the expansive *La Grand* judgment of 2001.

The international community gave the United States some time to implement the *LaGrand* judgment. However, after two years, Mexico remained unhappy about the treatment of its nationals. By this point there was no ambiguity about whether the Court would rule. Mexico filed suit in 2003, which ultimately led to the *Avena* ruling.

A clear pattern is apparent: as the Court issued more muscular rulings, states filed more ICJ lawsuits. Of course, it is not possible to provide statistical analysis to support this claim: the ICJ simply doesn't hear enough cases to permit a large-n analysis of case filings. Additionally, we cannot assess whether these rulings increased domestic litigation. Data on such lawsuits are not available, and any empirical study would need to control for attempts by the United States to implement the ICJ's judgment. However, it is clear that litigation at the international level continued as the ICJ grew stronger.

Compliance

United States reactions to the ICJ rulings also demonstrate how a stronger court can generate more compliance. It was relatively simple for the United States to implement its interpretation of the 2001 *LaGrand* ruling. The ICJ did not rule on domestic legal procedures, so the United States did not have to consider the legal and political implications of changing the procedural default rule. The ICJ ordered the United States to review and reconsider the convictions and sentencing of foreign nationals, but the ICJ did not impose constraints on these reviews and the United States believed that state clemency boards provided adequate review.

After *LaGrand*, the United States attempted to boost VCCR compliance and prevent future violations. The United States State Department's public education campaign for law enforcement officials explained the VCCR and instructed officials to notify foreign nationals of their right to consular notification and assistance within 72 hours of their arrest. This campaign certainly did not impose major costs on the United States government. Yet within the limits of a federal system of government, little else was possible to prevent future violations of the VCCR.

In contrast, the *Avena* judgment of 2004 dramatically increased the costs of abiding by the Court's rulings. In this judgment, the Court reiterated its earlier findings from the *LaGrand* case. It also ruled that the effort by the United States to prevent future VCCR violations satisfied Mexico's request for "guarantees and assurances of non-repetition."[93] However, the Court found that state-level clemency boards did not provide adequate reviews of the individual criminal cases. The ICJ ordered the United States to provide judicial review of the cases.

This put the United States government in an awkward position. All of the affected Mexican nationals had already exhausted state-level legal procedures. Even if a state wanted to review these cases again for VCCR claims, it was unclear how they could do so. If a state did not want to review these cases, then any attempt by the Bush administration to force a state to do so could trigger lawsuits over executive authority and states' rights. In contrast, if federal courts reviewed these cases for VCCR claims, then they would be breaking the procedural default rule, opening the floodgates to other cases. In the most extreme possible scenario, federal courts might have to review all criminal cases, regardless of whether the cases involved the VCCR, to provide equal treatment.

The United States government decided that the best of the bad alternatives was to try to force state courts to review the cases. In early 2005 President George W. Bush issued an executive order that stated:

> I have determined ... that the United States will discharge its international obligations under the decision of the International Court of Justice ... by having State courts give effect to the [*Avena*] decision in accordance with general principles of comity.[94]

Bush was heavily criticized. Many states, including Texas, refused to implement Bush's order. Shortly after the executive order was issued, a spokesman for the Texas Attorney General stated:

> The State of Texas believes no international court supercedes the laws of Texas or the laws of the United States. We respectfully believe the executive determination exceeds the constitutional bounds for federal authority.[95]

Some observers went even further, accusing Bush of "siding with Mexico over the American court system."[96] This tension came to a head three years later in the *Medellin* case.

Jose Ernesto Medellin was a Mexican national covered by the *Avena* ruling. As mentioned in Chapter 1, he was sentenced to death in Texas after being convicted of murder. Medellin had already exhausted state court proceedings by the time of Bush's 2005 order. Nonetheless, Medellin asked the Texas Court of Criminal Appeals to review his conviction and sentence in light of VCCR violations. The Texas court refused to reopen the case. Medellin then took his case to the United States Supreme Court and sued Texas for violating both the ICJ ruling and Bush's executive order.

The political stakes were high. A Supreme Court ruling that required Texas to reopen the case would have drastic repercussions for states' rights. Additionally, any ruling that limited the procedural default rule could open the door to an untold number of appeals in other criminal cases. Nonetheless, the Bush administration submitted an *amicus* brief in support of Medellin, arguing that Bush's executive order was binding on the Texas state courts. Texas prevailed. First, the Supreme Court found that ICJ rulings were not enforceable in domestic courts. Second, the Court argued that President Bush lacked the authority to order state courts to provide review and reconsideration of the *Avena* cases.

Mexico, upset by the ruling, returned to the ICJ. Its only remaining tactic, given the Court's procedures, was to request an interpretation of the 2004 *Avena* ruling.[97] Mexico argued that the Supreme Court ruling ensured that the United States would not abide by the ICJ's ruling. The ICJ ruled that Mexico and the United States agreed about the interpretation of the 2004 ruling: everyone understood that the United States had to provide judicial review and reconsideration. Additionally, the Court ruled that it lacked the authority to review violations of the previous judgment. Mexico's ICJ case was definitively over.

The attempts of the United States to comply with the VCCR illustrate my theoretical arguments. Before the *LaGrand* judgment, the United States exerted little effort to ensure that arrested foreign nationals could notify their consulate of their arrest. After the *LaGrand* ruling, the United States made a good faith effort to prevent future VCCR violations through its public education campaign, and it believed that state clemency boards provided adequate review and reconsideration of death penalty cases.

Stability

The 2004 *Avena* judgment changed the political calculations of the United States about its future behavior. Near the end of the judgment, the Court clarified that the United States must provide judicial review for foreign nationals from all VCCR members. The Court wrote that "the fact that in this case the Court's ruling has concerned only Mexican nationals cannot be taken to imply that the conclusions reached by it in the present Judgment do not apply to other foreign nationals finding themselves in similar situations in the United States."[98] The Court could not order the United States to provide judicial review for nationals of countries that had not yet sued the United States. However, the Court's statement clearly indicated that it would issue similar rulings in any future lawsuits: not only would the United States be in violation of the VCCR, it would also be expected to provide judicial review.

Since the United States federal government has limited control over the conduct of state and local law enforcement officers, future violations of the VCCR might occur. The Bush administration recognized that the *Avena* ruling raised the cost of these possible future violations. Before 2004, the United States believed that it was only obligated to prevent future violations and provide some form of review for those violations that did occur. These requirements were easily satisfied without major policy changes. After 2004, the United States knew that it would be expected to provide judicial review for future violations. The United States government knew that it would not be able to implement the ICJ's new requirement of judicial review because of the design of its federal and state judicial systems. The ICJ ordered the United States to enact a remedy that it simply could not afford.

The response of the United States was clear: instead of trying to comply with the VCCR and settle disputes when violations occurred, the United States decided to leave the Court's jurisdiction. On March 11, 2005, the Bush administration notified the United Nations that the United States was withdrawing from the Optional Protocol of the VCCR.[99] The United States continued to be bound by the VCCR. However, by exiting from the Optional Protocol, the United States removed itself from the Court's jurisdiction over future VCCR disputes.

Alternative Explanations

The behavior in this case is consistent with my theoretical argument, but perhaps this behavior can also be explained by power politics. Perhaps the United States—the world's most powerful country—left the ICJ because it didn't want its power to be constrained. In one sense, this is a plausible explanation. By asserting stronger delegation and obligation, the Court increased the cost of remaining a member of the Court. The United States simply could not comply with the ICJ's increasingly strict conditions, and believed that it would lose future ICJ rulings. The United States could no longer afford to remain a member of the club.

However, what is particularly striking about the consular relations cases is that the United States supported the substantive law and worked so hard to abide by the Court ruling, even after leaving the Court's jurisdiction. As detailed above, President Bush ordered state courts to implement the ICJ's *LaGrand* ruling despite concerns that this would violate the principle of federalism. Additionally, while President Bush lacked the ability to compel the United States Supreme Court to rule in Medellin's favor, his administration did file an *amicus* brief to support Medellin's case over three years after the United States had left ICJ jurisdiction. Finally, the Bush administration clearly supported the substantive law that the Court was overseeing because the United States remained a member of the VCCR.

This support was also reflected in the United States Congress. A few months after the Supreme Court's *Medellin* ruling, Representative Howard Berman introduced a bill called the *Avena Case Implementation Act of 2008*.[100] This bill allowed an individual to obtain "appropriate relief" if her consular notification rights were violated, including potentially "the vitiation of the conviction or sentence," but the bill languished in the House Judiciary Committee.[101] A few years later, Senator Patrick Leahy introduced a more detailed bill called the *Consular Notification Act of 2011* with the support of the Obama administration.[102] This bill never became a law, but Leahy publicized the issue during a July 2011 hearing of the Senate Judiciary Committee entitled "Fulfilling Our Treaty Obligations and Protecting Americans Abroad," which provoked extensive national press coverage. Leahy emphasized the importance of respecting the VCCR, stating:

> This bill . . . is about protecting Americans when they work, travel, and serve in the military in foreign countries. It is about fulfilling our obligations and upholding the rule of law. And it is about removing a significant impediment to full and complete cooperation with our international allies on national security and law enforcement efforts that keep Americans safe. We must bring the United States into compliance with our legal obligations. We cannot continue to ignore the treaty and expect other countries to honor it.[103]

Long after the United States left the ICJ's jurisdiction over the VCCR, support for the treaty itself continued.

***

We do not yet know what long-term impact the consular relations cases will have on perceptions of the ICJ. Since the United States withdrew from ICJ jurisdiction under the Optional Protocol, there have been no other cases involving individual rights under the VCCR. The legal basis for these cases was the Vienna Convention of Consular Relations, but the motivating political force behind the cases was opposition to the death penalty. Very few countries now use the death penalty, so it is unlikely that we will see future cases on this exact same topic. Nonetheless, these rulings are significant for future litigation in two major ways.

First, they demonstrate that the ICJ is now willing to create individual rights from traditional inter-state treaties. Paraguay's decision to use the VCCR to challenge the death penalty was a major legal innovation. The ICJ did not rule directly on the validity of the death penalty, which many states believe is a violation of international human rights law. However, the VCCR cases were broadly interpreted at both the international and domestic level as a statement of international opposition to the death penalty. It is likely that states will try to adopt similar tactics at the ICJ in the future, using inter-state treaties to try to create and protect individual rights.

Second, these cases suggest that the ICJ is now willing to venture into the growing field of human rights law. Since the 1990s, states have increasingly used the ICJ to challenge inter-state violations of humanitarian law, such as genocide during international conflicts.[104] However, few states have used the ICJ to litigate human rights law.[105] This reluctance to bring human rights claims was caused in part by the ICJ's unwillingness to rule in the *South West Africa* case. The consular relations cases suggest that the Court's attitude has changed. In 2009, Belgium sued Senegal at the ICJ under the UN Convention Against Torture. Belgium argued that Senegal had violated its treaty commitment to prosecute Hissene Habre, the former leader of Chad, for war crimes and torture. As of this writing, litigation continues. But the ICJ has consistently ruled in favor of Belgium, and has ordered Senegal to either prosecute Habre or extradite him to Belgium for trial.[106] The ICJ has only been willing to support human rights arguments on the basis of written treaties, and not customary law.[107] Nevertheless, states may be able to use the ICJ in the future to uphold human rights claims.

Regardless of how the ICJ will behave in the future, the consular relations cases clearly illustrate my argument. As the ICJ issued successively stronger rulings, litigation increased. States became more willing to challenge the United States as they became more confident that the ICJ would rule in these cases and that these rulings would affect the behavior of the United States. Second, as the Court grew stronger, United States compliance with the VCCR increased as the State Department worked to prevent future treaty violations. However, when the Court ordered that the United States must provide judicial reviews, the cost of remaining under ICJ jurisdiction became too high. President Bush ordered state courts to review the criminal cases and supported Medellin in his attempts to appeal his case in a state court. Even though the United States government supported the VCCR, it could no longer afford to remain under ICJ jurisdiction.

4.6 Conclusion

As Henkin (1979, 9) famously observed, assessments of the strength or effectiveness of international law are inherently subjective and often driven by "differences in perspective." The ICJ is weaker than many other international courts, such as the GATT/WTO Dispute Settlement System. There is limited delegation to the ICJ because jurisdiction and standing rules are highly restrictive. Additionally, there is limited obligation to the ICJ rulings because the Court lacks effective formal enforcement mechanisms. Nonetheless, there have been key points in the ICJ's history at which the Court used jurisprudence to modestly change its own strength. The case studies above show that these changes affected the behavior of member states.

In the notorious *South West Africa* cases, the ICJ issued a judgment in 1966 that weakened its ability to hear decolonization cases. Not only did this hinder a resolution to the South West Africa dispute, it also ruled out future litigation over other colonial territories, including Southern Rhodesia, Angola, and Mozambique. The ICJ's judgment coincided with increased noncompliance by the Union of South Africa, which administered South West Africa. The Court's judgment did not decrease ICJ stability because states that made unilateral declarations before 1966 continued to accept ICJ jurisdiction.

In the consular relations cases, the ICJ issued a series of rulings that increased the Court's strength. As the Court grew stronger, more states sued the United States. The United States initially attempted to meet the Court's demands, but as the demands of the Court grew larger, the United States eventually renounced the Court's jurisdiction over consular relations cases.

These cases illustrate and support my theoretical framework, yet it is worth asking: Why is the International Court of Justice still so weak in comparison to other international courts? My theory suggests that one factor is that the ICJ oversees a relatively imprecise body of law. Additionally, the court does not have a voluminous record of past jurisprudence. Stronger courts—such as the WTO dispute settlement system and the European Court of Justice—hear far more cases than the ICJ, creating precedent and reducing future uncertainty about how these courts will rule in future cases.

When a court oversees imprecise laws, states are less certain about the likely outcome of litigation. This informational problem makes it more difficult for countries to reach negotiated solutions to their disputes. Strengthening the ICJ beyond its current limits would likely exacerbate the effects of incomplete information and increase costly litigation. To offset these effects, it is necessary to accompany institutional change with revisions to the body of law overseen by the court. In order for a strong court to be effective, it must oversee a body of law that is clear and precise. Such precision is currently lacking in the immense number of multilateral treaties overseen by the ICJ.

Of course, supporters of the ICJ might argue that if we make the ICJ stronger, then the Court can increase precision over time as it builds up a body of case law and becomes more active in hearing disputes. Over the long-run, this enhanced precision may allow the Court to grow more effective. How one evaluates such a policy proposal ultimately depends upon how one evaluates the short-term costs of enhanced litigation and instability against the possible long-run benefits of precision. As shown above, even small changes in the Court's jurisprudence have dramatically changed the way that states interact in the shadow of the ICJ. The consular relations rulings prompted the United States to completely withdraw from the ICJ's jurisdiction over the VCCR even though politicians in the United States from diverse political backgrounds have repeatedly emphasized the fundamental importance of the VCCR to the foreign policy of the United States.[108]

It is probably unrealistic to expect that if the ICJ is made stronger, then precision will naturally follow of its own accord. It is far more likely that a dramatic strengthening of the Court would lead to a massive exodus from its jurisdiction before the Court can build a body of case law. This does not mean that international law is doomed to failure. Rather, it means that the details of institutional design matter.

5

Strengthening the GATT/WTO Dispute Settlement System

5.1 Introduction

The shift from the GATT to the WTO in 1995 is arguably the most complex and important change ever in the design of an international organization. States renegotiated their legal commitments and created a new institution that is dedicated to trade liberalization. One key component in this shift was the transformation of the dispute settlement system.

The GATT dispute settlement system (DSS) was largely diplomatic and consisted of informal norms that evolved slowly from 1947 to 1979. By 1980, the GATT had developed norms that granted very low delegation and obligation to the DSS. There were six different dispute settlement systems from 1980 to 1994. The main DSS covered disputes arising under the GATT itself, while the other five covered optional issue-specific add-on agreements. These optional agreements created a complex web of legal commitments and overlapping jurisdiction among the six systems. When states designed the WTO, all members had to accept the same legal commitments, and only one DSS could hear WTO disputes. This new legalistic regime granted high delegation and obligation to the WTO DSS. The transformation from the GATT to the WTO did not occur because internal actors changed the way that states perceived the legal regime, as in the ICJ rulings in Chapter 4. The transition to the WTO occurred after long and arduous negotiations over many aspects of the multilateral trade regime, and all of the changes in institutional design became effective at the same time.

My theory shows that when a court grows stronger, states are less likely to settle their disputes because strong courts increase the importance of uncertainty about how the court will rule. States can capture the benefits of a strong court, such as enhanced compliance, and avoid some of its costs if they increase the precision of the law. So when rational actors want to enhance international cooperation, an increase in court strength should be matched by an increase in the precision of the regime's rules.

In this chapter, I examine the relationship between strength and precision to both illustrate and assess the plausibility of my theory. I argue that the creation of the WTO in 1995 significantly strengthened delegation and obligation to the trade regime's dispute settlement system and simultaneously enhanced the precision of international trade law. I examine GATT and WTO laws on three important issues: safeguards, subsidies and countervailing duties, and antidumping duties. I show that the transition to the WTO dramatically enhanced precision in the coverage of legal commitments, the definition of treaty terms, and the rules for domestic and international procedures. Of course, current WTO law still contains many ambiguities. Nevertheless, the shift from the GATT to the WTO dramatically enhanced the precision of trade law. While this analysis does not definitively prove that strength caused precision, it does support my theory's key implication. I first provide a brief overview of the GATT/WTO. I then discuss how my theoretical argument applies to this institution and my methodological strategy for assessing my theory. Next I detail how the shift from the GATT to the WTO enhanced delegation and obligation to the DSS. Finally, I examine legal texts to show that WTO rules are more precise than their GATT predecessors and I discuss a possible alternative explanation for this precision.

5.2 Overview of the GATT/WTO

International trade took a back-seat to other international issues during the early 1940s. States did not begin multilateral trade negotiations until 1946. During these negotiations, states wrote two separate treaties: the General Agreement on Tariffs and Trade of 1947 (GATT), and the Havana Charter of 1948.[1] The GATT focused on substantive legal commitments. It included broad legal principles to govern international trade, and contained detailed lists of each state's tariff concessions. The Havana Charter created a new institution to oversee the GATT. In 1947, twenty-three states agreed to implement the GATT immediately on a provisional basis, pending the completion of the Havana Charter.[2]

However, the Havana Charter never went into effect. By the late 1940s, the United States Senate grew tired of the proliferation of new international organizations—such as the United Nations, the International Monetary Fund, and the World Bank—and refused to ratify the Havana Charter. The Truman administration eventually bowed to Congressional opposition and announced in 1950 that it would no longer seek Senate approval.[3] The international community quickly abandoned the Havana Charter.

States created a set of binding trade commitments in the GATT, but had no formal institution to oversee and manage these commitments. Over time, GATT commitments grew deeper as members pledged to lower tariffs and reduce nontariff barriers to trade.[4] Members gradually developed an institutional structure, including a secretariat, a committee system, and a dispute settlement system. States did not embed this structure in a formal treaty, but GATT members slowly developed a *de facto* institution from 1947 to 1979.

The mature GATT era began in 1980 when many GATT members signed a complex system of optional agreements known as the Tokyo Codes. These agreements addressed a host of issues, including dispute settlement, antidumping duties, and subsidies and countervailing duties. All GATT members continued to be bound by GATT rules. The Tokyo Codes were only binding amongst GATT members that chose to sign them and thereby increase their trade commitments. Critics dubbed this system "GATT *à la carte*" because members could pick and choose which rules they followed. This system created a complex web of legal commitments in which different rules applied to different pairs of members. It grew so complicated that GATT members decided to create a common set of rules for international trade.[5] States began a series of negotiations, known as the Uruguay Round, to strengthen the multilateral trade regime.

The World Trade Organization (WTO) replaced the informal GATT institution when the Uruguay Round agreements went into effect in 1995. These agreements dramatically expanded the scope of trade law to new issues (such as services, intellectual property, and investment), and refined preexisting laws (such as rules on safeguards, subsidies and countervailing duties, and antidumping duties). Additionally, the Uruguay Round increased both delegation and obligation to the dispute settlement system.

The GATT/WTO definition of a trade dispute is relatively broad. A dispute occurs anytime there is a "nullification or impairment" of "any benefit accruing to [a member] directly or indirectly under [GATT]."[6] So if one member adopts a policy that is relevant to its GATT/WTO commitments, then any other member that is hurt by this policy can file a complaint with the DSS. Many disputes are caused by blatant violations of treaty commitments, while others are caused by principled disagreements over the meaning of legal commitments. That is, two states may wish to comply but differ in their interpretation of what compliance entails. The WTO Secretariat acknowledges that:

> [t]he precise scope of the rights and obligations contained in the WTO Agreement is not always evident from a mere reading of the legal texts. Legal provisions are often drafted in general terms so as to be of general applicability and to cover a multitude of individual cases, not all of which can be specifically regulated. (WTO 2004, 3)

It is not surprising that GATT/WTO rules are sometimes unclear because they are written during complex multilateral negotiations. As in the theoretical framework above, GATT/WTO rules place limits on trade policy, but states are often uncertain about whether their specific actions are legally permissible.

States used the GATT/WTO dispute settlement system more as the international trade regime evolved. Figure 5.1 shows that during the early GATT period of 1947 to 1979, when dispute settlement was informal and diplomatic, states filed relatively few disputes. When the mature GATT era began in 1980, states increased their use of the DSS. This trend continued under the WTO. Of course, as the GATT/WTO evolved, new states joined the trade regime. It is difficult to say whether the increase in DSS use was caused by the evolution of the GATT/WTO institution, changes in substantive trade commitments, or increases in the scope of issues and the number of members. Nonetheless, dispute settlement is clearly a key component of the multilateral trade regime.

Bargaining plays an important role in all of these trade disputes (Busch and Reinhardt 2000; Davis 2003). Both the GATT and WTO encourage settlement of trade disputes, rather than litigation. GATT scholars consistently reiterate that "the GATT has always been mainly a forum for negotiation" (Trebilcock and Howse 1995, 399). Similarly, the WTO Secretariat stresses that:

> Although the dispute settlement system is intended to uphold the rights of aggrieved Members and to clarify the scope of the rights and obligations, ... the primary objective of the system is not to make rulings or to develop jurisprudence ... [T]he priority is to settle disputes, preferably through a mutually agreed solution that is consistent with the WTO Agreement. (WTO 2004, 6)

Figure 5.1: GATT/WTO Disputes over Time

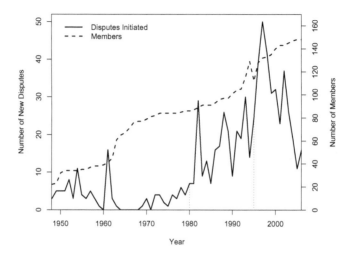

Source: GATT data compiled from Busch and Reinhardt (2003), Hudec (1993), and Reinhardt (1996). WTO data compiled from Horn and Mavroidis (2011).

DSS litigation occurs only if states cannot negotiate a settlement.

5.3 Strength and Precision: Theory and Hypotheses

When two players negotiate in the shadow of a court, their bargaining behavior will be affected by their beliefs about how the court will behave if it makes a ruling on the merits. If players have common beliefs about how the court will act, then they should be able to negotiate a settlement that both prefer to litigation. However, settlement becomes more difficult when disputants have differing beliefs about how the court will act. When a court grows stronger, the court becomes more willing and able to rule on the merits, and the court's rulings have a larger effect on political outcomes. This increase in delegation and obligation heightens the importance of uncertainty about how the court will rule on the merits. The overall effect of delegation and obligation is thus to reduce the likelihood of settlement. Precision has the opposite effect. As laws become more precise, disputants have more accurate and similar beliefs about how judges will rule and it is easier for them to settle, rather than litigate, their disputes.

Delegation and obligation also have complex effects on compliance with treaty rules and the stability of a cooperative regime. If a state faces a relatively low cost of cooperation, then increasing the cost of dispute settlement makes compliance more likely. Strong courts thus increase compliance with legal rules. However, if a state has a very high cost of cooperation, then increasing the cost of dispute settlement makes it more difficult for a state to temporarily violate its treaty commitments and remain a member of the regime. Strong courts thus decrease the stability of legal regimes.

The ICJ chapter above examined internal change and showed how unexpected changes in jurisprudence affected state behavior. Rulings in the *South West Africa* and consular relations cases changed delegation and obligation to the ICJ for future related cases. These changes in court strength affected settlement, compliance, and stability in the ways predicted by Propositions 2, 6, and 7.

In contrast, sometimes states create external change by redesigning a treaty regime with an eye to its expected consequences. This occurred during the 1995 transition from the GATT to the WTO. Unlike the unexpected ICJ rulings, the changes to the GATT/WTO dispute settlement system resulted from prolonged negotiations that allowed states to consider the long-term effects of changes in the legal regime. Additionally, all three dimensions of legal design changed simultaneously during the transition from the GATT to the WTO. We can therefore only assess the validity of my theory for the GATT/WTO by examining the main implication of my theory: when rational states deliberatively decide to strengthen an adjudicative body like the DSS, they should simultaneously increase the precision of law. In this chapter, I first examine the ways in which the 1995 transition from the GATT to the WTO strengthened the dispute settlement system of the multilateral trade regime. I then examine whether this transition coincided with an increase in the precision of trade law.

The transition to the WTO dramatically changed trade law, incorporating new issues and developing jurisprudence for pre-existing issues. To my knowledge, there are no areas of trade law that became less precise in the transition. However, to be confident of the explanatory value of my theory, I use four criteria to select the legal issues on which I assess my arguments. First, I only examine issues that existed prior to 1995. It would make no sense to examine new issues—such as services, intellectual property, or investment—because there was no baseline level of imprecision that needed to be adjusted in response to the new DSS rules. Second, I focus on issues that were salient in the 1980s and

1990s, when states were negotiating the Uruguay Round agreements. For example, I do not examine GATT provisions that were written in response to 1940s colonialism. Since these provisions were irrelevant in the 1990s, GATT members made no attempt to revise these laws when they designed the WTO. Third, I do not examine areas of law that were highly precise prior to 1995. Some areas of international trade law—such as most-favored nation and national treatment, and the elimination of quantitative restrictions—were sufficiently clear by 1995 that no increase in precision was needed. Finally, I focus on issues that are commonly litigated in the WTO.

This last criterion stacks the deck against my theory. Imprecise laws, by their very nature, create more uncertainty than precise laws. And because uncertainty makes negotiations more difficult, imprecise laws should generate more litigation than precise laws. Stated differently, disputes that involve imprecise laws are more likely to go to trial. This selection effect implies that if we look at trade issues that are often litigated, then we are examining trade issues with relatively imprecise laws. My theory implies that the transition to the WTO should have coincided with an increase in precision. So by looking at commonly litigated issues, I am examining laws that should be difficult for my theory to explain. I am seeking precision in the laws that are least likely to be precise.

Additionally, by focusing on commonly litigated issues, I can be confident that I am analyzing legal areas that states care about for economic or political reasons. And because of their importance, these are issues that any plausible theory of institutional change would need to explain. Three issues satisfy these criteria: safeguards, subsidies and countervailing duties, and antidumping duties. Section 5.5 contains detailed analysis of these three complex areas of law, but some simplified definitions and examples may be helpful to readers at this point.

States can impose *safeguards* if an unforeseen event causes an import surge that harms a domestic industry. For example, a fashion trend in the late 1940s increased the popularity of women's felt hats with fur trimmings. United States milliners could not compete effectively with foreign producers because these hats were labor-intensive and the United States had relatively high labor costs. The United States increased its tariff on these hats so that milliners would be protected from foreign competition. The United States viewed its tariff as legitimate under GATT safeguard rules, but Czechoslovakia—a major exporter of these hats to the United States—disagreed and filed a complaint.[7] Table 5.1 shows that safeguard disputes were relatively rare during the mature GATT era. However, safeguard disputes have become more

Table 5.1: Types of Trade Disputes

Dispute Type	Mature GATT (1980–1994)		WTO (1995–2010)	
	Number	Percentage	Number	Percentage
Safeguards	4	2%	40	10%
Subsidies and Countervailing Duties	30	12%	88	21%
Antidumping	19	8%	85	20%
Total Disputes	245*	–	419	–

* Unable to code 50 GATT cases because of lack of documentation. GATT percentages are based on the full number of 245 disputes.
Source: GATT data compiled from Hudec (1993) and archival records in the Stanford GATT Digital Archive (http://gatt.stanford.edu). WTO data from Horn and Mavroidis (2011).

common and now make up about 10 percent of WTO disputes.

A GATT/WTO member can impose *countervailing duties* if a domestic industry is harmed by a subsidized import. For example, the United States and Canada have a long-standing dispute over softwood lumber. Both countries allow lumber companies to purchase logging rights on government-owned lands. However, Canada charges below-market prices, so lumber production costs are significantly lower in Canada than in the United States. The United States argues that Canada has granted a subsidy that harms the United States lumber industry, so the United States has imposed a countervailing duty that raises the price of Canadian lumber. Canada has filed multiple disputes at the WTO to challenge the legality of the duty.[8] Disputes over subsidies and countervailing duties made up 12 percent of mature GATT disputes, but now make up 21 percent of WTO disputes.

Finally, a member can impose an *antidumping duty* if a domestic industry is harmed by an imported good that is "dumped"—sold below its normal value. Antidumping disputes usually involve complex economic arguments about how to calculate a good's export price and its normal value. These calculations are particularly difficult when goods are imported from a non-market economy. For example, the European Union imposed an antidumping duty on Chinese leather shoes in 2006. China later filed a complaint at the WTO and challenged the EU's methods for calculating the normal value of the shoes.[9] Antidumping disputes made up 8 percent of GATT disputes, and have increased to be 20 percent of WTO disputes.

In sum, these three areas of law are important in the multilateral trade regime. As shown in Table 5.1, over half of WTO disputes involve safeguards, subsidies and countervailing duties, or antidumping duties. My goal in the rest of this chapter is to show that changes in the design of the DSS coincided with increases in the precision of these three legal issues. I argue that strength coincides with precision.

Before proceeding, I should note that the GATT/WTO dispute settlement system has its own distinct terminology. In the GATT/WTO, complainants (not "plaintiffs") can file a dispute against a respondent (not a "defendant"). These disputes are heard by panels (not "courts"), and panel members (not "judges") write reports (not "rulings"). Additionally, the WTO has an Appellate Body (not an "appeals court") at which disputants can challenge a panel report. Both the GATT and the WTO avoid legalist terms and prefer settlements to litigation. Nevertheless, since at least 1980 a panel's primary purpose has been to evaluate factual claims and legal arguments.[10] In this sense, the DSS is an international court in practice, if not in name.[11]

5.4 Strengthening the Dispute Settlement System

Legalization has been the dominant theme of GATT and WTO development. The GATT dispute settlement system began in 1947 as a diplomatic process, in which disputants conducted informal negotiations, known as consultations. Dispute settlement procedures evolved gradually over the subsequent decades. By 1980—the beginning of the mature GATT—members had established a system of informal norms for dispute settlement. This system was relatively weak because GATT voting rules ensured that there was low delegation to panels and low obligation to panel reports. After a series of ineffective minor reforms, states revamped the entire dispute settlement system under the WTO Dispute Settlement Understanding, which took effect in 1995.

The WTO DSS has high delegation to adjudicatory panels and obligation to panel reports. By 1980, GATT members had six different dispute settlement systems. The WTO consolidated these into a single DSS. The WTO also changed the DSS voting procedure, which ensured that respondents could not block dispute settlement. Finally, the WTO created an Appellate Body and detailed procedures for the implementation of DSS reports.

Early Years of the DSS (1947–1979)

The Havana Charter created elaborate dispute settlement rules for the proposed International Trade Organization.[12] Members could refer their disputes to internal committees, nonbinding arbitration, or even the International Court of Justice. However, when the United States Senate refused to ratify the Charter, the international community was left with little guidance on how to resolve trade disputes. The primary mechanism for settling trade disputes during the early years of GATT was thus informal negotiations. The GATT required that each member "afford adequate opportunity for consultation" during a trade dispute.[13] If disputants could not negotiate a "satisfactory solution" on their own, then the dispute could be referred to the member-states as a whole—called the Contracting Parties (CP)—which could consult with individual disputants.[14] If both types of consultations failed, then the GATT specified that a member could make "written representations or proposals," followed by another round of negotiations.[15]

The GATT did not contain any formal procedures for dispute settlement beyond consultations, but an informal DSS slowly evolved from 1947 to 1979.[16] Dispute settlement initially consisted of mediation by the Chairman of the CP or a special working party. Over time, these working parties evolved into panels with *ad hoc* procedures. These panels reviewed legal arguments and wrote nonbinding reports with recommendations. These reports could then be adopted by the CP as binding legal documents.

Throughout this process, the CP used a consensus voting rule: all GATT members had to agree for the CP to take action. Any GATT member—including the respondent—could veto the involvement of the CP in a dispute. A respondent had to both consent to the adjudicative process and voluntarily accept its punishment.[17]

While the GATT DSS did develop slowly from 1947 to 1979, this did not occur in a routinized and predictable fashion. The *ad hoc* nature of dispute settlement ensured that procedures developed for one case did not necessarily apply to others. Even if a panel ruling in one case asserted greater delegation and obligation to the DSS, the ruling did not necessarily apply to how the DSS would operate in the future. It is thus not possible to assess the plausibility of my theory by examining cases from this period. Unlike the ICJ cases above, individual rulings did not change beliefs about how the DSS would function in future cases. Indeed, this lack of consistency is what motivated the GATT members in the 1970s to develop a consistent set of dispute settlement procedures. Hudec (1993, 38) wrote that: "attempts to use [the DSS] seemed to have lurched from crisis to crisis. There was simply not a very strong underlying consensus about the legitimacy of the procedure." One objective of the Tokyo Round negotiations of 1973 to 1979 was "to strengthen the panels by elaborating their procedures and increasing the predictability of their outcome" (Trebilcock and Howse 1995, 385).

Figure 5.2: Mature GATT Dispute Settlement System (1980–1994)

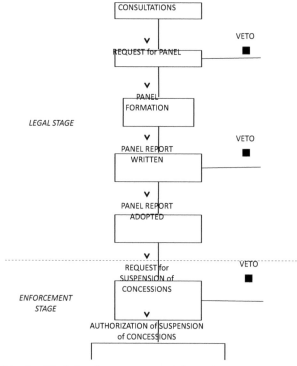

Source: This simplified flowchart was created from the Tokyo Understanding of 1979.

Mature GATT DSS (1980–1994)

A key outcome of the Tokyo Round negotiations was the Tokyo Understanding, which codified dispute settlement procedures.[18] This document was not legally binding on GATT members, but its procedures quickly became standard practice.[19] This codification marked the beginning of a new period in dispute settlement that scholars call the "mature GATT period." Figure 5.2 shows the basic outline of the mature GATT dispute settlement system.

Procedures

During the mature GATT period, the DSS began with a legal stage. The first step in the DSS was informal negotiations. These consultations could be conducted with or without the assistance of a mediator or working party. However, if the disputants could not reach a mutually agreed solution, then the complainant could request that the CP form a panel. Any state, including the respondent, could veto this request. If a panel was formed under a CP vote, its responsibility was to "make an objective assessment of the matter before it."[20] The Tokyo Understanding did not establish any binding deadlines or rules of procedures, instead requiring that "[p]anels set up their own working procedures."[21] After the panel released its written report, the CP could then decide whether to adopt the panel report, thereby granting it legal status. Once again, any state could veto this action.

If a panel report was adopted but the respondent refused to change its behavior, then an enforcement stage began. The complainant could once again refer the dispute to the CP and request authorization to suspend concessions. However, this was considered an extreme response. The Tokyo Understanding emphasized that "[i]n the absence of a mutually agreed solution, the first objective of the [CP] is usually to secure the withdrawal of the measures concerned."[22] Not a single case progressed all the way to authorization of the suspension of concessions during the mature GATT era.[23]

Weaknesses

As shown in Table 5.2, one of the first weaknesses of the mature GATT was the proliferation of multiple dispute settlement systems. The Tokyo Understanding codified the procedures of the GATT's primary DSS. However, the optional Tokyo Codes created new trade rules for issues such as antidumping and countervailing duties. Five of these codes created new dispute settlement systems, but disputes could also be submitted to the GATT DSS.[24] Many disputes involved alleged violations of multiple trade agreements. For example, in 1986 New Zealand disputed the legality of United States duties on imported copper rod and wire.[25] New Zealand argued that the United States had violated GATT Article VI, the Tokyo Antidumping Code, and the Tokyo Subsidies Code, so the dispute fell under the jurisdiction of three different dispute settlement systems. The optional Tokyo Codes created a situation in which "dispute settlement procedures were fragmented ... [and] disputes would occur over which procedure to use"

Table 5.2: Evolution of the Dispute Settlement System

DSS Text	Mature GATT (1980–1994)	WTO (1995–present)
DSS Text	Tokyo Understanding	Dispute Settlement Understanding
Number of Systems	Six*	One
Panel Formation	Consensus**	Negative Consensus
Panel Report Adoption	Consensus	Negative Consensus
Implementation	No Info	Detailed Procedures
Suspension of Concessions	Consensus	Negative Consensus

* In addition to the GATT DSS, the Tokyo Codes established additional issue-specific dispute settlement systems in the areas of: subsidies and countervailing duties, technical barriers, government procurement, customs valuation, and antidumping duties.

** Some Tokyo Codes required automatic formation of panels for issue-specific procedures. However, the consensus voting rule remained in place for the GATT DSS.

(Jackson 2000, 177). Cases could be delayed *ad infinitum* using legal arguments about which DSS (if any) should adjudicate a particular dispute. The existence of six different systems weakened delegation to GATT adjudication because overlapping jurisdictions limited the ability of an individual DSS to rule on a case.

The second major weakness was the consensus voting rule. This rule allowed the respondent to block adjudication anytime that CP action was required. As shown in Figure 5.2, the respondent could veto CP action at three key junctures. First, any member could file a complaint against another member, but all CP had to agree to form a panel. So the respondent could end the dispute settlement process by vetoing the formation of a panel. This limited delegation to the DSS. Next, even if the respondent allowed a panel to hear the case, the respondent could veto the adoption of the panel report if it disagreed with the panel's findings or recommendations. Such a veto ensured that the panel report did not become a binding legal document. This reduced obligation to the DSS because it limited the impact of the DSS on final political outcomes. Finally, if the respondent did not want to implement an adopted panel report, it could veto the complainant's request to suspend concessions. Once again, this limited obligation to the DSS.

It is difficult to quantify the impact of the consensus voting rule on trade disputes because of selection effects. When two states were involved in a trade dispute, both understood the GATT process and voting rule. There was little purpose for a state to file a complaint if it believed that its trading partner would exercise its veto. A leader might sometimes find it beneficial to file a case purely to signal support to domestic interest groups (Allee and Huth 2006*a*). However, in the majority of circumstances, there is little reason for a state to file a dispute if it knew that the dispute would be blocked.

The final major weakness of the GATT DSS was that it lacked formal procedures for implementation of an adopted panel report. The way to implement a report is often clear: the respondent must withdraw the offending measure. However, disputes over implementation are common. For example, a respondent might contend that changing its trade policies is (temporarily) impossible. Alternatively, the original trade policy may be replaced with a new measure to which the complainant also objects. The GATT contained no guidance on how to handle implementation disputes. If a complainant was not satisfied with the respondent's actions, then the complainant's only options were to either seek authorization to suspend concessions or file a new dispute. This absence of an implementation process weakened obligation to the DSS.

Transition to the WTO

The weakness of the GATT dispute settlement system was optimal for the context in which it was created. By 1947, the postwar enthusiasm for multilateralism had waned in many countries, including the United States. GATT member governments valued the flexibility that the GATT provided through legal ambiguity and weak institutionalization (Barton et al. 2006; Jackson 2000). However, this institutional design grew problematic over time. In late 1982, GATT ministers declared that "the multilateral system ... is seriously endangered." One of the primary causes of their gloom was an increase in trade protectionism that sparked a "growing number and intensity of disputes." The ministers identified two primary causes: a "deep and prolonged crisis in the world economy" and continuing "differences of perception regarding ... rights and obligations under the GATT."[26] Both the United States and EC actively tried to strengthen the DSS by changing the consensus voting rule (Hudec 1993, 165). However, the final Ministerial Declaration of 1982 stated that "no major change is required in [the Tokyo] framework." GATT members clarified a few minor details of the Tokyo Understanding, but did not make any significant reforms and "reaffirmed that consensus will continue to be the traditional method of resolving disputes."[27] In 1982, the GATT membership as a whole clearly did not believe that a stronger DSS would enhance the precision of trade law.

Two years later, GATT members returned to the subject of the DSS. The final results were modest. Members granted the Secretary-General the power to appoint panelists if disputants couldn't agree to a panel composition within 30 days. They also urged panels to create procedural deadlines to make the DSS more expeditious.[28] Meanwhile, dispute settlement was included as one of the official subjects of the Uruguay Round trade negotiations, which began in 1986.[29] Some states wanted to strengthen the powers of the DSS, while others were opposed to further legalization of the GATT (Hudec 1993, 200). As a short-term compromise, GATT members adopted an interim DSS agreement in 1989 called the Improvements to the GATT Dispute Settlement Rules and Procedures ("Improvements").[30]

The 1989 Improvements created new legal disputes. They stated that the CP "agree that the existing rules and procedures of the GATT in the field of dispute settlement shall continue."[31] For example, the document explicitly stated that the consensus voting rule still applied to the adoption of panel reports.[32] However, the Improvements did not explicitly assert that the consensus rule still applied to panel formation. The 1989 text stated:

> If the complaining party so requests, **a decision to establish a panel or working party shall be taken** at the latest at the Council meeting following that at which the request first appeared on an item on the Council's regular agenda, **unless** at that meeting **the Council decides otherwise**.[33]

Some GATT members believed that this text removed the consensus voting rule for panel formation. They argued that the text specified that a panel would be formed automatically by the CP unless there was a consensus to not form a panel. However, other states believed that no change had been made in the panel formation process. This provision became a new source of conflict until the WTO was created in 1995 (Hudec 1993, 232–233).

WTO DSS (1995–present)

The WTO Dispute Settlement Understanding (DSU) revolutionized trade adjudication.[34] Despite being a compromise between advocates and opponents of legalization, Van den Bossche (2005, 52) describes

Figure 5.3: WTO Dispute Settlement System (1995–present)

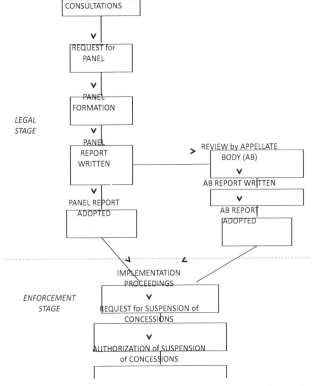

Source: This simplified flowchart was created from the WTO Dispute Settlement Understanding.

the DSU as "arguably the single most important achievement of the Uruguay Round negotiations." Unlike the fragmented Tokyo system, all WTO members "signed and ratified the WTO Agreement as a single undertaking, of which the DSU is a part" (WTO 2004, 8). Members could no longer choose their legal commitments *à la carte*. States had to accept all of the revised rules to become a member of the WTO. Figure 5.3 shows a simplified flowchart of the WTO dispute settlement system.[35]

Procedures

As in the GATT, the legal stage begins with the filing of a complaint, followed by consultations. WTO publications stress that: "the DSU provides a framework in which the parties to a dispute must always at least attempt to negotiate a settlement" (WTO 2004, 6). If disputants are unable to reach a mutually agreed solution, then the complainant can request a panel. As in GATT, a panel hears the case and writes a report that summarizes its findings and recommendations. If either party disagrees with part of the panel report, it may request review by the Appellate Body, which hears the case again and issues its own report. This appellate report can then be adopted. If neither party requests appellate review, then the initial panel report can be adopted.

After a report is adopted, the enforcement stage begins. If an adopted report states that the respondent has nullified or impaired GATT benefits, then the respondent must "bring [his trade] measure into conformity with the covered agreements" or compensate the complainant.[36] Panels and the Appellate Body rule on whether a violation has occurred, but they do not specify how the respondent must behave. There are thus often disputes over how to implement a report. The DSU includes elaborate implementation procedures. Finally, if a respondent refuses to follow the rulings, the complainant can request authorization to suspend concessions.[37]

Strengths

Table 5.2 shows the ways in which the transition to the World Trade Organization strengthened the DSS. First, the DSU reduced the number of dispute settlement systems. The DSU specifies that the WTO has only one dispute settlement system. As the WTO Secretariat clearly states: "The dispute settlement system is compulsory. All WTO [m]embers are subject to it" (WTO 2004, 8). Procedures vary slightly for some specialized legal issues.[38] However, there is no confusion regarding which body is empowered to adjudicate WTO disputes. Complainants can no longer choose between multiple venues for dispute settlement, ensuring that respondents can no longer argue that the DSS lacks jurisdiction over a case. The DSU strengthened delegation by creating a unified DSS with clear authority and jurisdiction to rule on all WTO disputes.

Second, the DSU removed the consensus rule for dispute settlement. Instead of allowing any state—including the respondent—to veto CP decisions, states are now bound by a negative consensus voting rule.[39]

Dispute settlement continues unless all GATT members—including the complainant—agree to stop the process.[40] As shown in Figure 5.3, the respondent cannot veto the formation of a panel, the adoption of a report, or an authorization to suspend concessions. The dispute settlement process can only stop if the complainant drops its case. In the overwhelming majority of cases, this only occurs if the respondent changes its behavior, thus removing the legal basis for the case, or if the disputants negotiate an agreement. For this reason, many scholars describe the steps in the WTO DSS as automatic.[41] The new negative consensus rule strengthened both delegation and obligation to the DSS.

Finally, the DSU strengthened obligation to the DSS by creating implementation rules. The DSU specifies that if removal of a measure is not immediately possible, then the complainant is entitled to temporary compensation. Additionally, it creates an adjudicatory process for disputes about the legality of replacement measures.[42] These rules have created new ways in which the complainant can use a DSS report to change final political outcomes.

The Appellate Body (AB) was created in part to offset some of the political and legal consequences of enhanced legalization. Under the GATT system, if a dispute proceeded to litigation and a disputant disagreed with part of the panel report, it could veto the adoption of the report. Since the transition to WTO eliminated this veto power, states believed that the reformed DSS needed an institutional framework in which a state could challenge an adverse ruling. The Appellate Body was intended to serve this purpose. The AB doesn't offset the effect of the change in voting rules because a state cannot veto AB proceedings or reports. However, it does give states an additional opportunity to plead their case if they disagree with a panel report. Since the WTO operates using *de facto* precedent, the AB should enhance the precision of trade law over time by creating additional and more refined jurisprudence (Palmeter and Mavroidis 2004; Pelc forthcoming).

Overall, the shift from the GATT to the WTO dramatically increased the strength of the DSS. Delegation increased because the WTO DSS has a greater willingness and ability to decide cases than its predecessor. Obligation increased because WTO adjudication has a greater influence on final political outcomes than the GATT DSS.

5.5 Increasing the Precision of International Trade Law

The initial weaknesses of the GATT DSS were optimal in the late 1940s, when GATT members want to preserve their flexibility to respond to domestic political interests. Barton et al. (2006) note that strengthening of the GATT DSS went hand-in hand with enhanced precision of trade rules. While GATT members were initially willing to permit noncompliance with trade rules in order to ensure the stability of the regime, the expansion of GATT membership over time changed the political calculus. Members grew increasingly concerned that the institutional weakness of the GATT "granted new members ... license to ignore the spirit of the rules," and "[i]ncreased legalization led members to specify with greater detail aspects of the trade contract" (Barton et al. 2006). As the DSS grew stronger in 1995, international trade law grew more precise in three areas: safeguards, subsidies and countervailing duties, and antidumping duties.

Safeguards

Safeguards are one way that GATT/WTO members can deviate from their treaty commitments. A GATT/WTO member may violate its previous commitments if unforeseen developments cause an import surge that threatens a domestic industry. States usually implement safeguards through tariff increases or import quotas. If a GATT/WTO member is harmed by another member's safeguard, it can challenge the safeguard's permissibility through the DSS. For example, Czechoslovakia challenged the United States tariff on fur-trimmed felt hats by arguing that the import surge had not caused injury to United States milliners.

During the mature GATT era, the only source of safeguards law was Article XIX of the GATT, which contained four paragraphs.[43] It stated:

> If, as a result of unforeseen developments and of the effect of the [GATT] obligations, ... any product is being imported ... in such **increased quantities** ... as to cause or threaten **serious injury** to domestic producers in that territory of like or directly competitive products, the [GATT member] shall be free ... to suspend the obligation in whole or in part or to withdraw or modify the concession.[44]

Article XIX is notorious for its imprecision. Lee (2005, 18) argues: "The lack of specific and detailed regulations in Article XIX turned out to be a major problem in the discipline of safeguards, since the provisions of Article XIX did not provide sufficient guidelines for a series of important and practical issues in the application of a safeguard measure."

Table 5.3: Major Changes in Safeguards Law

Type	Item	GATT (1947–1994)	WTO (1995–present)
Definitions	Import surge	Ambiguous	Clear definition with criteria
	Serious injury	Ambiguous	Clear definition with criteria
Procedures	Investigation	No info	Required
	Monitoring	Informal CP powers	Committee on Safeguards
Form	Magnitude	No info	Limited
	Duration	No info	Limited
	Selectivity	Ambiguous	Non-discriminatory
	Voluntary export restraints	No info	Prohibited

GATT members attempted to create new safeguards rules during the Tokyo Round negotiations.[45] GATT members agreed that Article XIX was not sufficiently clear or detailed to regulate the growing demand for safeguards in the 1970s. However, members could not agree on a new set of safeguards rules. They were only able to write a nonbinding understanding that slightly enhanced the ability of developing countries to use safeguards for economic development.[46] In the years following the Tokyo Round, GATT members agreed that they needed "to bring into effect a comprehensive understanding on safeguards to be based on the principles of [GATT]."[47] Article XIX reform became an official objective of the Uruguay Round negotiations.

These negotiations ultimately resulted in the WTO Safeguards Agreement.[48] This nine page document has revolutionized safeguards law by dramatically increasing precision in three categories: definitions, procedures, and the form of safeguards. Table 5.3 provides a schema of the major changes in safeguards law.

One of the major sources of imprecision in the GATT was the definition of an import surge and serious injury. These terms are the basis of all safeguards law because they determine when a member can impose safeguards. Article XIX referred to "increased quantities" of imports, but did not specify criteria for identifying import surges. GATT members disagreed about whether the safeguard clause required an absolute or relative increase in imports (or both). Similarly, the GATT was unclear about what constituted serious injury. This was a major issue in the fur-trimmed felt hats dispute. Most milliners produced a wide variety of both men's and women's hats, so the United States could not demonstrate that the increased imports caused a decline in firm profits. Instead, the United States argued that the imports caused an overall decline in aggregate employment in the hat industry. Czechoslovakia countered that many different factors affected the hat industry during this time period, including changes in the production of men's hats. Additionally, Czechoslovakia argued that even if aggregate employment declined, the number of skilled laborers probably increased because the United States production of fur-trimmed felt hats increased. The GATT panel ultimately agreed that the United States's employment argument was inconclusive, but found that the United States hat industry had nevertheless experienced serious injury because the imported hats cost less than their domestic counterparts.[49]

The WTO Safeguards Agreement clarifies the definition of both an import surge and serious injury. The text declares that an import surge occurs if there is either an "absolute or relative" increase in imports.[50] It also includes a list of factors that states must consider when determining injury, including: sales levels, capacity utilization, and employment levels. Finally, it states that "[w]hen factors other than increased imports are causing injury to the domestic industry at the same time, such injury shall not be attributed to increased imports."[51]

GATT Article XIX also lacked precision about procedures for imposing and monitoring safeguards. It required members to notify the CP prior to restricting trade. However, members were not required to conduct an investigation or provide evidence to the GATT that safeguards were needed. GATT members had no constraints on their decision-making process for imposing safeguards. As with all GATT provisions, a state that imposed a safeguard was required to consult with other members if a dispute arose, and the CP could intervene and facilitate negotiations. However, Article XIX did not authorize the CP to monitor safeguards.

In contrast, the WTO Safeguards Agreement contains more detailed procedures. It increases the transparency of state decision-making by requiring states to conduct a public investigation prior to imposing trade protection. It also creates a specialized body to monitor state behavior.

Finally, GATT Article XIX was very imprecise in limiting the form of safeguards. The text contained no limits on the magnitude or duration of trade restrictions. Members could suspend trade concessions "to the extent and for such time as may be necessary to prevent or remedy" an import surge.[52] The importing country decided for itself what was necessary.

The WTO Safeguards Agreement limits the magnitude of safeguards by stating that WTO members "shall apply safeguard measures only to the extent necessary to prevent or remedy a serious injury and to facilitate adjustment."[53] If quotas are used, the Agreement specifies how levels shall be chosen. Additionally, it requires progressive liberalization of safeguards over time. The Safeguard Agreement limits the duration of safeguards to eight years. Once a safeguard is removed, it cannot be reapplied until the passage of a specified period of time.

GATT members disagreed about another aspect of the form of safeguards: whether safeguard measures could be applied selectively to other states. In the late 1970s and early 1980s, automobile manufacturers in the United States and Europe were under siege from a surge in imported Japanese cars. Japanese car manufacturers had substantially lower production costs than their competitors, and the 1979 oil crisis, which drove fuel prices to unprecedented highs, increased demand for the small fuel-efficient cars produced by Toyota, Honda, and Nissan (Clark and Fujimoto 1991, 58–60; Weiss, Hogan, Chai, Meigher, Jr. and Cuneo 1996, 278). Many European countries imposed safeguards on Japanese cars, but not on cars imported from other countries (Bronckers 1985, 111–156). Were such selective safeguards permissible under GATT? The answer to this question depended on how one interpreted the GATT's requirement of most-favored nation (MFN) treatment. MFN requires that if a GATT member extends a benefit to one GATT member, then it must extend the same benefit to all other GATT members. Each member is entitled to the most favorable treatment that is granted to any other member.[54]

Opponents of selectivity argued that if a state imposed a safeguard on imports from some GATT members but not others, then the MFN standard was violated. Under this interpretation, a selective safeguard on Japanese cars would have violated the GATT because would not have treated Japan as favorably as Italy treated other car exporters. In contrast, advocates of selectivity noted that the safeguards clause allowed a threatened state to "suspend [its] obligations."[55] In addition to increasing tariffs or imposing a quota, they argued, a state could suspend its MFN commitment. The debate on this issue was so divided that GATT members were unable to negotiate a new Safeguards Code during the Tokyo Round (Bronckers 1985, 135). The WTO's Safeguard Agreement definitively settled the debate: selective safeguards are not permitted in the WTO. Safeguards must be nondiscriminatory and "applied to a product being imported irrespective of its source."[56]

Finally, members were unsure about the legality of a new form of trade restrictions: voluntary export restraints. The global economic decline of the 1970s tempted many leaders to safeguard their industries by raising tariffs or imposing quotas. However, trading partners were entitled to compensation under Article XIX. Any member that was injured by a safeguard—including the source of the import surge—could suspend "substantially equivalent concessions."[57] To avoid paying such compensation, many states shifted to a new form of protection from import surges: voluntary export restraints.

In a voluntary export restraint (VER), an exporter voluntarily limited the amount of a good that it sold in a foreign market.[58] Importers did not directly violate their GATT commitments because the exporter restricted the supply of goods, not the importer. These agreements were made between governments, industry groups, or both.

For example, the United States could have imposed a safeguard on Japanese cars in the late 1970s and early 1980s. However, the United States and Japan instead signed an VER in May 1981 in which Japan voluntarily limited the number of automobiles that it exported to the United States. This restriction kept the price of cars artificially high in the United States market, and temporarily protected the United States automobile industry as it shifted to production of smaller cars (such as the Chevrolet Nova), adopted new production technologies, and waited for the oil crisis to pass. Meanwhile, Japanese auto manufacturers increased their profits by charging prices significantly above their own marginal cost of production.

GATT members disagreed about whether VERs were permissible under GATT. Quantitative restrictions were being voluntarily imposed by the exporter, not the importer. So VERs were not explicitly covered by Article XIX. The GATT contained no legal provision that banned or regulated VERs. Nonetheless, experts believed that "many and probably most [VERs were] more than likely inconsistent with the obligations of GATT."[59] The WTO Safeguards Agreement removed this ambiguity by prohibiting all voluntary export restraints involving governments. It did not prohibit VERs between industries, but WTO members could not "encourage or support" such export restrictions.[60]

Overall, the transition from the GATT to the WTO enhanced the precision of safeguards law. This new agreement clarified legal definitions, created new procedures for investigating and monitoring safeguards, and restricted the form of safeguards.

Subsidies and Countervailing Duties

Governments often provide subsidies—specialized benefits or assistance—to their industries. The GATT defines a subsidy quite broadly as "any form of income or price support" provided by a government.[61] There are two types of subsidies: export subsidies and domestic subsidies. Export subsidies "are granted only to products when they are exported" (Jackson 1997, 279). In contrast, domestic subsidies "are granted for the benefit of products regardless of whether those products are exported or not" (Jackson 1997, 280). Subsidies usually lower—directly or indirectly—the market price of a good. If a GATT/WTO member imports a subsidized good, then it is more difficult for domestic producers to compete.

GATT/WTO members can impose countervailing duties (CVDs) if a domestic industry is harmed by subsidized imports.[62] These additional duties offset any "subsidy bestowed directly, or indirectly, upon the manufacture, production or export of any merchandise."[63] To impose a CVD, a state must first establish that an injury has occurred because of a foreign subsidy, and then determine the size of the subsidy so that it imposes a CVD of the appropriate magnitude. Subsidies and CVDs are routinely challenged in the DSS.

When the mature GATT era began in 1980, there were two sets of rules for subsidies and countervailing duties: the GATT and the Tokyo Subsidies Code.[64] While some GATT members chose to join the Code, others did not. The WTO has consolidated its rules in the Agreement on Subsidies and Countervailing Measures (the "SCM Agreement").[65] As shown in Table 5.4, the transition from the mature GATT to the WTO enhanced precision in five areas: the coverage of legal commitments, the definition of a subsidy, the regulation of subsidies, the use of CVDs, and the procedures for dispute resolution.

One major source of ambiguity during the mature GATT was the coverage of legal commitments. Any country that joined the GATT was subject to its rules. However, when the GATT was signed in 1947, its members believed that the Havana Charter would soon take effect. Many countries, including the United States, did not want to go through the domestic ratification process twice. So members adopted the GATT rules using an executive agreement known as the Protocol of Provisional Application. Signatories needed to ensure that the new GATT rules did not conflict with pre-existing domestic trade laws because neither the Protocol nor the GATT itself were ratified by a domestic legislature. So negotiators included a loophole in the Protocol called the "grandfather clause." This clause specifies that certain

Table 5.4: Major Changes in Countervailing Duties Law

Type	Item	GATT (1947–1994)	Tokyo (1980–1994)	WTO (1995–present)
Coverage	Members covered?	Most*	Some (optional)	All
Definition	What is a subsidy?	Undefined	Examples provided	Defined
Subsidies Regulation	Export: primary products	Prohibited if not equitable share	Prohibited if not equitable share, or materially lowers prices	Prohibited**
	Export: non-primary products	Prohibited if price distortion	Prohibited	Prohibited
	Domestic	No info	Allowed	Allowed, unless adverse effects or contingent on use of domestic goods
CVDs	Investigation procedures	No info	Some rules	Detailed rules
	Injury standard	Imprecise	Factors specified	Expanded description
	Size of subsidy	No info	No info	Detailed rules
Disputes	System	GATT	GATT or Tokyo	WTO

* Some countries exempt under the grandfather clause of the Protocol of Provisional Application.
** Subsidies on agricultural products are excluded from the prohibition.

portions of the GATT—including rules on subsidies and countervailing duties—only applied "to the fullest extent not inconsistent with existing legislation."[66] For example, when GATT was signed, the United States already had domestic laws about CVDs.[67] So the United States was exempt from GATT rules in this area until 1980, when it signed the Tokyo Subsidies Code and rewrote its domestic CVD laws. The GATT rules thus applied to most members, but not to all.

The optional Tokyo Subsidies Code exacerbated this imprecision. Some GATT members signed the Code, while others chose not to accept the additional rights and responsibilities. However, GATT requires its members to provide most-favored nation (MFN) status to all other GATT members. This created a legal puzzle: were Code members required to extend their optional concessions to all GATT members under the MFN standard? The United States and many other states argued that those who refused to sign the optional codes were not entitled to the benefits conferred by these codes (Hudec 1993, 120–123). In contrast, the GATT CP declared that MFN privileges extended to the new Tokyo codes: GATT members could not selectively withhold Tokyo concessions from non-Tokyo members.[68] The United States refused to accept this declaration with respect to the new Subsidies Code. Hudec (1993, 486–487) wrote: "the [United States] government concluded that the code granted too many exceptions to developing countries, and so took the position that it would not grant developing countries the benefit of Subsidies Code concessions unless they gave an additional bilateral commitment on eliminating export subsidies." Those countries that did not make additional concessions on subsidies would not gain the benefit of the United States concessions on CVDs. This led to GATT litigation between the United States and India when the United States refused to require an injury test for CVDs placed on Indian exports.[69] Over time, frustrations mounted about the implications of having optional GATT agreements.

This issue was resolved when states created the WTO. Since the WTO agreements were treated as a single undertaking, every WTO member is subject to the SCM Agreement: there are no grandfather clauses and no member may selectively opt out of SCM commitments. Of course, the decision to create a single undertaking had another key benefit: it allowed states to link issues together in a way that expanded the scope and depth of legal commitments (Davis 2003; Steinberg 2002). The WTO agreements clarified the coverage of legal commitments since states can no longer disagree about which legal commitments apply to which members. All WTO members are covered by the SCM Agreement.

The second source of ambiguity was the definition of a subsidy. The GATT did not contain a definition of the term, so members could avoid GATT regulations by declaring that a challenged policy was not a subsidy. Additionally, disagreement about the definition of subsidy led to disputes about the legality of CVDs. In the late 1950s and early 1960s many developed countries agreed on a list of specific policies that they considered to be subsidies.[70] However, most developing countries refused to accept these guidelines, and the developed countries continued to have disputes over the term. For example, many GATT members, such as the EC and Japan, imposed taxes on goods sold within their markets, but exempted exported goods. In the late 1970s, the U.S. Customs Court ruled that these exemptions were subsidies, thereby allowing the United States to impose CVDs on these products. Japan filed a complaint at the GATT and argued that its tax exemption was not a subsidy.[71]

The Tokyo Code attempted to clarify the definition of subsidy by including an "illustrative and nonexhaustive" list of subsidies.[72] Nevertheless, states continued to disagree about what was a subsidy. Bourgeois (1988, 229) wrote that this imprecision led "to increased, if not almost total, reliance on unilateral [CVDs]" by importers of subsidized products, instead of effective international regulation. Additionally, because the Code was two-track—that is, CVD restrictions were contained in a different section of the Code than subsidy regulations—members debated whether the subsidy examples provided in the regulatory section of the Code also applied to the CVD portion of the agreement (Jackson 1997, 288; Jackson 2000, 94). This ambiguity was never fully resolved. Trebilcock and Howse (1995, 128) wrote: "The main weakness in the Code is that there is no clear definition of a countervailable subsidy. Because of the Code's silence on this issue, countries are given a great deal of latitude in defining 'subsidy' for countervailing duty purposes."

The WTO's SCM Agreement contains a detailed definition of a subsidy that has reduced, although not eliminated, conflict between states.[73] A subsequent WTO panel wrote that: "the inclusion of this detailed and comprehensive definition of the term 'subsidy' is generally considered to represent one of the most important achievements of the Uruguay Round in the area of subsidy disciplines."[74]

The third area of imprecision was the regulation of subsidies. GATT regulations were relatively lax. The GATT separated subsidies into three classes that each had a different legal standard: domestic subsidies, export subsidies for primary products, and export subsidies for non-primary products. Domestic subsidies were not mentioned in the GATT at all. The Tokyo Subsidies Code later clarified that domestic subsidies were permissible.

Under GATT, export subsidies for primary products—such as farm, fishery, and mineral products—were allowed, but the GATT required that:

> such [a] subsidy shall not be applied in a manner which results in [the subsidizing nation] having more than an **equitable share** of world export trade in that product.[75]

However, the GATT text did not instruct members on how to determine what is an "equitable share." The treaty specifies that members should consider the share of trade during a "previous representative period," but there were no restrictions on how this representative period should be determined. The treaty also allowed states to consider unspecified "special factors." The Toyko Subsidies Code was slightly stricter: export subsidies for primary products were prohibited if they violated the equitable share standard or materially lowered prices. However, both the GATT and the Tokyo Code were plagued by uncertainty about the meaning of "equitable share" (Jackson 1997, 286).

For example, in the 1950s France had an elaborate agricultural price control system in which wheat and wheat flour producers sold their goods to a government agency, which then resold the goods on the domestic and world market.[76] French wheat and wheat flour exports soared in the mid-1950s. In 1952, French exports of wheat and wheat flour constituted 0.5 and 5.8 percent, respectively, of the world total. By 1955, French exports had risen to 10.9 and 14.1 percent of the world market.[77] Australia, another major wheat exporter, filed a GATT complaint. The GATT panel found that the French system constituted an export subsidy, and then considered whether France had "more than an equitable share of world export trade."[78] France argued that World War II was a special factor that reduced wheat exports in the 1940s and early 1950s, so the panel should treat the late 1930s as the previous representative period. The panel ultimately ruled against France.

Export subsidies for non-primary products—such as manufactured goods—were prohibited under GATT if they created a price distortion in which the exported good was sold "at a price lower than the comparable price charged for the like product in the domestic market."[79] The Tokyo Subsidies Code went a step further and banned all export subsidies on non-primary products. This ban led to disputes about whether a subsidized good was a primary product. For example, in the early 1980s the United States was involved in a dispute with the European Community over subsidies for pasta exporters.[80] The United States argued that pasta was a non-primary good, so the EC subsidies were prohibited under the Tokyo Subsidies Code. However, the EC claimed that it was subsidizing pasta producers for the cost of the durum wheat, a primary product, used to make pasta. A GATT panel ultimately ruled in favor of the United States, finding that "durum wheat incorporated in pasta products could not be considered as a separate 'primary product' and that the EEC export refunds paid to exporters of pasta products could not be considered to be paid on the export of durum wheat."[81] However, this conclusion was so divisive within the broader membership that the GATT never adopted the panel report (Hudec 1993, 494).

The WTO dramatically simplified the regulation of most subsidies by banning all non-agricultural export subsidies.[82] States no longer need to debate the meaning of terms like "equitable share." In contrast to the GATT and the Tokyo Code, the WTO restricts the use of some domestic subsidies. A domestic subsidy is prohibited if it requires "the use of domestic over imported goods."[83] All other domestic subsidies are classified according to whether they are "specific to an enterprise or industry or group of enterprises or industries."[84] For example, subsidies that promote Pennsylvania steel production are specific, while educational and infrastructure spending are not. If a domestic subsidy is specific, then it is prohibited if it creates "adverse effects to the interests of other members."[85] The SCM Agreement contains detailed criteria for determining whether a subsidy is specific, and a definition of adverse effects. All other domestic subsidies are permitted by the WTO.

The mature GATT period also had ambiguous rules about the use of countervailing duties. A GATT member could impose CVDs if the effect of foreign subsidization was "to cause or threaten **material injury** to an established domestic industry, or ... to retard materially the establishment of a domestic industry." The GATT contained no guidelines or restrictions on how a member investigated claims that a subsidy has caused material injury. Similarly, it did not provide a definition of material injury, but it did outline some circumstances in which a state cannot claim material injury.[86] Finally, the GATT provided no rules about how states should determine the size of a subsidy. CVDs could not exceed the amount necessary to offset the harm caused by a foreign subsidy. However, the lack of constraints on determining the size of a subsidy left GATT members with tremendous discretion in the choosing the magnitude of their CVDs.

The Tokyo Code modestly enhanced precision on these issues. It specified basic procedures that states must use during CVD investigations. In particular, it mandated that the importer and exporter must hold consultations before a formal investigation began. The Code also specified factors for determining whether a countervailable injury has occurred, including the volume of imports, the effect of the subsidy on prices, and the impact of the subsidy on industry-specific measures (such as output, investment return, cash flow, and employment levels). However, the Code contained no guidelines for determining the size of the subsidy.

The WTO's SCM Agreement contains more detailed rules about the use of CVDs. First, it contains precise restrictions on CVD investigations. Public notice provisions have been strengthened and final determinations must now be subject to domestic judicial review. WTO members are required to immediately terminate CVD investigations if there is not support from a sufficiently large portion of the affected industry or if subsidies are sufficiently small. The agreement contains elaborate new procedures for the collection, presentation, and consideration of evidence, and gives WTO members the right to submit information to investigating authorities. The SCM Agreement also has greater detail on the determination of injury. It includes new standards for establishing whether there is a threat of material injury, and new restrictions on assessing the cumulative effect of subsidies across multiple countries. Finally, the SCM Agreement contains guidelines for determining the size of a subsidy. WTO members still contest how these rules apply to non-market economies, yet the SCM Agreement is a significant improvement on its predecessor agreements.

The last area of imprecision during the mature GATT era was dispute settlement. The Tokyo Subsidies Code created a new dispute settlement system that applied only to Code members. Under the new Code, subsidizing members could be required to compensate any other members who suffered negative externalities from a subsidy, even if the subsidy was allowed. So Code members could use this new specialized DSS to both challenge the legality of subsidies, and to secure compensation if a subsidy nullified or impaired their benefits. Tokyo members were entitled to consultations, and unresolved disputes could be referred to the new Subsidies Committee. The one major procedural change from the GATT dispute settlement system was the removal of the consensus rule for the formation of a panel. No disputant could veto the creation of a panel to hear a dispute under the Tokyo DSS. However, the consensus voting rule was preserved for all other decisions, including recommendations by the Committee and the authorization of the suspension of concessions.

At the same time, all members could use the GATT dispute settlement system for disputes involving the GATT. This created ambiguity about the relationship between the GATT DSS and the specialized Tokyo DSS. Both legal and policy experts worried that these dual systems could lead to conflict (McRae and Thomas 1983, 79–80; Bliss 1987, 41). For example, a disputant who was unhappy with the outcome of one set of procedures might seek a contradictory ruling from the other DSS. The Code did not specify how these two systems related to one another and what should be done if the same dispute were filed under both systems. Even if the two systems heard different cases, there was also concern that these two systems might develop conflicting legal interpretations and standards. Panelists at the GATT were not formally bound to prior reports by a doctrine of *stare decisis*. However, both panelists and states were careful to be respectful of prior reports. Jackson (2000, 38–42) has frequently referred to the GATT years as a constitutional period in which a body of trade law evolved via accumulated panel reports, rather than formal written treaties.

The WTO's SCM Agreement eliminated the Tokyo DSS. All disputes are covered by the WTO dispute settlement system. Disputants can no longer engage in forum-shopping across different adjudicatory institutions within the multilateral trade regime.[87]

Overall, the WTO regulations on subsidies and countervailing duties are substantially more sophisticated and precise than their GATT predecessors. Many challenges and imprecisions remain in the SCM Agreement. In particular, WTO has continued the earlier GATT practice of treating regulation and CVDs as separate issues. The overlapping legal standards are, at best, convoluted. However, observers are unified in noting that the WTO rules are "more fully elaborated" than previous versions and "a substantial improvement" on the GATT and Tokyo Subsidies Code (Trebilcock and Howse 1995, 38; Jackson 1997, 290).

Antidumping Duties

The final issue that I examine is antidumping (AD) duties.[88] Sometimes producers dump their goods—sell them "at less than [their] normal value"—in foreign markets.[89] Consumers in the importing country benefit from the low price of these goods. However, domestic producers that compete with imported goods are harmed by dumping if they are unable to match these prices. Dumping is permissible under GATT and WTO rules. Nonetheless, the GATT and WTO allow states to impose AD duties to protect domestic producers. Historically, the most frequent users of AD duties are the United States, EC, Australia, and Canada, but AD duties are now commonly used by developing countries such as China, India, and Mexico.

Exporters often challenge the permissibility of AD duties by arguing that their goods were not dumped, or that the importer's domestic producers have not experienced sufficient harm to warrant a restriction on trade. As mentioned in section 5.3, it is very difficult to determine the normal value of a good that is imported from a non-market economy. Since China's accession to the WTO in 2001, it has filed many disputes that challenge the methods that other countries use to determine the normal value of Chinese goods.

Table 5.5: Major Changes in Antidumping Duties Law

Type	Item	GATT (1947–1994)	Tokyo (1980–1994)	WTO (1995–present)
Coverage	Members covered?	Most*	Some (optional)	All
Definitions	Export price	Undefined	Guidelines	No change
	Normal value	Criteria specified	More detailed standards	Very detailed standards
AD Duties	Investigation procedures	No info	Some rules	Expanded rules
	Injury standard	Imprecise	Factors specified	Expanded rules
Disputes	System	GATT	Tokyo and GATT	WTO

* Some countries exempt under the grandfather clause of the Protocol of Provisional Application.

GATT antidumping law was articulated in Article VI, which stated that:

> dumping, by which products of one country are introduced into the commerce of another country at less than the **normal value** of the products, is to be condemned if it causes or threatens **material injury** in an established industry.[90]

During the mature GATT era, many GATT members joined the optional Tokyo AD Code, which created a second set of AD rules.[91] As shown in Table 5.5, the WTO Antidumping Agreement enhanced precision in four areas: the coverage of legal commitments, the definition of legal terms, the use of AD duties, and the procedures for dispute resolution.[92]

The evolution of AD coverage echoed that of subsidies and CVDs. Before the WTO, many members were exempt from GATT rules under the grandfather clause, and the Tokyo AD Code led to MFN disputes similar to those described above. These problems were resolved in 1995 when the WTO AD Agreement took effect. All WTO members are subject to the AD Agreement, so there are no more debates about the coverage of AD rules.

The mature GATT era also had imprecise definitions of export price and normal value. These definitions are very important for two reasons. First, they are the basis for determining whether dumping has occurred. Second, they establish limits on the size of AD duties.

These duties cannot exceed the difference between the export price and the normal value. This difference is usually referred to as the dumping margin. AD duties can only offset the injury caused by dumping; they cannot be used for punitive purposes.

Finger (1993, 30) writes: "[c]omparing home price with export price and then determining if any detected difference has caused injury to an industry in the importing country looks at first glance like a straightforward operation. But the operation's simplicity disappears quickly under any kind of scrutiny." For example, how should a government determine the export price or normal value of a good that is sold to multiple buyers at different prices? Similarly, how should a government estimate the costs of production for a good that is made in a non-market economy? How much profit should be added to this production cost to determine an overall constructed value? Numerous additional difficulties can arise if a firm is exporting its goods to a foreign affiliate or subsidiary, particularly when these exports are intermediate goods that are used to make other products (Jackson 1997, 251–252).

The GATT did not provide any guidance on how to determine the export price of a good. However, it did contain some modest criteria for determining the normal value of a good. The Tokyo rules refined the GATT text, but countries continued to dispute the proper method for determining normal value and export price. These definitions continue to be the basis for many WTO disputes, but the AD Agreement has clarified the earlier antidumping definitions. The WTO text on export prices is equivalent to the Tokyo AD Code. However, the WTO text contains extensive new rules on how members should calculate normal value. Additionally, the AD Agreement contains new rules on the "fair comparison" of normal value and export price.[93] These include restrictions on how countries convert currencies and compare weighted average prices.

The transition from the GATT to the WTO also enhanced the precision of rules on the use of AD duties. Before applying an AD duty, a GATT member first had to investigate whether dumping had occurred, but the GATT provided no constraints on these investigations. For example, United States antidumping rules in the 1960s—when AD duties became increasingly common—contained a complex sequence of procedures (Dale 1980, 14–15 and 71–72). Exporters criticized the United States because they believed that these procedures led to excessive delay, which was costly for exporters. United States importers were less likely to buy goods under investigation because they were uncertain about whether the government would impose an AD duty on these goods.[94] The Tokyo AD Code imposed some rules on AD investigations. But members still had tremendous discretion in how they conducted AD investigations, and most observers believed that these investigations were biased against imported goods.

In contrast, the WTO has expanded rules for AD investigations. The AD Agreement includes detailed constraints on the investigation process. Additionally, the text requires a minimum level of industry support and grants exporters enhanced rights to intervene at various stage of AD investigations. WTO members continue to have diverse procedures, but the increased precision of WTO rules has reduced uncertainty about domestic AD investigations.

To impose AD duties, members had to determine that an industry had experienced material injury. As with countervailing duties, the GATT provided no definition for material injury.[95] GATT members had tremendous discretion in determining whether a domestic industry had suffered sufficient harm to warrant AD duties. For example, the United States, which was exempt under the grandfather clause, required only "injury"—not "material injury"—for the use of AD duties. Additionally, United States law allowed for the segmentation of domestic markets, rather than requiring injury for a domestic industry as a whole. Such segmentation made it easier for investigators to demonstrate injury. The lack of clear and uniform law about the injury standard created inconsistency and uncertainty about the interpretation of the GATT AD regulations (Jackson 1997, 267; Dale 1980, 72).

The Tokyo AD Code contained some criteria for the injury standard. Signatories were required to consider the volume, effect, and impact of dumping, and to separate the impact of dumping from other factors that might be causing harm to an industry. The text also constrained a definition of domestic industry. But the Code was unclear on many questions. For example, Tokyo members lacked guidance about whether they could impose AD duties if the dumping margin or volume of dumped goods was small (Bierwagen 1990, 93). Additionally, the Tokyo text lacked clear guidelines on how members should treat goods that were dumped by multiple different exporting countries.[96] Did investigators need to prove that dumping by each exporting country caused material injury, or could they assess injury by examining the aggregate impact of a dumped good?

Although some ambiguities remain, the WTO has more detailed rules about injury. Investigating authorities must continue to consider the volume, effect, and impact of dumping, but the WTO rules contain a list of additional factors that "the authorities should consider" when determining injury.[97] The AD Agreement requires that investigations be automatically terminated if the dumping margin or volume of dumped goods is negligible, and restricts how members assess dumping by multiple exporters.

Finally, the transition to the WTO reduced uncertainty about dispute resolution. As with subsidies and CVD rules, AD rules were adjudicated by two different dispute settlement systems during the Tokyo period of the GATT. Under the WTO, only one DSS is permitted to consider alleged violations of the AD Agreement. States no longer have the option of choosing among multiple dispute settlement systems.

Antidumping disputes are common in the WTO, probably because the use of AD duties has risen dramatically. Nonetheless, antidumping rules are more precise than their predecessors in the coverage of legal commitments, the definition of legal terms, the use of AD duties, and the procedures for dispute resolution.

Alternative Explanations

The sections above—on safeguards, subsidies and countervailing duties, and antidumping duties—show that states increased the precision of international trade law during the transition from the GATT to the WTO. My theory provides one possible explanation for this behavior: rational states chose to increase precision, at least in part, because enhanced delegation and obligation to the DSS threatened the settlement of trade disputes and the stability of cooperation. However, an alternative explanation is possible: perhaps both the strengthening of the DSS and the increased precision were caused by a desire to promote trade liberalization. That is, perhaps states wrote more precise laws in order to close permissive loopholes in the original GATT text.[98]

Many of the legal changes detailed above support this view. For example, the WTO rules have severely constrained the use of subsidies. Similarly, the WTO rules for safeguards, countervailing duties, and antidumping duties all impose procedural requirements that were missing from the earlier GATT rules. These requirements have presumably constrained trade protection by states that previously lacked restrictive domestic procedures. However, the WTO's precision has not consistently supported trade liberalization. Some WTO rules are both more precise and more permissive of trade protectionism than their GATT predecessors.

One example in which the WTO's precise rules are more permissive is the compensation rules for safeguards. As discussed above, Article XIX of GATT 1947 allowed an importing state to impose safeguards if an import surge threatened a domestic industry. However, the importing country was required to compensate any exporting country that was harmed by the safeguard. Ideally, a country that imposed a safeguard on one good would compensate its trading partners by granting trade concessions on other goods that flowed between the two countries. If such compensation was not provided within ninety days, then the exporting country could retaliate by imposing its own trade barriers on goods from the safeguarding country.[99] As documented by Pelc (2009), such compensation was routine in the early decades of the GATT. The GATT safeguard rules were thus relatively restrictive. Even if an importing country satisfied the legal criteria in Article XIX and imposed a legitimate safeguard, it was required to compensate its partners.

In contrast, the WTO's Safeguards Agreement is more permissive. In many circumstances, WTO members are allowed to impose safeguards without providing any compensation for three years.[100] The permissiveness of the WTO's safeguards rule is no accident. As Bown (2002, 51) documents: "the safeguards provisions under the WTO were designed to be more attractive than their predecessor." While the transition from the GATT to the WTO dramatically increased the precision of trade rules, it did not always lead to rules that promoted trade liberalization. In some cases, states chose to write rules that were both precise and that promoted trade protection.

5.6 Conclusion

Strong international courts come with hidden costs. If two disputants have common beliefs about how a court will rule on their case, then they should always be able to reach a negotiated settlement, regardless of the court's strength. However, when two disputants have differing beliefs about how a court will rule, they are less likely to reach a settlement and more likely to go to trial. When a court is relatively weak—because it has low levels of delegation and obligation—uncertainty about the court's behavior plays only a small role in pre-trial negotiations. Uncertainty about how a court will rule is relatively unimportant if the court is unlikely to hear the case and if its ruling will have only a small impact on final political outcomes. However, when a court grows stronger, uncertainty becomes more important because the court is more likely to rule on the merits and its ruling will have a larger effect on political outcomes. Strong courts thus make it more difficult for states to settle their disputes via diplomatic negotiations. Precision has the opposite effect on state behavior. Precision reduces uncertainty about how a court will rule, which facilitates pre-trial settlement.

A stronger court imposes a larger cost on a state that has violated its commitments and wishes to remain a member of the regime in the future. When it is relatively easy for a state to cooperate—because it has a low cost of cooperation—increasing the cost of dispute settlement makes compliance more likely. Strong courts thus enhance compliance with regime rules. However, when it is more difficult for a state to cooperate, compliance becomes infeasible. In such a situation, increasing the cost of dispute settlement makes the state more likely to exit the treaty regime. Strong courts thus reduce regime stability.

My discussion of the ICJ allowed me to assess some of these theoretical relationships by examining how unexpected rulings affected state behavior in the shadow of the court. However, one weakness of these examples is that they rely on relatively small and idiosyncratic changes in court behavior. Individual rulings had only a small effect because they only applied to cases that were similar to those on which the court ruled. These cases did not lead to major changes in institutional design.

In contrast, the transition from the GATT to the WTO in 1995 is perhaps the most important example ever of institutional change. Many of the factors that make the transition such an important example— including the prolonged and deliberative design process, and the sweeping reforms that were all implemented in 1995—make it impossible to directly test my arguments. Rather than testing Propositions 2, 6, and 7 from the theory, this chapter examined the plausibility of an implication of my argument: that strong courts should have precise laws.

The relationship between strength and precision is clear in the transition from the GATT to the WTO. The creation of the WTO in 1995 significantly strengthened delegation and obligation to the regime's dispute settlement system. Regime members can no longer unilaterally veto the formation of a panel, the adoption of a panel report, or the authorization to suspend concessions. This transition from a weak to a strong court was accompanied by enhanced precision of trade law. WTO agreements on safeguards, subsidies and countervailing duties, and antidumping duties are much more precise than their GATT predecessors for three reasons. First, a single set of rules now applies to all WTO members, rather than the complex web of *à la carte* rules from the mature GATT era. Second, the WTO agreements have increased the precision of legal definitions and procedural rules at both the domestic and international level. Finally, the elimination of the specialized Tokyo dispute settlement systems has ensured that all disputes are adjudicated under a common set of rules. In sum, enhanced delegation and obligation to the GATT/WTO went hand-in-hand with enhanced precision of international trade law.

6

Designing International Courts

6.1 Introduction

International institutions can help states to cooperate by reducing transaction costs and uncertainty about state behavior (Keohane 1982, 1984). By delegating authority to international bodies, states can shift issues and disputes from the political to the technocratic realm (Johns and Pelc 2014b). International law facilitates cooperation by specifying rules for appropriate behavior and creating formal and informal institutions that determine the consequences for rule violations. Institutions can help states to reduce uncertainty by monitoring state behavior, yet they also create a new source of uncertainty: uncertainty about how the institution will behave. Courts can determine if a member has committed a legal violation and how the international community should respond to a violation. Both delegation and obligation magnify the importance of uncertainty about how the court will rule. While litigation can provide public benefits by clarifying and developing jurisprudence, in any given case it represents a bargaining failure: rather than settling their dispute through diplomatic negotiations, states instead wage costly litigation. Strengthening international courts heightens the importance of uncertainty about how they will rule and hence makes pre-trial settlements less likely. In contrast, as the rules of a legal regime become more precise, uncertainty decreases and states are more likely to reach early settlements.

Cooperation creates opportunities for a state to violate its agreements, harming other states. When it is relatively easy for a state to cooperate, the temptation to violate is small enough that the state will always choose to either comply with regime rules or violate the rules and engage in dispute settlement. Strengthening international courts thus boosts compliance by increasing the cost of dispute settlement. In contrast, when cooperation is relatively difficult because a government faces intense political or economic pressure to violate a treaty, compliance is not feasible. A state will break the regime's rules and then either participate in dispute settlement or leave the regime altogether. Because stronger courts make dispute settlement more costly, strengthening international courts reduces the stability of international cooperation.

The design of a legal regime can change over time for both internal and external reasons. Sometimes judges try to internally change delegation or obligation to their court through jurisprudence. Unexpected rulings can change state beliefs about the court's future behavior. Chapter 4 examined two such examples from the International Court of the Justice. In the *South West Africa* case, the international community expected that the Court would condemn the Union of South Africa for maladministration of South West Africa. However, after a single judge recused himself, the Court issued a dramatic and unexpected ruling: the Court abruptly dismissed the case using reasoning that limited its ability to hear future decolonization cases. This ruling was a self-inflicted wound that haunted the ICJ for decades. No future colonial disputes were filed at the ICJ, the Union of South Africa increased its defiance of international law, and the membership of the Court remained stable. In contrast, ICJ judges issued rulings in the consular relations cases of 1998–2004 that progressively strengthened delegation and obligation to the Court. The United States initially tried to comply with the relevant law. However, as the Court grew stronger, litigation against the United States increased and the cost of remaining within the regime grew higher. Eventually, the United States exited the jurisdiction of the Court.

While court strength can sometimes change for idiosyncratic reasons, such as the recusal of a single judge in the ICJ's *South West Africa* case, at other times states will negotiate complex changes to the design of an institution. Chapter 5 examined an external change by analyzing the transition from the GATT to the WTO in 1995. When states redesigned the multilateral trading regime, they changed a voting rule for dispute settlement and required that members treat all WTO agreements as a single undertaking. These changes dramatically increased delegation and obligation to the dispute settlement system. At the same time, GATT members completely rewrote the substantive laws that the DSS oversees. Chapter 5 showed that the strengthening of the DSS coincided with a systematic attempt to increase the precision of trade law on three important issues: safeguards, subsidies and countervailing duties, and antidumping duties.

My theoretical arguments identify the hidden costs of legalization, but they do not suggest that we should abandon the enterprise of legalization. Some cooperation is better than none, so any court, regardless of its design, is better than having no court whatsoever. What my arguments suggest is that design matters: the attributes of a legal regime shape how states cooperate. The relevant question is not *should we have courts?*—it is *how should we design courts to promote international cooperation?* Individual states will evaluate the trade-offs between settlement, compliance, and stability differently. Each state's political and economic situation will affect how it balances the benefits of short-term compliance against costs of long-term instability and reduced settlement. No institutional design is optimal across all circumstances. Nonetheless, my theoretical argument has policy implications for the design of international law and courts. These implications do not uniformly support or oppose legalization. We must adopt a more nuanced perspective.

6.2 Policy Implications

Stronger Courts Are Not Always Better

Strong international courts have both positive and negative effects on international cooperation. Courts with high levels of delegation or obligation ultimately result in high dispute settlement costs for treaty violators. If a state finds it relatively easy to cooperate, strong courts increase compliance. However, if a state is experiencing tough times, then the benefits of cooperation are relatively low compared to the costs and the state may be best off by leaving the regime. Exit is more likely in regimes with strong courts. Weak courts do not have the same ability to compel compliance. However, they have two important benefits: they facilitate the early settlement of disputes and they increase the stability of the cooperative regime. States are less likely to leave weak courts during tough times, which can make states more willing to join the cooperative regime if they anticipate future instability (Rosendorff and Milner 2001). Weak courts can sometimes be more effective than strong courts in promoting international cooperation.

The International Court of Justice is often lambasted for its controversial 1966 ruling that dismissed the *South West Africa* dispute. African nations subsequently refrained from joining the Court and submitting cases to it. However, consider the alternative: suppose the ICJ had heard the case. Before 1966, African nations with black-majority rule were optimistic that the Court would help abolish white-minority rule in other parts of Africa. Successful intervention by the Court in the *South West Africa* dispute would likely have had two key effects. First, Court intervention would have encouraged new lawsuits about the African territories still under white-minority rule. Second, intervention would have opened the door to new lawsuits about prior colonial administration. The ICJ could not risk offending the developed European nations—most of which were current or former colonial powers—that were the base of the ICJ's support. It is easy for us to look back and lament the ICJ's timidity in 1966. However, we should realize that the ICJ probably would not exist today if it had become a forum for anti-colonial activism in the 1960s. Such activism probably would have created a mass exodus from the Court by developed countries.

Australia's behavior in 2002 demonstrates how the fear of litigation can prompt a state to exit from a court's jurisdiction. As discussed in Chapter 2, Australia was sued at the ICJ by Portugal in the 1990s over maritime delimitations in the Timor Gap. Australia was able to have the case dismissed because both Indonesia and Portugal claimed authority over the East Timor and Indonesia refused to participate in the suit. However, when East Timor gained independence in 2002, it became an independent state that could file cases at the ICJ on its own behalf. Australia feared that East Timor would renew litigation over the Timor Gap, so Australia withdrew from the Court's jurisdiction over maritime disputes shortly before East Timor's official date of independence.

Large sections of this book focus on how the dispute settlement system (DSS) grew stronger during the 1995 transition from the General Agreement on Tariffs and Trade (GATT) to the World Trade Organization (WTO). However, we should remember that the weak GATT was a highly effective institution during the aftermath of World War II, when most states were experiencing tough political and economic times. The reconstruction of Europe and the demise of colonialism were slow processes that often made trade liberalization a very costly endeavor. A strong and highly legalized trade court would probably not have survived these difficult times. When reassessing the history of GATT, Jackson (2000, 170) argued that the GATT dispute settlement rules "worked better than might be expected, and some could argue that in fact they worked better than those of the [ICJ] and many other international dispute procedures." Similarly, Barton et al. (2006, 27) conclude that: "the irony of the [GATT] trade regime may be that its remarkable success is attributable to a lack of a strong and defined structure ... the regime's greatest strength may have been its flexibility, allowing the reconciliation of domestic interests in its member states with the general purpose of trade liberalization."

Some trade experts believe that the 1995 transition to the WTO made the DSS too strong. Pauwelyn (2005, 6) has written that "the world trade system is out of balance ... [and has] become too rigid or legalized to respond to valid flexibility demands of representative politics." He argued that disputants should be allowed to veto judicial rulings that they dislike. This would create a partial return to the weaker GATT-era procedures that allowed any state, including the defendant, to veto the adoption of a panel report. Pauwelyn's view is supported somewhat by statistical analysis of international trade. Kucik and Reinhardt (2008) examine the relationship between WTO membership and antidumping procedures, which are domestic laws that allow a government to sometimes violate its trade commitments without abrogating the WTO treaty itself. Commentators often believe that the WTO's permissive attitude towards antidumping laws indicates that it is too weak in enforcing international trade obligations. However, Kucik and Reinhardt find that new members of the WTO are more likely to adopt antidumping procedures than non-members. Additionally, the presence of antidumping procedures makes a country more likely to join the WTO. This suggests that membership in a cooperative institution is facilitated by weakness in the corresponding international court. The WTO's permissive attitude towards antidumping procedures may promote the stability of the multilateral trading regime.

When will weak courts be more effective than strong courts? If law is imprecise, then states will be very uncertain about how the court will behave and this uncertainty will forestall pre-trial settlement. Since strong courts further exacerbate this effect, weak courts will probably be more effective when they adjudicate a broad range of disputes that involve undeveloped areas of international law. This can include disputes over customary international law, which lacks the precision of treaty law, or disputes over legal issues with little existing jurisprudence. For example, the ICJ adjudicates on a huge number of cases involving diverse states and open legal questions. States are usually uncertain about how the Court will rule in part because it is constantly asked to rule on new legal questions, such as whether a treaty that regulates consular relations also creates individual rights. The second factor that will affect whether a weak court is optimal is the feasibility of exit from the legal regime. Strong courts raise the cost of dispute settlement, which makes exit more attractive when a state finds compliance extremely difficult. If exit is not a feasible option, then states can design stronger courts without the fear that they will create instability. But weak courts are best when it is easy for states to leave the legal regime.

States should therefore design weak institutions when they want to promote broad multilateral cooperation on new issue-areas. This seems especially apparent in the ongoing attempts by developed countries to coordinate their financial regulations. Financial regulation is a relatively new issue in international politics that has taken on increasing importance with the rise of multinational corporations. The international community has attempted to promote cooperation by writing a series of agreements called the Basel Accords. The most recent agreement, the Basel III Accord, was written in response to the global financial crisis of 2007–2008. The Basel Accords are non-binding agreements that set common regulatory standards. The institution that oversees these agreements, known as the Basel Committee, is extremely weak and has no formal dispute settlement procedures. While international lawyers may lament the weak (if not nonexistent) legalization of Basel, my theory suggests that the design of the Basel Committee is probably optimal. Lawyers can speak meaningfully about international trade law and international investment law, but there is nothing to say about international finance law because it does not exist. Given the absence of precise rules and the multilateral nature of this issue, the Basel III Accord is probably best suited to weak institutionalization. Stronger courts are not always better.

Strong Courts Should Be Nested in Broader Political Institutions

The international system is fundamentally anarchic because there is no central authority that can compel states to behave in a certain way. International institutions must therefore be self-enforcing: their rules must be designed to ensure that states want to both become and remain members of the institution. A strong court can enhance cooperation in the short-term by increasing compliance with international rules, but in doing so, it also reduces long-term cooperation by decreasing the likelihood that states will want to be members of the regime. States can offset this cost if they make exit from a court more costly. One way to increase the cost of exit—and thereby enhance a court's stability—is to nest a court in a broader political institution that provides its members with cooperative benefits. If membership in the legal regime is linked to benefits that are provided by a broader political institution, then exit becomes more costly.

Such nesting is one important explanation for the success of the European Court of Justice (ECJ). The ECJ is a body of the European

Union, meaning that a state cannot leave the jurisdiction of the ECJ unless its also exits the EU as a whole. Because the EU promotes cooperation on so many economic and social issues, an EU member is unlikely to exit the institution as a whole merely to satisfy short-term political pressure for a single treaty violation. The design of the ECJ shows that while the international system is anarchic, states can create order if they link membership in an international court to membership in other cooperative institutions. By linking the judicial function of courts to the benefits of political institutions, states can forestall exit from an international court, making the international system more closely resemble domestic political systems.

Scholars of domestic courts need not worry that individuals will leave a court's jurisdiction, yet they do recognize that domestic courts face challenges in establishing their authority (Staton 2004; Vanberg 2005). A government can uphold the rulings of a domestic court in a way not possible in the international context, yet governments choose how actively to support and uphold a domestic court's jurisdiction and rulings. International and domestic courts therefore share many similarities and lie along a continuum of judicial authority (Carrubba 2009; Hafner-Burton, Victor and Lupu 2012; Staton and Moore 2011). By linking the ECJ to the broader EU, states have made the European system more closely resemble a domestic government. Exit has been so effectively forestalled that the modern ECJ more closely resembles a federal court than an international organization and many scholars question whether we should even classify it as an international organization (Pollack 2005).

Of course, this nesting doesn't solve all of the challenges of cooperation. Even if states want to remain members of the institution, they will still be tempted to violate their treaty obligations. When a political leader is under intense political and economic pressure, she may still choose to violate her commitments and then participate in dispute settlement, rather than fully comply. Nevertheless, neither scholars nor states view instability as a problem at the ECJ.

While the ECJ is a prominent example of successful nesting, we should remember that there are limits to this tactic. Nesting can be effective only if two conditions are met: exit from the court must ensure exit from the broader institution, and the broader institution must provide significant benefits to its members. Few examples satisfy these two criteria. For example, it is very simple for a state to exit from the ICJ's jurisdiction under a unilateral declaration or a compromissory clause. In most circumstances, a state must only send an official notice to the UN Secretary-General.[1] Since ICJ jurisdiction is not a condition of UN membership, a state that exits ICJ jurisdiction incurs few costs. And even if UN membership were directly linked to ICJ jurisdiction, the broader benefits that are provided by the UN are relatively insignificant when compared to the EU.

Strong Courts Need Precise Laws

Institutions can change for many different reasons. Some IR scholars argue that institutions are designed by rational actors to solve specific cooperation problems (Koremenos, Lipson and Snidal 2001), while others note that many international courts are created and changed for reasons that are seemingly irrational. Alter (2012) argues that diffusion has been driving the proliferation of regional courts. Many regional organizations in Africa, Asia, and Latin America have transplanted the designs of the ECJ and the WTO dispute settlement system, even if these designs are not appropriate for their political context.[2] My theoretical argument examines how changes in the design of an institution affect the behavior of rational states, but I neither assume nor believe that rationality alone can explain the design of all international courts. Nonetheless, even if a model does not perfectly describe the origins of institutions, it can prescribe ways to make institutions more effective.

Strong courts exacerbate the impact of uncertainty during trade disputes. States become more likely to litigate, rather than to resolve their disputes through diplomatic negotiations. As I argued in chapter 3, rational actors can offset this negative effect if they increase the precision of law, and thereby reduce uncertainty about how the court will behave. Stronger courts need more precise laws.

This implication is most apparent in the transition to the World Trade Organization dispute settlement system. During the early decades of the GATT, its members developed informal procedures for dispute settlement that they later codified in the Tokyo Understanding of 1979. The DSS during the mature GATT period of 1980 to 1994 was very weak. Delegation to the DSS was low because any GATT member, including the defendant, could block panel formation. Obligation to the DSS was also low because any member could veto the adoption of a panel report. Additionally, many of the GATT's substantive rules—such as rules on safeguards, countervailing duties, and antidumping duties—were very imprecise. States were uncertain about the interpretation and application of many areas of GATT law. When states created the WTO in 1995, they strengthened both delegation and obligation to the dispute settlement system. Both panel formation and the adoption of panel reports became a quasi-automatic process. WTO designers also increased the precision of many areas of trade law, including safeguards, countervailing duties, and antidumping duties. Of course, states still have disputes over the interpretation and application of the new WTO agreements. However, my theory suggests that WTO members would have litigated even more if the WTO designers had not revised the GATT's substantive laws.

Uncertainty, and the litigation that it generates, hinders membership in strong courts. For example, the International Criminal Court has very high delegation and obligation. The United States has not joined the ICC for many different reasons. Many policy-makers in the United States fear that the Court will be used to prosecute United States military leaders. Additionally, some scholars view the ICC as an attempt by middle powers to assert control over the United States, while others believe that the existence of the ICC will prolong the rule of despots (Gilligan 2006; Goldsmith 2003; Goldsmith and Krasner 2003). Yet another factor that has prevented United States membership in the ICC is uncertainty about the substantive law that will be enforced by the Court.

Many treaties have established basic principles of humanitarian law, such as the 1948 Genocide Convention, but activists have pushed the ICC into new areas for which it lacks precise laws. For example, feminists have pushed the International Criminal Court to prosecute sexual violence, such as rape and sexual slavery, as a war crime (Engle 2005; Halley 2008). The International Criminal Tribunals for Rwanda and the Former Yugoslavia (ICTR/ICTFY), which were forerunners and models for the ICC, were presented with many sexual violence cases. However, neither of these two courts could invoke established treaty law, custom, or jurisprudence on the treatment of sexual violence under international law (Schomburg and Paterson 2007, 123).[3] Jurists of the ICTR and ICTFY made the controversial decision to expand the application of existing humanitarian law by ruling that rape can be prosecuted as genocide and a crime against humanity.[4] The Rome Statute, which created the International Criminal Court, includes a few modest sentences that define rape and sexual slavery as war crimes, but the ICC lacks detailed criteria or procedures for determining when sexual violence rises to the level of a war crime.[5] The ICTR and ICTFY rulings suggest that when confronted with a case that is not covered by existing humanitarian law, ICC jurists may apply existing law in unexpected ways.

Similarly, ICC members have been using the Review Conference of the Rome Statute, a bureaucratic body associated with the ICC, to develop new laws. One hotly contested political issue is the legal definition of the crime of aggression.[6] In 2010, the Review Conference adopted procedures that could allow the ICC to investigate and prosecute aggression as a war crime beginning in 2017, but there is tremendous uncertainty about how the ICC will define acts of aggression.[7] For example, states are uncertain about how the ICC would view acts such as the 1999 NATO intervention in Kosovo (Paulus 2009). This intervention was not approved by the UN Security Council, but nevertheless received broad international support from NATO members, the EU, and Serbia's neighboring countries. Is such an intervention an illegal act of aggression? One key reason why the United States has not become a member of the ICC is that the United States does not know what rules the Court will enforce. To promote cooperation, a strong court, like the ICC, needs precise laws.

Specialized Courts Will Be More Effective than General Courts

My theoretical argument treats delegation, obligation, and precision as separate dimensions of the law. However, there may be dynamic relationships between these dimensions over time. The conflict model showed that both delegation and obligation increase the likelihood of litigation rather than settlement. In the short term, litigation is inefficient for the disputants because both would be better off if they could reach a negotiated settlement and avoid litigation costs. However, litigation can benefit all of the members of a regime if it allows a court to clarify the meaning of the law (Fiss 1984). Additionally, if judges are biased in favor of institutional values—such as trade liberalization, regional integration, or environmental protection—then litigation can uphold and reinforce institutional values in ways that political settlements may not (Benvenisti 2004). While litigation creates private costs for disputants, it creates public benefits for other members of the institution (Johns and Pelc 2014a). When delegation or obligation increase, the short-term costs of increased litigation may be outweighed by the long-term benefit of increased precision. However, this dynamic relationship between strong courts and precise laws can only hold if rulings change beliefs about how the court will behave in future cases.

As discussed in chapter 3, the design of an international court is often a compromise between countries with common and civil law systems. Under common law systems, courts are bound by *stare decisis*, which is the principle that past legal rulings should serve as a precedent for future legal rulings. However, judges who operate within civil law systems are not bound by precedent. They are expected to make rulings based purely on current statutes and litigant behavior, and without reference to previous legal rulings. Accordingly, neither the ICJ nor the WTO dispute settlement system is formally bound by previous rulings when it hears new disputes. However, in practice both of these courts are exceptionally deferential towards prior jurisprudence. International courts regularly cite and rely upon the logic and interpretations of previous rulings (Bhala 1998-1999; Lupu and Voeten 2012; Pelc forthcoming). Most international courts thus display some level of *de facto*, if not *de jure*, *stare decisis*.

Delegation and obligation can only enhance long-term precision if the Court rules repeatedly on related legal questions over time. The value of an individual ruling in creating precedent is therefore a function of its legal, political, and economic context. If the court hears a large variety of cases involving a diverse set of actors and treaties, then the impact of any given ruling is likely to be small, simply because the court is unlikely to return to the same kind of case in the future. General courts—which oversee many different issue-areas—will find it difficult to develop precise laws since they must rule on a large and diverse set of questions. In contrast, if a court oversees law for a single issue-area, such as trade or investment, it is more likely to adjudicate similar cases in the future and any given ruling should have a more important long-term effect on precision. This suggests that specialized courts—which oversee a single issue-area—will be more successful in increasing precision over time by building up a large body of jurisprudence on a narrow set of legal questions. Specialized courts will be more effective than general courts.

The WTO dispute settlement system is a perfect example of a specialized court that has developed relatively precise rules for the interpretation and application of treaty texts over time. For example, when two WTO members are involved in a dispute over antidumping duties, they can develop relatively accurate and similar beliefs about how a panel will rule by looking at both the text of the WTO Antidumping Agreement and the extensive case law that has developed from previous antidumping cases. This precision is facilitated in part by a large industry of trade law specialists who are consulted by both disputants and the WTO itself (Pauwelyn 2002).

In contrast, the ICJ is a general court that oversees treaties on a huge range of issue-areas. When Paraguay sued the United States under the VCCR, it had little information about how the court would behave. Both Paraguay and the United States could examine the text of the VCCR itself and attempt to infer how the court would behave based upon its interpretations of other treaties. However, they lacked a body of case law on which they could base their assessments.

ICJ members now have more precise information about how the ICJ would likely rule in future consular cases involving the arrest of foreign nationals. But these cases are unlikely to occur because the Court has moved on to disputes in other unrelated issue-areas.

This suggests that the legalization of international politics will be most successful when it occurs via specialized, issue-specific legal institutions. One promising trend in international law is therefore the development of institutions like the International Center for the Settlement of Investment Disputes (ICSID), an adjudicatory body that is housed at the World Bank. ICSID was created in 1966 as an international venue in which individual investors can challenge foreign governments for alleged expropriation and discriminatory treatment. In its early years, ICSID played only a small role in the international system because most treaties that protected foreign investment were written prior to 1966.[8] However, the 1990s saw a surge in the number of new bilateral investment treaties, most of which allow foreign investors to file legal claims at ICSID (Allee and Peinhardt 2010, 2011). ICSID has since become the primary venue for investment disputes, allowing it to develop a large and detailed body of jurisprudence on the interpretation of bilateral investment treaties.

Additionally, general courts may be more effective if they focus on specialized areas of law. For example, the Andean Court of Justice (ACJ) is the judicial institution of the Andean Community, an organization that promotes regional integration in Latin America. The ACJ ostensibly is a general court with the ability to rule on conflicts between the laws of the Andean Community and its members. In terms of its case-load, the Court is one of the most active in the world, falling behind only the European Court of Justice and the European Court of Human Rights (Helfer, Alter and Guerzovich 2009). Yet the overwhelming majority of its jurisprudence has focused on a single issue: intellectual property rights. Even though the Andean Community has laws on a broad range of trade and investment issues, Alter and Helfer (2010, 580) note that: "It is a striking fact that of the 1,338 ATJ preliminary rulings between 1984 and 2007, only thirty-five involve subjects other than intellectual property." The ACJ may appear to be an important and effective general court, but its influence is overwhelmingly limited to a very narrow and specialized area of law.

In contrast, many recent developments in international law are likely to prove highly problematic. Both states and judges themselves are often eager to push successful international courts into new issue-areas. In recent years the purview of the WTO dispute settlement system has grown to include a broader array of economic issue-areas, including foreign investment and intellectual property rights. Many states are keen to also use the WTO to litigate cases on labor rights and environmental protection, even though the WTO lacks the clear statutory authority to do so.[9] Similarly, the European Court of Human Rights has recently begun to rule on intellectual property disputes (Helfer 2008a). Legal scholars are divided in their opinions on such expansions. Some scholars are optimistic that these institutions will be effective in these new issue-areas, while others argue that such mission-creep will likely be problematic, particularly in large multilateral institutions like the WTO (Brewster 2011b; Pauwelyn 2004; Steinberg 1997). My theory suggests that expanding the purview of highly specialized trade and human rights courts into broader areas of law is more likely to harm the effectiveness of these courts than it is to promote international cooperation.

Limited Membership Agreements May Harm Cooperation More than They Help

When states cannot negotiate multilateral agreements with a broad membership, they often attempt to promote international cooperation by writing limited membership agreements (LMAs), such as bilateral investment treaties and preferential trade agreements, that are intended to promote cooperation amongst a limited group. These agreements have proliferated rapidly in recent decades (Elkins, Guzman and Simmons 2006; Jo and Namgung 2012).

Supporters of LMAs argue that these agreements are beneficial because some international cooperation is preferable to none. For example, shortly after the formation of the WTO in 1995, its members began a new round of trade negotiations known as the Doha Round. WTO members have tried to use these negotiations to further deepen their trade commitments. However, the Doha Round has been unsuccessful because of stalemate among its members. The United States has responded to the multilateral stalemate by negotiating new preferential trade agreements (PTAs). In 2012 alone, the United States ratified new bilateral PTAs with Colombia, Korea, and Panama. As of this writing in early 2014, the United States is negotiating two major PTAs: the Transatlantic Trade and Investment Partnership with the European Union; and the Trans-Pacific Partnership with a diverse set of countries with borders on the Pacific Ocean, like Australia, Chile, Singapore, and Vietnam.

Supporters of LMAs also argue that by promoting cooperation among a limited membership, outsiders and domestic constituencies may change their perceptions about the benefits of international cooperation and become more willing to engage in multilateral cooperation (Downs, Rocke and Barsoom 1998; Mansfield and Milner 1999). In international trade, many policy experts believe that the proliferation of successful PTAs may persuade other countries to support the Doha Round negotiations.[10] LMAs may promote long-term cooperation if they persuade non-members to cooperate in multilateral venues.

However, bilateral and regional agreements come with a cost. The proliferation of limited membership agreements means that states often have overlapping and conflicting legal commitments. This creates uncertainty that hinders the early settlement of disputes and fuels costly litigation. Additionally, overlapping agreements open the door to jurisprudential conflicts between courts with overlapping jurisdictions.[11] Limited membership agreements may harm cooperation more than they help.

Recall the GATT *à la carte* system that was discussed in Chapter 5. All GATT members were bound by the legal commitments established in the original 1947 treaty. However, many GATT members chose to accept additional legal obligations by signing the optional Tokyo Codes, which took effect in 1980. So multiple sets of GATT rules simultaneously regulated international trade until the creation of the WTO in 1995. GATT members disagreed about whether the most-favored nation (MFN) principle, which requires that if a member extends a benefit to another WTO member it must extend the same benefit to all other WTO members, applied to the Tokyo Codes. Some GATT members believed that all members were entitled to Tokyo benefits, even non-signatories, while other members believed that states that refused to join the Tokyo Codes could be excluded from the benefits created by these Codes. The creation of the WTO in 1995 resolved this issue because it was created as a single undertaking, meaning that WTO members were required to accept all WTO agreements. They could no longer pick-and-choose their commitments.

The recent proliferation of preferential trade agreements has led to new conflicts with WTO rules. Article XXIV of the GATT allows members to sign PTAs, which implies that benefits provided to PTA members do not need to be extended to all WTO members. There is thus a tension between the most-favored nation principle, which is a core tenet of the multilateral trade regime, and PTAs. One WTO panel report noted that this relationship "has not always been harmonious" and has led to trade disputes.[12]

For example, Turkey has signed multiple trade agreements with the European Communities (EC) since 1963 that gradually developed into a Turkey-EC customs union.[13] As part of this process, Turkey negotiated new agreements with its trading partners in the early 1990s so that its textile rules would match those of the EC. India, a major textile exporter, refused to participate in these negotiations, prompting Turkey to impose unilateral restrictions on textile imports from India in 1996. India quickly filed a WTO dispute against Turkey, arguing that Turkey had violated multiple WTO rules.[14] Turkey argued that it should be exempt from these rules under Article XXIV because it was changing its laws to form a Turkey-EC customs union. Both the WTO panel and Appellate Body ruled against Turkey, stating that "Article XXIV does not allow Turkey to adopt, upon the formation of a customs union with the European Communities, quantitative restrictions ... which were found to be inconsistent with" WTO rules.[15] This created a legal quandary: Turkey had to violate either WTO rules by changing its textile laws, or its PTA with the EC by not changing its laws.

Similar complications plague bilateral investment treaties (BITs). These treaties usually grant most-favored nation status, but they vary in their dispute settlement provisions. As mentioned above, most modern BITs grant investors the right to file a complaint at the International Center for the Settlement of Investment Disputes (ICSID). However, BITs signed before the 1990s often do not contain this clause.[16] Even if a treaty does grant access to ICSID, investment treaties vary in the conditions they place on ICSID lawsuits. For example, some BITs require that a foreign investor must first litigate her case in domestic courts, while others allow an investor to go straight to ICSID without any domestic litigation.[17] Many investors who have been unable to file lawsuits at ICSID under their home-country's BIT have argued that MFN provisions allow them to invoke ICSID clauses in a BIT signed by a different country.

For example, two Italian companies filed an ICSID case against Jordan in 2002. The Italian companies had completed work for the Jordanian government on a public contract. When the companies submitted their final bill, the government refused to pay the full amount charged by the companies. The Italy-Jordan BIT granted most-favored nation status, but contained ambiguous language about investor access to ICSID. However, Jordan had previously granted clear ICSID jurisdiction to United States investors in a BIT between Jordan and the United States. The Italian companies argued they too should have access to ICSID because the MFN clause of the Italy-Jordan BIT ensured that Italian investors could not be treated less favorably than United States investors. Put more simply, the Italian companies tried to sue Jordan using a treaty that Italy had not signed. The legal validity of this tactic is an open question. As of this writing, ICSID has issued contradictory rulings about whether an investor can use a MFN clause to gain access to ICSID.[18] The vast web of overlapping bilateral investment treaties creates ambiguity about legal commitments and dispute settlement procedures.

These examples illustrate the complexity of using limited membership agreements to promote international cooperation. Globalization has made states more connected, and the growth of international law has created complex and overlapping sets of rules that regulate international relations. This interconnectedness enhances our need for inclusive cooperative agreements. Treaties with a broad membership have a multiplier effect on cooperation because they create more consistent—and hence more precise—rules than can be created by a network of overlapping bilateral and regional agreements. Multilateralism is more than just the sum of its parts.

6.3 Conclusion

International courts must solve fundamental problems of both conflict and cooperation. They must resolve disputes that arise over the interpretation and application of the law, and their existence and design must promote both compliance and the stability of cooperation over time. Legal regimes are designed with an eye to both enhancing cooperation today among current members of a regime and ensuring that these states cooperate in the future by remaining members of the regime.

The design of a legal regime affects international cooperation. Delegation and obligation increase the cost of dispute settlement for a defendant and therefore promote compliance for those states that find cooperation to be relatively easy. However, delegation and obligation also reduce the stability of a cooperative regime by making it more costly for a state to remain a member of the regime during tough times. International law faces a trade-off between the competing priorities of short-term compliance and long-term stability.

When a dispute occurs, states will always be somewhat uncertain about how a court will interpret the law. Both delegation and obligation increase the importance of this uncertainty, which decreases the probability that states can negotiate an early settlement. Precision has the opposite effect. When laws are made more precise, disputants have less uncertainty about how the court will rule and it is easier for them to resolve their conflicts without actually using the court. This suggests that when states increase the strength of a court, they should also increase the precision of the laws on which the court rules.

While the focus of this book has been on international courts, many of my arguments hold for international organizations in general. Most scholars believe that international organizations facilitate cooperation by reducing transaction costs and providing information to their members (Keohane 1982, 1984). However, we should remember that international organizations change the *form* of transaction costs and uncertainty, rather than eliminating them altogether. An international organization can reduce uncertainty about appropriate behavior and the behavior of its members, yet it also creates a new source of uncertainty: uncertainty about the organization's actions and authority. As an organization has more power, this uncertainty becomes more important. States are less likely to reach diplomatic solutions on their own and more likely to rely on institutional dispute settlement. In most international organizations, dispute settlement is a costly process that often drags on for years, if not decades. These costs are probably less than the cost of military violence, trade wars, and other forms of conflict. Additionally, international organizations may lead to more just or fair outcomes. However, international organizations are not costless: they reduce the value of cooperation if they prolong disputes that could be settled through diplomatic negotiations. Strong international organizations can exacerbate the problems that they are intended to solve. Sometimes weakness is a virtue.

A

Appendix

A.1 Conflict Game

Table A.1 shows model notation, and Figure A.1 shows the game tree with payoffs. Assume that case quality, π, is distributed according to density function f on the interval $[\pi_L, \pi_H]$ where $0 < \pi_L < \pi_H < 1$. Let $x : [\pi_L, \pi_H] \to [0,1]$ denote the plaintiff's strategy, where $x(\pi)$ is the demand chosen by type π. Let $t : [0,1] \to [0,1]$ denote the defendant's strategy, where $t(x)$ is the probability that the defendant rejects demand x and the case goes to trial. Delegation is represented by parameter q, which is the probability that the court rules on the merits. Obligation is

Table A.1: Model Notation

Court Attributes	
q	Delegation: probability the court will issue a substantive ruling on the merits
r	Obligation: how much a favorable court ruling benefits the winner
p	Precision: measure of uncertainty about how the court will rule
Information (Types)	
π	Case quality: probability the plaintiff wins if the court rules on the merits
τ	Cost of cooperation
Strategies	
x	Settlement demand
t	Probability of trial
e	Effort
C	Compliance: choose effort at or above the mandated minimum
S	Dispute Settlement: violate the agreement, but then participate in dispute settlement
X	Exit: violate the agreement and leave the cooperative regime
Preferences	
L	Loss to the plaintiff from the defendant's prior action
a	Bargaining outcome if the court does not rule on the merits
b	Bargaining outcome if the court rules and the defendant wins
k	Cost of litigation

Figure A.1: Conflict Model with Mathematical Notation

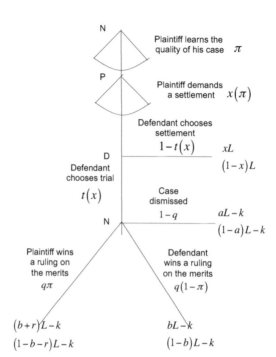

represented by parameter r, which is each player's benefit from winning, rather than losing, a ruling on the merits, where $0 < b < a < b + r < 1$. I derive the fully separating weak Perfect Bayesian Equilibrium that satisfies the refinement of universal divinity.[1]

Proof of Proposition 1

In a fully separating equilibrium, each type, π, makes a unique demand, $x(\pi)$. Let $\pi(x)$ denote the inverse function for equilibrium demands. After observing an on-the-equilibrium-path demand, the defendant's belief about the plaintiff's type is: $\mu(x(\pi)) = \pi$.

The expected utility from trial for the plaintiff and the defendant, respectively, is:

$$\begin{aligned} T_P &= [(1-q)a + qb + q\pi r]L - k \\ T_D &= L - [(1-q)a + qb + q\pi r]L - k \end{aligned}$$

The defendant is indifferent between settlement and trial iff:

$$(1-x)L = E[T_D] \quad \Leftrightarrow \quad x = (1-q)a + qb + q\pi(x)r + \frac{k}{L}$$

This demand is always positive, and is less than 1 for small k or large L. The defendant's beliefs are correct in equilibrium, so the optimal demand strategy is:

$$x^*(\pi) = (1-q)a + qb + q\pi r + \frac{k}{L} \tag{A.1}$$

The plaintiff's expected utility from a demand x is:

$$
\begin{aligned}
EU_P(x|\pi) &= t(x)T_P + [1-t(x)]xL \\
\frac{\partial EU_P(x|\pi)}{\partial x} &= t'(x)T_P + [1-t(x)]L - t'(x)xL = 0 \\
\Leftrightarrow \quad x &= \frac{T_P}{L} + \frac{1-t(x)}{t'(x)} \tag{A.2}
\end{aligned}
$$

Both (A.1) and (A.2) must hold in equilibrium, so:

$$
\begin{aligned}
(1-q)a + qb + q\pi r + \frac{k}{L} &= \frac{T_P}{L} + \frac{1-t(x)}{t'(x)} \\
\Leftrightarrow \quad t'(x)\left(\frac{2k}{L}\right) &= 1 - t(x) \\
\Rightarrow \quad t(x) &= 1 - \exp\left(\frac{-xL}{2k} + \theta\right)
\end{aligned}
$$

Note that:

$$
\begin{aligned}
0 \le t(x) \quad &\Leftrightarrow \quad \exp\left(\frac{-xL}{2k} + \theta\right) \le 1 \Leftrightarrow \theta \le \frac{xL}{2k} \\
t(x) < 1 \quad &\Leftrightarrow \quad 0 < \exp\left(\frac{-xL}{2k} + \theta\right)
\end{aligned}
$$

The latter always holds. By universal divinity, $\theta = \frac{x^*(\pi_L)L}{2k}$, and the defendant always chooses a trial for $x > \max\{x^*(\pi)\}$ and settles for $x < \min\{x^*(\pi)\}$. So we have the following equilibrium:

$$
\begin{aligned}
x^*(\pi) &= (1-q)a + qb + q\pi r + \frac{k}{L} \\[2mm]
t^*(x) &= \begin{cases} 0 & \text{for } x < x^*(\pi_L) \\ 1 - \exp\left(\frac{-[x-x^*(\pi_L)]L}{2k}\right) & \text{for } x \in [x^*(\pi_L), x^*(\pi_H)] \\ 1 & \text{for } x^*(\pi_H) < x \end{cases} \\[2mm]
\mu^*(x) &= \begin{cases} \pi_L & \text{if } x < x^*(\pi_L) \\ \pi(x) & \text{if } x \in [x^*(\pi_L), x^*(\pi_H)] \\ \pi_H & \text{if } x^*(\pi_H) < x \end{cases}
\end{aligned}
$$

So demands are strictly increasing in case quality, and the probability of trial is strictly increasing in the plaintiff's demand.

The equilibrium probability of trial, given π, is:

$$t^{*}\left(x^{*}\left(\pi\right)\right) = 1 - \exp\left(\frac{-qr\left(\pi - \pi_{L}\right)L}{2k}\right)$$

Proof of Proposition 2

Delegation increases the probability of trial:

$$\frac{\partial t^{*}\left(x^{*}\left(\pi\right)\right)}{\partial q} = \exp\left(\frac{-qr\left(\pi - \pi_{L}\right)L}{2k}\right)\left[\frac{r\left(\pi - \pi_{L}\right)L}{2k}\right] > 0$$

So delegation decreases the probability of settlement.

Obligation increases the probability of trial:

$$\frac{\partial t^{*}\left(x^{*}\left(\pi\right)\right)}{\partial r} = \exp\left(\frac{-qr\left(\pi - \pi_{L}\right)L}{2k}\right)\left[\frac{q\left(\pi - \pi_{L}\right)L}{2k}\right] > 0$$

So obligation decreases the probability of settlement.

Proof of Proposition 3

Let p denote the precision of the law, and suppose that $\pi \sim U\left[\pi_{L}, \pi_{H} - p\right]$. Then the *ex ante* probability of trial is:

$$T^{*} = \int_{\pi_{L}}^{\pi_{H}-p}\left[1 - \exp\left(\frac{-qr\left(\pi - \pi_{L}\right)L}{2k}\right)\right]\left(\frac{1}{\pi_{H} - p - \pi_{L}}\right)d\pi$$

and:

$$\frac{\partial T^{*}}{\partial p} = \int_{\pi_{L}}^{\pi_{H}-p}\left[1 - \exp\left(\frac{-qr\left(\pi - \pi_{L}\right)L}{2k}\right)\right]\left(\frac{1}{\left[\pi_{H} - p - \pi_{L}\right]^{2}}\right)d\pi$$

$$- \left[1 - \exp\left(\frac{-qr\left(\pi_{H} - p - \pi_{L}\right)L}{2k}\right)\right]\left(\frac{1}{\pi_{H} - p - \pi_{L}}\right) < 0$$

$$\Leftrightarrow \int_{\pi_{L}}^{\pi_{H}-p}\left[1 - \exp\left(\frac{-qr\left(\pi - \pi_{L}\right)L}{2k}\right)\right]f(\pi)d\pi$$

$$< \left[1 - \exp\left(\frac{-qr\left(\pi_{H} - p - \pi_{L}\right)L}{2k}\right)\right]$$

$$\Leftrightarrow \exp\left(\frac{-qr\left(\pi_{H} - p - \pi_{L}\right)L}{2k}\right) < \int_{\pi_{L}}^{\pi_{H}-p}\exp\left(\frac{-qr\left(\pi - \pi_{L}\right)L}{2k}\right)f(\pi)d\pi$$

Note that for any π:

$$\exp\left(\frac{-qr\left(\pi_{H} - p - \pi_{L}\right)L}{2k}\right) \leq \exp\left(\frac{-qr\left(\pi - \pi_{L}\right)L}{2k}\right)$$

$$\Leftrightarrow \frac{qr\left(\pi - \pi_{L}\right)L}{2k} \leq \frac{qr\left(\pi_{H} - p - \pi_{L}\right)L}{2k} \quad \Leftrightarrow \quad \pi \leq \pi_{H} - p$$

This holds for all values of π, which implies that $\frac{\partial T^{*}}{\partial p} < 0$. So precision decreases the probability of trial, and increases the probability of settlement.

Proof of Proposition 4

The plaintiff's expected utility from the conflict subgame (prior to the realization of π) is:

$$
\begin{aligned}
U_P &= \int_{\pi_L}^{\pi_H - p} \left\{ t^* \left(x^* \left(\pi \right) \right) T_P + \left[1 - t^* \left(x^* \left(\pi \right) \right) \right] x^* \left(\pi \right) L \right\} f(\pi) d\pi \\
&= \left[(1 - q) a + qb + qE\left[\pi \right] r \right] L - k \\
&\quad + 2k \int_{\pi_L}^{\pi_H - p} \exp \left(\frac{-qr \left(\pi - \pi_L \right) L}{2k} \right) f(\pi) d\pi
\end{aligned}
$$

The defendant's expected utility from the conflict subgame is:

$$
\begin{aligned}
U_D &= \int_{\pi_L}^{\pi_H - p} \left\{ t^* \left(x^* \left(\pi \right) \right) T_D + \left[1 - t^* \left(x^* \left(\pi \right) \right) \right] \left[1 - x^* \left(\pi \right) \right] L \right\} f(\pi) d\pi \\
&= L - \left[(1 - q) a + qb + qE\left[\pi \right] r \right] L - k
\end{aligned}
$$

If the next condition holds, then delegation increases the plaintiff's expected utility:

$$
\begin{aligned}
\frac{\partial U_P}{\partial q} &= \left(b - a + E\left[\pi \right] r \right) L \\
&\quad - rL \int_{\pi_L}^{\pi_H - p} \exp \left(\frac{-qr \left(\pi - \pi_L \right) L}{2k} \right) \left(\pi - \pi_L \right) f(\pi) d\pi > 0 \\
\Leftrightarrow \quad E\left[\pi \right] &- \int_{\pi_L}^{\pi_H - p} \exp \left(\frac{-qr \left(\pi - \pi_L \right) L}{2k} \right) \left(\pi - \pi_L \right) f(\pi) d\pi > \frac{a - b}{r}
\end{aligned}
$$

and decreases the defendant's expected utility:

$$
\frac{\partial U_D}{\partial q} = \left[a - b - E\left[\pi \right] r \right] L < 0
$$

Obligation always increases the plaintiff's expected utility:

$$
\begin{aligned}
\frac{\partial U_P}{\partial r} &= qE\left[\pi \right] L - qL \int_{\pi_L}^{\pi_H - p} \exp \left(\frac{-qr \left(\pi - \pi_L \right) L}{2k} \right) \left(\pi - \pi_L \right) f(\pi) d\pi \\
&= qL \int_{\pi_L}^{\pi_H - p} \left[\pi - \exp \left(\frac{-qr \left(\pi - \pi_L \right) L}{2k} \right) \left(\pi - \pi_L \right) \right] f(\pi) d\pi \\
&= qL \int_{\pi_L}^{\pi_H - p} \left\{ \pi \left[1 - \exp \left(\frac{-qr \left(\pi - \pi_L \right) L}{2k} \right) \right] \right. \\
&\quad \left. + \pi_L \exp \left(\frac{-qr \left(\pi - \pi_L \right) L}{2k} \right) \right\} f(\pi) d\pi > 0
\end{aligned}
$$

and decreases the defendant's expected utility:

$$\frac{\partial U_D}{\partial r} = -qE[\pi]L < 0$$

If $\pi \sim U[\pi_L, \pi_H - p]$, then precision always increases the plaintiff's expected utility:

$$\frac{\partial U_P}{\partial p} = 2k \int_{\pi_L}^{\pi_H - p} \exp\left(\frac{-qr(\pi - \pi_L)L}{2k}\right)\left(\frac{1}{[\pi_H - \pi_L - p]^2}\right)d\pi$$

$$-2k \exp\left(\frac{-qr(\pi_H - \pi_L - p)L}{2k}\right)\left(\frac{1}{\pi_H - \pi_L - p}\right) > 0$$

$$\Leftrightarrow \quad \exp\left(\frac{-qr(\pi_H - \pi_L - p)L}{2k}\right) < \int_{\pi_L}^{\pi_H - p} \exp\left(\frac{-qr(\pi - \pi_L)L}{2k}\right)f(\pi)d\pi$$

and has no impact on the defendant's expected utility:

$$\frac{\partial U_D}{\partial p} = 0$$

***

To simplify the analysis of the cooperation game, suppose that we allow states to negotiate after an alleged violation has occurred, but before the conflict game begins. Then the plaintiff will accept any offer σ prior to observing π iff:

$$\sigma L \geq U_P$$

So the minimal acceptable offer is: $\sigma L = U_P$. The defendant is willing to make this offer iff:

$$U_D \leq L(1 - \sigma) = L - U_P \quad \Leftrightarrow \quad 0 \leq 2k\left[1 - \int_{\pi_L}^{\pi_H - p} \exp\left(\frac{-qr(\pi - \pi_L)L}{2k}\right)f(\pi)d\pi\right]$$

So efficient settlement of the dispute is possible. The transfer that will be paid is: $\sigma L = U_P$. By Proposition 4, σ is increasing in delegation, obligation, and precision.

A.2 Cooperation Game

Suppose that each state's cost parameter, τ, is independently and identically distributed according to density function h, where $\tau \sim U[0, T]$ for large T. I suppress the index for player and time for the sake of clarity. Let $e : [0, T] \to \mathbf{R}_+$ denote a state's effort strategy, where $e(\tau)$ is the state's effort when it has cost τ. Let $u(e)$ denote each player's utility from effort level $e \geq 0$ such that $u' > 0$, $u'' < 0$, $\lim_{e \to 0} u' = \infty$, and $\lim_{e \to \infty} u' = 0$. So each player i's one-period utility is:

$$U_i(e_i, e_j, \tau_i) = u(e_i) + u(e_j) - \tau_i e_i$$

Let e_C denote the minimum effort level. If $e_j < e_C$, then player i's losses are: $L(e_j) = u(e_C) - u(e_j)$. I refer to $\sigma \in (0, 1)$ as court strength in the main text.

Then player j's expected cost from violating the agreement and then participating in dispute settlement is: $\sigma L\left(e_j\right)$.

Proof of Proposition 5

Define χ_C as the continuation payoff from both players remaining within the cooperative regime. Define χ_N as the continuation payoff from cooperation absent a regime. So:

$$\chi_N \equiv \frac{1}{1-\delta}\int_0^T [2u(y(\tau)) - \tau y(\tau)]\, dH(\tau)$$

I begin by deriving the optimal effort level for each action profile: compliance (C), dispute settlement (S), and exit (X). Let τ_S denote the type that is indifferent between compliance and dispute settlement. Let τ_X denote the type that is indifferent between dispute settlement and exit.

A player's expected utility from the three action profiles is:

$$
\begin{aligned}
EU(C|\tau) \;=\; & u(e) - \tau e + \int_0^T u(e(\tau))dH(\tau) + \int_{\tau_S}^{\tau_X}\sigma L(e(\tau))\,dH(\tau)\\
& + H\left(\tau_X\right)\delta\chi_C + [1 - H\left(\tau_X\right)]\delta\chi_N\\
\Rightarrow\quad & e_C\left(\tau\right) = \begin{cases} y(\tau) & \text{if } \tau \le u'(e_C)\\ e_C & \text{if } u'(e_C) < \tau \end{cases}\\[2mm]
EU(S|\tau) \;=\; & u(e) - \tau e - \sigma L(e) + \int_0^T u(e(\tau))dH(\tau) + \int_{\tau_S}^{\tau_X}\sigma L(e(\tau))\,dH(\tau)\\
& + H\left(\tau_X\right)\delta\chi_C + [1 - H\left(\tau_X\right)]\delta\chi_N\\
\Rightarrow\quad & e_S(\tau) = y\left(\frac{\tau}{1+\sigma}\right) < e_C \;\Leftrightarrow\; (1+\sigma)\,u'(e_C) < \tau\\[2mm]
EU(X|\tau) \;=\; & u(e) - \tau e + \int_0^T u(e(\tau))dH(\tau) + \int_{\tau_S}^{\tau_X}\sigma L(e(\tau))\,dH(\tau) + \delta\chi_N\\
\Rightarrow\quad & e_D(\tau) = y(\tau) < e_C \;\Leftrightarrow\; u'(e_C) < \tau
\end{aligned}
$$

To compare expected utility from actions C and S, define for $(1+\sigma)\,u'(e_C) < \tau$:

$$
\begin{aligned}
\Delta_S \;\equiv\; & EU(C|\tau) - EU(S|\tau)\\
= \; & u(e_C) - \tau e_C - u\left(y\left(\frac{\tau}{1+\sigma}\right)\right) + \tau y\left(\frac{\tau}{1+\sigma}\right) + \sigma L\left(y\left(\frac{\tau}{1+\sigma}\right)\right)\\
= \; & (1+\sigma)\left[u(e_C) - u\left(y\left(\frac{\tau}{1+\sigma}\right)\right)\right] + \tau\left[y\left(\frac{\tau}{1+\sigma}\right) - e_C\right]
\end{aligned}
$$

Note that: $e_S\left(\tau = (1+\sigma)\,u'(e_C)\right) = e_C$, and

$$
\begin{aligned}
\frac{\partial\Delta_S}{\partial\tau} \;=\; & -(1+\sigma)u'\left(y\left(\frac{\tau}{1+\sigma}\right)\right)y'\left(\frac{\tau}{1+\sigma}\right)\frac{1}{1+\sigma}\\
& + \tau y'\left(\frac{\tau}{1+\sigma}\right)\frac{1}{1+\sigma} + y\left(\frac{\tau}{1+\sigma}\right) - e_C\\
= \; & y\left(\frac{\tau}{1+\sigma}\right) - e_C < 0
\end{aligned}
$$

So $EU(C|\tau) < EU(S|\tau)$ for $(1+\sigma)\,u'(e_C) < \tau$, which means that $\tau_S = (1+\sigma)\,u'(e_C)$.

To compare expected utility from actions S and X, define for $(1+\sigma)\,u'(e_C) < \tau$:

$$
\begin{aligned}
\Delta_X &\equiv EU(S|\tau) - EU(X|\tau) \\
&= (1+\sigma)u\left(y\left(\frac{\tau}{1+\sigma}\right)\right) - u(y(\tau)) - \sigma u(e_C) + \tau\left[y(\tau) - y\left(\frac{\tau}{1+\sigma}\right)\right] \\
&\quad + \delta H\left(\tau_X\right)(\chi_C - \chi_N)
\end{aligned}
$$

and note that:

$$
\begin{aligned}
\frac{\partial \Delta_X}{\partial \tau} &= (1+\sigma)u'\left(y\left(\frac{\tau}{1+\sigma}\right)\right)y'\left(\frac{\tau}{1+\sigma}\right)\frac{1}{1+\sigma} \\
&\quad - u'(y(\tau))y'(\tau) + \tau\left[y'(\tau) - \frac{y'\left(\frac{\tau}{1+\sigma}\right)}{1+\sigma}\right] + \left[y(\tau) - y\left(\frac{\tau}{1+\sigma}\right)\right] \\
&= y(\tau) - y\left(\frac{\tau}{1+\sigma}\right) < 0
\end{aligned}
$$

So X strictly dominates S for sufficiently large values of τ.

Finally, note that for $u'(e_C) < \tau$:

$$
\begin{aligned}
\tilde{\Delta} &\equiv EU(C|\tau) - EU(X|\tau) \\
&= u(e_C) - \tau e_C - u(y(\tau)) + \tau y(\tau) + \delta H\left(\tau_X\right)(\chi_C - \chi_N) \\
\frac{\partial \tilde{\Delta}}{\partial \tau} &= -e_C - u'(y(\tau))y'(\tau) + \tau y'(\tau) + y(\tau) = y(\tau) - e_C < 0
\end{aligned}
$$

So a necessary and sufficient for equilibrium existence is:

$$
\tilde{\Delta}((1+\sigma)u'(e_C)) > 0
$$

Note that:

$$
\frac{\partial \tilde{\Delta}((1+\sigma)u'(e_C))}{\partial \sigma} = u'(e_C)\left[y((1+\sigma)u'(e_C)) - e_C\right] < 0
$$

because $(1+\sigma)u'(e_C) > u'(e_C)$, and

$$
\tilde{\Delta}((1+\sigma)u'(e_C))(\sigma = 0) = \delta H\left(\tau_X\right)(\chi_C - \chi_N) > 0
$$

So this equilibrium holds for σ sufficiently small.

Consider the continuation value from future cooperation:

$$
\chi_C = \int_0^T [2u(e(\tau)) - \tau e(\tau)]dH(\tau) + \delta H\left(\tau_X\right)^2 \chi_C + \delta[1 - H\left(\tau_X\right)^2]\chi_N
$$

Then:

$$
\chi_C - \chi_N = \frac{\alpha}{1 - \delta H\left(\tau_X\right)^2}
$$

where:

$$\alpha \equiv \int_{u'(e_C)}^{(1+\sigma)u'(e_C)} [2u(e_C) - \tau e_C] \, dH(\tau)$$

$$+ \int_{(1+\sigma)u'(e_C)}^{\tau_X} \left[2u\left(y\left(\frac{\tau}{1+\sigma}\right)\right) - \tau y\left(\frac{\tau}{1+\sigma}\right) \right] dH(\tau)$$

$$- \int_{u'(e_C)}^{\tau_X} [2u(y(\tau)) - \tau y(\tau)] \, dH(\tau)$$

So the equilibrium cutpoint τ_X is implicitly defined by:

$$\lambda \equiv (1+\sigma)u\left(y\left(\frac{\tau_X}{1+\sigma}\right)\right) - u(y(\tau_X)) - \sigma u(e_C)$$

$$+ \tau_X \left[y(\tau_X) - y\left(\frac{\tau_X}{1+\sigma}\right) \right] + \frac{\delta H(\tau_X)\alpha}{1 - \delta H(\tau_X)^2} = 0$$

Proof of Proposition 6

$$\frac{\partial \tau_S}{\partial \sigma} = u'(e_C) > 0$$

Proof of Proposition 7
By the implicit function theorem:

$$\frac{\partial \tau_X}{\partial \sigma} = -\frac{\lambda_\sigma}{\lambda_{\tau_X}}$$

Note that:

$$\lambda_\sigma = u\left(y\left(\frac{\tau_X}{1+\sigma}\right)\right) - u(e_C) + \left[\frac{\delta H(\tau_X)}{1 - \delta H(\tau_X)^2} \right] \frac{\partial \alpha}{\partial \sigma}$$

$$\text{where } \frac{\partial \alpha}{\partial \sigma} = - \int_{(1+\sigma)u'(e_C)}^{\tau_X} \left[y'\left(\frac{\tau}{1+\sigma}\right) \frac{\tau^2(1-\sigma)}{(1+\sigma)^3} \right] dH(\tau)$$

As σ grows larger, $(1+\sigma)u'(e_C) \to \tau_X$, so $\frac{\partial \alpha}{\partial \sigma} \to 0$. This ensures that $\lambda_\sigma < 0$ for sufficiently large values of σ (which still satisfy the existence requirement).

Next:

$$\lambda_{\tau_X} = y(\tau_X) - y\left(\frac{\tau_X}{1+\sigma}\right) + \frac{\delta h(\tau_X)\left[1 + \delta H(\tau_X)^2\right]\alpha}{\left[1 - \delta H(\tau_X)^2\right]^2}$$

$$+ \frac{\delta H(\tau_X)}{1 - \delta H(\tau_X)^2} \frac{\partial \alpha}{\partial \tau_X}$$

where:

$$\frac{\partial \alpha}{\partial \tau_X} = h(\tau_X) \left[2u\left(y\left(\frac{\tau_X}{1+\sigma}\right)\right) - \tau_X y\left(\frac{\tau_X}{1+\sigma}\right) - 2u'(y(\tau_X)) + \tau_X y(\tau_X) \right]$$

So $\frac{\partial \alpha}{\partial \tau_X}$ is small, and $\lambda_{\tau_X} < 0$. So overall, $\frac{\partial \tau_X}{\partial \sigma} < 0$ for sufficiently large σ.

Notes

Chapter 1

1. This litigation is discussed in extensive detail in chapter 4.

2. On foreign investment, see United Nations Conference on Trade and Development (2012), *World Investment Report, 2012: Towards a New Generation of Investment Policies.*

3. On trade, see World Trade Organization (2012), *World Trade Report, 2012: Trade and Public Policies: A Closer Look at Non-Tariff Measures in the 21st Century.* On migration flows, see United Nations Secretary-General (2012), "International Migration and Development," General Assembly document A/67/254, 3 August.

4. Here I build upon the framework created in the 2000 special issue of *International Organization* on legalization, particularly Abbott et al. (2000). I discuss these dimensions at greater length in Chapter 2.

5. The European Court of Justice has perhaps been more successful than the WTO in promoting its own form of international cooperation. However, its task has been easier because its members have much more in common, both politically and economically. Many scholars regard it as a federal court than an international court (Pollack 2005).

Chapter 2

1. For an introductory text on the use of game theory in law, see Baird, Gertner and Picker (1994). For an overview of other major approaches to international law scholarship, see Cali (2010, 73–86).

2. The essays in Oye (1986) provide an excellent overview of early rational choice scholarship on international cooperation. These ideas have been introduced into legal scholarship relatively recently, in work such as Ginsburg and McAdams (2003) and Goldsmith and Posner (2005).

3. See Ginsburg and McAdams (2003, 1252) and Goldsmith and Posner

(2005), who use the term "coincidence of interest" to describe such situations.

4. The well-known prisoners' dilemma is a collaboration problem.

5. High tariffs raise the domestic price of goods and services, which is harmful to consumers. However, most political economists argue that politicians place more weight on the concerns of import-competing industries than on those of consumers. See Grossman and Helpman (1994, 1996).

6. These arguments have recently appeared in legal scholarship (Guzman 2002, 2007; Norman and Trachtman 2005). However, political scientists have made these arguments since at least the 1980s (Axelrod 1985; Oye 1985).

7. See also Morrow (2002) on the role of common conjecture in international law, and Goldstein and Keohane (1993) on ideas in foreign policy.

8. This is the definition that is used by economists, who believe that dynamic- or time-inconsistency creates commitment problems.

9. This is the definition that is used by most legal scholars and political scientists.

10. However, increasing the cost of a treaty violation does not always promote cooperation. Hollyer and Rosendorff (2011) argue that accession to a human rights treaty can be a costly signal that a leader wants to violate human rights.

11. For example, investors will not send their capital to a foreign state if that state will expropriate. A bilateral investment treaty can increase foreign investment if the state credibly pledges to protect foreign property. If the state subsequently violates the treaty, then investors lose their capital. Investors would have better off without a bilateral investment treaty because they would have sent their capital elsewhere.

12. DSU, Article 3.7.

13. See Dispute Settlement System Training Module, Chapter 6.2, "Consultations." This can be accessed at: http://www.wto.org/english/tratop_e/dispu_e/disp_settlement_cbt_e/signin_e.htm.

14. For recent discussions of the distinction between effectiveness and compliance, see Raustiala (2000) and Martin (2013).

15. See Simmons (1998, 2010) for overviews of the large literature on treaty compliance.

16. See Helfer (2002) for an account of this litigation.

17. Helfer (2002, 1872).

18. Vienna Convention on the Law of Treaties, Art. 2, para. 1(d). Reservations are also sometimes called understandings or declarations.

19. On constraints, see Brownlie (2008, 612–615). For the legal debate on reservations, see Bradley and Goldsmith (2000) and Swaine (2006).

20. *East Timor* (Portugal v. Australia).

21. See ICJ, *Declarations Recognizing the Jurisdiction of the Court as Compulsory*, Australia, para. (b).

22. This conceptualization of legal regimes was first developed in Abbott et al. (2000) and Goldstein et al. (2000).

23. *European Communities–Regime for the Importation, Sale and Distribution of Bananas* (Complainants: Ecuador; Guatemala; Honduras; Mexico; United States).

24. In my coding, 74 percent of ICJ cases had a jurisdictional challenge.

25. For example, see White (1999).

26. For example, see the *Barcelona Traction* and *South West Africa* cases.

27. For a more extensive introduction to these three classes of rulings, see Brownlie (2008). For a detailed analysis of judicial economy in international law, see Busch and Pelc (2010).

28. This basis of jurisdiction is commonly referred to as acceptance of compulsory jurisdiction under Article 36 (2) of the ICJ Statute. See Gill (2003, 74–77).

29. See *Case Concerning Military and Paramilitary Activities in and Against Nicaragua* (Nicaragua v. United States of America), Order of 4 October 1984.

30. For example, see D'Amato (1987).

31. *South West Africa* Case, Judgment of 18 July 1966, p. 51.

32. Janis (1987, 144). See Falk (1967) for the reaction of a contemporary observer who was also surprised by the ruling. This case—and the unexpectedness of the 1966 ruling—is discussed in much greater length below in Chapter 4.

33. *Case Concerning the Northern Cameroons*, Judgment on Preliminary Objections, 2 December 1963, p. 29.

34. Ibid., pp. 37 and 38.

35. *Nuclear Tests Case*, Order on Interim Measures of Protection of 22 June 1973.

36. See *Nuclear Tests Case*, Order on Interim Measures of Protection of 22 June 1973. See also Stiles (2000) and Flora Lewis, "France, Reportedly Urged by China, Going Ahead With A-Test," *New York Times*, 3 July 1973; Nan Robertson, "French Clergy, Army Clash Over A-Tests," *New York Times*, 18 July 1973; and Robert Trumbull, "Tests Criticized, France Quits Pacific Parley," *New York Times*, 18 September 1973.

37. The ICJ can rule on reparations, but this procedure has only been utilized once in the history of the court. See *Corfu Channel*, Judgment of 15 December 1949.

38. Venezuela argued that the United States regulation violated the national treatment standard and could not be justified under the Article XX exceptions to normal WTO rules.

39. See *United States–Standards for Reformulated and Conventional Gasoline - Status Report by the United States*. WT/DS2/10 and WT/DS2/10/Add.7.

40. For example, see *North Sea Continental Shelf*, Judgment of 20 February 1969.

41. For example, see *Case Concerning the Gabcikovo-Nagymaros Project*, Judgment of 25 September 1997, para. 155(2)(B).

42. Jennifer L. Rich, "U.S. Admits That Politics Was Behind Steel Tariffs," *New York Times*, 14 March 2002.

43. Paul Meller, "Europe Is Set To End Threat On Steel Tariffs," *New York Times*, 26 September 2002. At the time, Florida was governed by Jeb Bush, the brother of President Bush, and South Carolina had a contentious Senate election caused by the retirement of Senator Strom Thurmond.

44. See *Land and Maritime Boundary between Cameroon and Nigeria*, Judgment on the Merits of 10 October 2002.

45. For accounts of Nigerian domestic reactions to the ruling, see "Nigeria Sends More Soldiers to Bakassi Warships," *Africa News*, 11 October 2002; "Bakassi representatives vow to remain in Nigeria despite world court ruling," *BBC Summary of World Broadcasts*, 11 October 2002; "Cameroon; Nigerian Troops on Red Alert, Bakassi Indigenes Vow to Stay," *Africa News*, 13 October 2002; "World Briefing Africa: Nigeria: Cameroon Dispute Deepen," *New York Times*, 19 October 2002; and Will Connors, "Nigeria Turns Over Disputed Land to Cameroon," *New York Times*, 15 August 2008.

46. Quoted in Paulson (2004, 450).

47. Anonymous source quoted in Ade Obisesan, "Nigerians slam own govt over loss of land to Cameroon," *Agence France Presse*, 11 October 2002.

48. For example, see "UN, UK, France mount 'intense pressure' on Nigeria over Bakassi Peninsula," *BBC Worldwide Monitoring*, 18 June 2002; "Cameroon; Bakassi: Nigeria Bound By ICJ's Ruling, Says Britain," *Africa News*, 25 October 2002; "Cameroon; Bakassi: EU Gives Nigeria, Cameroun N55m for Demarcation," *Africa News*, 23 October 2003; and Paulson (2004, 451).

49. "Nigeria; Under Intensive UN Mediation, Countries Sign Accord Ending Border Dispute," *UN News Service*, 12 June 2006.

50. See *Agreement between the Republic of Cameroon and the Republic of Nigeria Concerning the Modalities of Withdrawal and Transfer of Authority in the Bakassi Peninsula.* 12 June 2006.

51. The final transfer of Bakassi occurred on 14 August 2008.

52. See also Simmons (2002).

53. In one of Davis' interviews, Joshua Bolton, the White House chief of staff in 2002, stated that "The WTO ruling helped politically to set the timing for bringing [the steel safeguards] to an end" (Davis 2012, 35).

54. See *Subsidies on Upland Cotton*, Appellate Body Report of 3 March 2005.

55. Senator Barney Frank claimed that "the Obama administration apparently feels compelled to preserve our right to subsidize American cotton farmers by extending that subsidy to Brazilian cotton farmers." See Jeff Flake, "Congressmen Flake, Kind, Ryan, and Frank Send Letter to President Obama Regarding U.S.-Brazil Trade Dispute," Press Release, 28 December 2012.

56. See the recent 2008 United States Supreme Court ruling in *Medellín v. Texas*. This ruling is discussed in greater detail in Chapter 4 below.

57. See *Lawrence v. Texas*, Opinion of 26 June 2003; and *Roper v. Simmons*, Opinion of 1 March 2005.

58. *Roper v. Simmons*, Opinion of 1 March 2005.

59. This began as two separate cases filed by the Federal Republic of Germany ('Germany') against Denmark and the Netherlands. The ICJ joined the two proceedings into a single case in 1968.

60. See *North Sea Continental Shelf*, Judgment of 20 February 1969, para. 15.

61. *North Sea Continental Shelf*, Judgment of 20 February 1969, para. 101.

62. For example, recent disputes such as *EC–Hormones* and *United States–Shrimp* have pitted trade liberalization against the legitimate interests of states in protecting public safety and wildlife. The WTO will also likely face litigation in coming years over the legal validity of carbon taxes applied to imported goods and other climate change policies (Blustein 2009, 280–281).

63. Optional Protocol to the International Covenant on Civil and Political Rights, Art. 5, para. 4.

Chapter 3

1. This chapter uses verbal, rather than mathematical, arguments. Readers who are interested in the mathematical models can consult the Appendix.

2. These arguments expand on some of my previous research in Gilligan, Johns and Rosendorff (2010). I thank my coauthors for allowing me to reiterate some of the arguments from our earlier work.

3. In this book, I assume that the plaintiff has private information and makes a demand. Suppose instead that the defendant has private information. Propositions 1–3 all continue to hold because the key assumption driving these results is that the informed player chooses the demand. However, Proposition 4 does not necessarily hold. So if the defendant is the player with private information, then Propositions 5–7 require an additional assumption: that delegation and obligation increase the plaintiff's expected utility from dispute settlement and decrease the defendant's expected utility.

4. The defendant knows the distribution of the plaintiff's type.

5. See *Application of the Convention on the Prevention and Punishment of the Crime of Genocide*, Judgment of 26 February 2007, and Marlise Simons, "Genocide Court Ruled for Serbia Without Seeing Full War Archive," *New York Times*, 9 April 2007.

6. Note that I am implicitly assuming that the plaintiff will proceed to litigation when the defendant rejects his demand. So in my model, either litigation costs are sufficiently low or the plaintiff's loss is sufficiently large that the threat of litigation is always credible. I set aside the issue of legal capacity (Busch, Reinhardt and Shaffer 2009).

7. Readers can interpret this as an exogenous effect, or as the endogenous outcome of a bargaining subgame that is treated as a reduced form. See Johns (2012) for the latter approach.

8. The Appendix contains additional information about my solution concept and refinements for off-the-equilibrium path beliefs. Readers who wish to see the full class of equilibria, including pooling and semi-separating equilibria, can consult Gilligan, Johns and Rosendorff (2010).

9. Regardless of off-the-equilibrium path beliefs, there does not exist a Perfect Bayesian Equilibrium in which the defendant is more likely to accept larger demands.

10. This response to off-the-equilibrium-path demands is consistent with off-the-equilibrium-path beliefs that satisfy the refinement of universal divinity. Details are in the Appendix.

11. The Appendix contains mathematical details about how I model

precision.

12. I adopt this perspective because after a violation has occurred, each state knows whether it will be the plaintiff and defendant for the subgame. When we nest this subgame in a broader model of cooperation, we can then take into account a state's uncertainty about whether it will be a plaintiff or a defendant in subsequent interactions. For Proposition 4, I must make an additional (but reasonable) assumption on the distribution of case quality relative to other parameters. Readers can see the Appendix for details.

13. For example, see Alter (2003), Busch and Reinhardt (2000), and Hudec (1993).

14. This model builds on Johns (2014), Rosendorff and Milner (2001), and Rosendorff (2005). This two-player model is easily extended to a multilateral agreement. I use the simpler model here to provide the reader with clearer exposition and analysis.

15. This kind of uncertainty differs from the uncertainty in the conflict game. Increasing the precision of a legal regime will not affect uncertainty about the future costs of cooperation. States will be uncertain about future political and economic pressure to violate even if precision reduces uncertainty about the legal consequences of a violation.

16. Details of the utility function and other aspects of the model are included in the Appendix. The results also hold if states have a constant marginal benefit from effort and increasing marginal costs.

17. So my framework is a generalization of the standard Prisoner's Dilemma.

18. In the discussion subsection below, I discuss the robustness of the model to alternative punishments.

19. It is never rational for a state to exit the regime if it has complied or participated in dispute settlement.

20. Pelc (2011, 2013a) shows that such excess effort is common in international trade: states often impose tariffs that are lower than their treaty tariff binding.

21. Below I discuss the robustness of the model to limited punishments and renegotiation.

22. I thank Bob Keohane for suggesting the importance of this topic.

23. Barton et al. (2006, 73): "The negotiating history behind the move to legalization of GATT/WTO dispute resolution suggests that it was not intended to lead to expansive judicial lawmaking." See also Goldstein and Steinberg (2008, 2009) and Steinberg (2004).

24. The model builds on previous work in Carrubba (2005).

25. I thank an anonymous reviewer for suggesting this interpretation and argument.

26. Hafner-Burton, Helfer and Fariss (2011) show that governments frequently suspend human rights commitments during crises. They examine derogations, which allow a government to violate its commitments without abrogating a treaty. While this book focuses on international courts, much of its argument can apply to derogations because they impose costly notification and monitoring requirements on states.

27. Of course, states may sometimes want to design a court to promote other objectives, such as to increase their own political power or constrain that of other states.

Chapter 4

1. The ECJ, like many international and domestic courts, often rules on cases that involve general principles of international law. However, as documented by Higgins (2003), the ECJ relies upon ICJ jurisprudence when determining the meaning and application of these principles.

2. Ethiopia and Liberia filed separate lawsuits that the Court later joined into a single case. South West Africa was the territory that makes up modern-day Namibia.

3. A detailed history of the founding of the ICJ and its predecessors is available in Gill (2003).

4. I use the Ginsburg and McAdams (2003) typology to describe these cases.

5. For example, see *Armed Activities on the Territory of the Congo* (Democratic Republic of the Congo v. Rwanda/Uganda/Burundi), *Legality of Use of Force* (Serbia and Montenegro v. Belgium, et al.), and *Application of the Convention on the Prevention and Punishment of the Crime of Genocide* (Croatia v. Serbia).

6. For example, see *Interhandel* (Switzerland v. United States of America) and *Barcelona Traction, Light and Power Company, Limited* (Belgium v. Spain).

7. The Court occasionally uses the term "interim measures" or "preliminary measures." I refer to all of these orders as "provisional measures."

8. The Court can also rule on jurisdiction and admissibility during the merits stage. Two other stages exist but are rarely used: the Court can determine reparations, and the Court can reinterpret or revise an earlier ruling.

9. This account is a brief introduction to sources of law and modes of interpretation in the ICJ. Readers who want detailed treatments of these topics can consult Brownlie (2008, 3–29, 630–636), Cassese (2005, 153–212), and Shaw (2008, 69–128, 932–938). For the sources of law,

see Article 38(1) of the Statute of the International Court of Justice.

10. More detailed discussions of ICJ jurisdiction and admissibility are provided by: Brownlie (2008, 710–720), Gill (2003, 67–89), and Shaw (2008, 1064–1086).

11. Many cases invoke more than one form of jurisdiction. For example, it is very common for applicants to invoke both unilateral declarations and compromissory clauses when trying to establish jurisdiction of the Court.

12. Data coded by author from Court records. Unilateral declarations are often referred to as the acceptance of compulsory jurisdiction. However, it is important to note that: (1) the consent of the state making the unilateral declaration is required; and (2) states frequently include reservations limiting the scope of jurisdiction with regard to a particular type of disputes, set of actors, and/or period of time. See Articles 36(2) and 36(5) of the ICJ Statute.

13. See Article 40(1) of the ICJ Statute.

14. See Article 38(5) of the Rules of the Court.

15. Early in the Cold War, the United States often used this process to initiate cases against the USSR and its satellite states, which always refused the invitation. This practice became so burdensome that the Rules of the Court were amended in 1978 to ensure that no Article 38(5) cases were entered in the Court's docket unless the respondent accepted the invitation to establish jurisdiction. As of this writing, only two cases have been successfully initiated under Article 38(5). Both are recent cases involving France: *Certain Criminal Proceedings in France* (Republic of the Congo v. France) and *Certain Questions of Mutual Assistance in Criminal Matters* (Djibouti v. France).

16. Data collected by author from Court filings.

17. *Case Concerning Military and Paramilitary Activities in and Against Nicaragua* (Nicaragua v. United States of America).

18. During ICJ proceedings, a Nicaraguan official posited that the instrument may have been lost on a ship that was sunk in early World War II.

19. Emphasis added.

20. Article 96 of the UN Charter also gives the ICJ the authority to issue advisory opinions to organs or specialized agencies of the United Nations. See Gill (2003) for a discussion of this role of the Court.

21. See UN Charter, Article 94 (2).

22. Some African states were nominally independent in the 1960s, but governed under white-minority rule. To distinguish these two groups, I use the term "African bloc" to refer to states under black-majority

rule. ICJ litigation was a prominent topic of the 1960 Second African States Conference in Addis Ababa. See Gill (2003, 138–139).

23. South Africa gained its independence from England in 1910, when the Union of South Africa joined the British Commonwealth. In 1961, the Union left the Commonwealth and became the Republic of South Africa. ICJ proceedings in 1960–1966 referred exclusively to the "Union" (rather than the "Republic") because the case involved actions taken before 1960. For the sake of simplicity, I also use the name "Union of South Africa" throughout this chapter even when discussing events that took place after 1961.

24. See *South West Africa Cases*, Order of 20 May 1961. Sources vary in whether they refer to this as a single case or two separate cases.

25. Covenant of the League of Nations, Article 22.

26. For comprehensive overviews of the mandate system, see Callahan (1999, 2004).

27. *Mandate for German South Africa*, Articles 2 and 4. Available in Baum (1976).

28. UN Charter, Chapter XII, Article 76, para. (b).

29. See UN General Assembly Resolutions 141 (III) and 227 (III).

30. See UN General Assembly Resolution 1060 (XI) and 1142A (XI). See also "Report of the Committee of South Africa." General Assembly Official Records: Fifteenth Session, Supplement No. 12 (A/4464).

31. Ethiopia and Liberia were chosen as complainants by the African bloc because they were the only states in the group that had been League of Nations members.

32. *South West Africa Cases*, Judgment of 21 December 1962, pp. 323 and 325.

33. *South West Africa Cases*, Judgment of 21 December 1962, p. 338.

34. *South West Africa Cases*, Judgment of 21 December 1962, p. 337.

35. *South West Africa Cases*, Judgment of 21 December 1962, p. 343.

36. *South West Africa Cases*, Judgment of 21 December 1962, p. 343.

37. See Gill (2003, 140) and *South West Africa Cases*, Dissenting Opinion of Judge Jessup, p. 328.

38. *South West Africa Cases*, Judgment of 18 July 1966, p. 19.

39. *South West Africa Cases*, Judgment of 18 July 1966, pp. 24 and 29.

40. *South West Africa Cases*, Judgment of 21 December 1962, p. 343.

41. *South West Africa Cases*, Dissenting Opinions of Judge Koretsky, p. 239, Judge Padilla Nervo, p. 443, and Judge Jessup, p. 325.

42. I make this conclusion based upon the subsequent 1966 votes of Tanaka and Padillo Nervo, who took over Cordova's seat as the representative for Mexico.

43. Dugard (1973) provides many details on the composition of the bench in 1966.

44. Zafrullah Khan served as an ICJ judge from 1954–1961, but then left the Court for three years to represent his country at the UN.

45. See ICJ Statute, Article 24.

46. Data was collected by the author from the annual ICJ Yearbook. Data is excluded from 1946–1956 because judges elected during this period would have had little to no opportunity to serve in political roles at the UN.

47. This is not the common view. Almost all detailed historical accounts of the *South West Africa* case highlight the difficult political context of the ruling and the internal machinations of the ICJ.

48. For example, see "A Desolate Land, But World Issue," *New York Times*, 16 May 1965.

49. Ballinger (1964, 46). Quoted in *South West Africa Cases*, Dissenting Opinion of Judge Koretsky, p. 242.

50. Max Frankel, "Crisis Seen Over South-West Africa," *New York Times*, 17 July 1966.

51. "South-West Africa Decision," *New York Times*, 18 July 1966.

52. "U.S. is Surprised by Africa Ruling," *New York Times*, 20 July 1966.

53. An international organization can request a nonbinding advisory opinion, but scholars question whether such opinions affect state behavior (Pomerance 1997).

54. *Case Concerning the Northern Cameroons*, Judgment on Preliminary Objections, 2 December 1963, p. 29.

55. Quoted in Raymond Daniell, "African Bloc Scores World Court Ruling and Plans Strategy," *New York Times*, 20 July 1966. See also "The World: Court Decision Stirs Up Africa," *New York Times*, 24 July 1966.

56. President Charles Stewart declared the ruling: "a complete justification of South Africa's sustained denial of any right to interfere by other states in the Republic's administration of South West Africa ... Any further attempt at interference by other means would spring from a spirit of persecution and should find no support from any respectable state or organization of states." See Falk (1967, 16).

57. Quoted in Drew Middleton, "South Africans Protest to U.S.," *New York Times*, 18 August 1966.

58. As described below, the UN Security Council did ask the ICJ for an advisory opinion on *South West Africa* in 1971. The Court also issued a 1975 advisory opinion on the legal status of Western Sahara

following decolonization. However, this case involved border claims and property rights, not the conduct of Spain during its colonial period.

59. See *Continental Shelf* (Tunisia/Libyan Arab Jamahiriya), which was filed in 1978. See also *Certain Phosphate Lands in Nauru* (Nauru v. Australia), filed in 1989, and *East Timor* (Portugal v. Australia), filed in 1991.

60. For example, the United States accepted ICJ jurisdiction in 1946 via a unilateral declaration. Over subsequent decades, the United States also signed many treaties that created ICJ jurisdiction under compromissory clauses, including the Optional Protocol to the Vienna Convention on Consular Relations (discussed below). The United States revoked its unilateral declaration in 1985. However, the United States remained subject to the Court's jurisdiction for certain treaties under preexisting compromissory clauses.

61. These states are: Liberia, Egypt, Sudan, Somalia, Uganda, Kenya, and Gambia.

62. Robert Conley, "Apartheid Move Faces Court Test," *New York Times*, 1 April 1964. See also "South-West Africa Gets Division Plan," *New York Times*, 28 January 1964.

63. See UN General Assembly resolution 2145 (XXI). See also Raymond Daniell, "49 Members Urge U.N. to Take Over South-West Africa," *New York Times*, 28 September 1966; Raymond Daniell, "League Mandate in Africa Ended by 114 to 2 in U.N.," *New York Times*, 28 October 1966; and "South Africans Defiant on Rule Over League Mandate Region," *New York Times*, 6 November 1966.

64. See UN General Assembly resolutions 2324 (XXII), 2440 (XXII), and 2346 (XXII). See also "30 Found Guilty in South Africa," *New York Times*, 27 January 1968; and "Contemporary Practice of the United States Relating to International Law," *American Journal of International Law*, 1969, pp. 312–336.

65. I thank an anonymous reviewer for suggesting this argument.

66. UN General Assembly resolution XXI of 27 October 1966.

67. See UN Security Council resolution 245 of 25 January 1968.

68. *Legal Consequences for States of the Continued Presence of South Africa in Namibia (South West Africa) notwithstanding Security Council Resolution 276*, Advisory Opinion of 21 June 1971, para. 133(1).

69. Quoted in "Contemporary Practice of the United States Relating to International Law," *American Journal of International Law*, 1970.

70. The legal name for the *Breard* case is technically the *Case Concerning the Vienna Convention on Consular Relations*. I refer to it as *Breard* in accordance with the ICJ's practice in the subsequent cases.

71. See *Case Concerning the Vienna Convention on Consular Relations* (Paraguay v. United States), Order of 9 April 1998.

72. See VCCR, Article 5.

73. For example, consider the circumstances of Angel Francisco Breard. As a national of Paraguay, he was arrested in the receiving state of the United States. The VCCR details the rights of consular officials of Paraguay, the sending state, to provide assistance to Breard.

74. Optional Protocol to the Vienna Convention on Consular Relations Concerning the Compulsory Settlement of Disputes (1963), Preamble. Compromissory clauses are often called optional protocols.

75. *LaGrand Case* (Germany v. United States), Judgment of 27 June 2001, para. 23.

76. *Case Concerning United States Diplomatic and Consular Staff in Tehran* (United States v. Iran).

77. See *LaGrand Case* (Germany v. United States), Judgment of 27 June 2001.

78. See *Case Concerning Avena and Other Mexican Nationals* (Mexico v. United States), Judgment of 31 March 2004.

79. *Vienna Convention on Consular Relations* (Paraguay v. United States of America), Order of 9 April 1998, para. 41, 1; and *LaGrand Case* (Germany v. United States), Order of 3 March 1999, para. 29, 1 (a).

80. For the court to issue an order of provisional measures, it only needs to have a *prima facie* basis for jurisdiction. This standard is lower than the standard that the Court uses in later litigation stages.

81. *LaGrand Case* (Germany v. United States), Judgment of 27 June 2001, para. 95 and 96.

82. *LaGrand Case* (Germany v. United States), Judgment of 27 June 2001, para. 109.

83. Emphasis added.

84. *LaGrand Case* (Germany v. United States), Judgment of 27 June 2001, para. 82.

85. Emphasis added.

86. *LaGrand Case*(Germany v. United States), Judgment of 27 June 2001, para. 86 and 85.

87. *LaGrand Case* (Germany v. United States), Judgment of 27 June 2001, para. 90.

88. *LaGrand Case* (Germany v. United States), Judgment of 27 June 2001, para. 125.

89. Paraguay dropped its case shortly after Breard's execution. Gossip abounds about why Paraguay did this. Unfortunately, we have no credible sources on this matter at this point in time.

90. Emphasis added. *LaGrand Case* (Germany v. United States), Judgment of 27 June 2001, para. 128(3).

91. See Shaw (2008, 171–174). For a more extensive discussion of the relationship between municipal and international law, see Shaw (2008, 129–194).

92. *Application for Revision of the Judgment of 11 September 1992 in the Case Concerning the Land, Island and Maritime Frontier Dispute* (El Salvador/Honduras: Nicaragua intervening)(El Salvador v. Honduras).

93. *Case Concerning Avena and Other Mexican Nationals* (Mexico v. United States), Judgment of 19 January 2009, para. 153(10).

94. White House, Office of the Press Secretary. "Memorandum for the Attorney General." Released on 28 February 2005.

95. Quoted in Adam Liptak, "U.S. Says It Has Withdrawn From World Judicial Body," *New York Times*, 10 March 2005.

96. See "U.S. Courts vs. World Court" in the House Congressional Record, H4214, 1 May 2007.

97. *Request for Interpretation of the Judgment of 31 March 2004 in the Case Concerning Avena and Other Mexican Nationals* (Mexico v. United States), Judgment of 19 January 2009.

98. *Case Concerning Avena and Other Mexican Nationals* (Mexico v. United States), Judgment of 19 January 2009, para. 151.

99. United Nations Archive. Reference: C.N.186.2005.TREATIES-1 (Depository Notification).

100. H.R. 6481 was introduced on 14 July 2008.

101. Avena Case Implementation Act of 2008 (H.R. 6481), Sec. 2, para. (a) and (b)(2).

102. S. 1194 was introduced on 14 June 2011. For the Obama administration's position, see "Consular Notification Compliance Act" in the Senate Congressional Record, S4215–4218, 29 June 2011.

103. Statement of Senator Patrick Leahy (D-Vt.), Chairman, Senate Committee on the Judiciary, "Fulfilling Our Treaty Obligations And Protecting Americans Abroad," 27 July 2011.

104. For example, see *Application of the Convention on the Prevention and Punishment of the Crime of Genocide* (Bosnia and Herzegovina v. Serbia and Montenegro), 1993–2007.

105. The ICJ decolonization cases, including *South West Africa* and *Northern Cameroons*, invoked human rights claims. However, many of cases that ostensibly involved human rights claims were actually conflicts over natural resources, including *Certain Phosphate Lands in Nauru* and *East Timor*.

106. See the rulings in *Questions Relating to the Obligation to Prosecute or Extradite* (Belgium v. Senegal).

107. For example, see *Arrest Warrant of 11 April 2000* (Democratic Republic of the Congo v. Belgium), Judgment of 14 February 2002, in which the ICJ refused to invalidate diplomatic immunity for a foreign minister accused of human rights violations. This stands in stark contrast to the changing international sentiment that was expressed in the Law Lords ruling for the Pinochet case.

108. See Brian Knowlton, "Texas Death Row Case Resonates to a Treaty," *New York Times*, 15 June 2011.

Chapter 5

1. Throughout this chapter I refer to both the GATT 1947 treaty and the trade regime that evolved from this agreement as "GATT." For a historical overview of the development of the GATT, see Jackson (1997, 31–78), Jackson (1998), and Pauwelyn (2005).

2. Protocol of Provisional Application of the GATT ("GATT PPA"), 30 October 1947, United Nations, *Treaty Series*, Vol. 55, p. 308. The distinction between an executive agreement and a ratified treaty does not matter for my theory as long as the agreement is believed to create legal commitments, as in the GATT.

3. In a press release on 6 December 1950, the Truman administration announced: "The interested agencies have recommended, and the President has agreed, that...the proposed Charter for an International Trade Organization should not be (re)submitted to the Congress." Quoted in Ostry (1997, 63).

4. The enhanced tariff commitments were made during the Annecy Round of 1949, the Torquay Round of 1951, the Geneva Round of 1956, the Dillon Round of 1960–1961, and the Kennedy Round of 1964–1967. Nontariff barriers became a prominent topic of GATT negotiations in the 1960s.

5. As in GATT, special provisions were made for developing countries. See Bown (2009) for an overview on this topic.

6. GATT 1947, Art. XXIII.

7. *United States–Withdrawal of a Tariff Concession under Article XIX (Fur Felt Hat Bodies)* (Complainant: Czechoslovakia).

8. For example, see *United States–Preliminary Determinations with Respect to Certain Softwood Lumber from Canada* (Complainant: Canada). See Dunoff (2007) for an overview of this dispute.

9. *European Union–Anti-Dumping Measures on Certain Footwear from China* (Complainant: China).

10. "[A] panel should make an objective assessment of the matter before it, including an objective assessment of the facts of the case and the applicability of and conformity with the [GATT]." *Understanding Regarding Notification, Consultation, Dispute Settlement and Surveillance* ("Tokyo Understanding"), GATT, BISD 26 Supp. 210–218 (1978–1979), para. 16.

11. Romano develops a taxonomy of international judicial institutions, and classifies both the ICJ and the GATT/WTO DSS as international courts. He argues that the GATT/WTO panel terminology reflects historical norms, and does not diminish the DSS's role as an international court (Romano 2011, 254).

12. See Chapter VIII of the Havana Charter.

13. GATT 1947, Art. XXII, para. 1.

14. GATT 1947, Art. XXII, para. 2.

15. GATT 1947, Art. XXIII, para. 1(c).

16. For an overview of this evolution, see Trebilcock and Howse (1995, 383–385).

17. Under certain very limited circumstances, the GATT permits the unilateral suspension of concessions. See GATT 1947, Art. XIX, para. 3(a), and Art. XXVIII, para. 3(b) and 4(d).

18. Understanding Regarding Notification, Consultation, Dispute Settlement and Surveillance ("Tokyo Understanding"), GATT, BISD 26 Supp. 210–218 (1978–1979).

19. See Jackson (1997, 75–78). Steinberg and Goldstein (2008) provide a critique of such *de facto* (or "behavioral") delegation to the GATT.

20. Tokyo Understanding, para. 16.

21. Tokyo Understanding, para. 10 and Annex, para. 6 (iv) and 16.

22. Tokyo Understanding, Annex, para. 4.

23. During the entire GATT period of 1947 to 1994, the suspension of concessions was authorized in only one case: a dispute between the Netherlands and the United States over dairy products in the early 1950s.

24. See Trebilcock and Howse (1995, 385). The five new dispute settlement systems were created by the Tokyo Codes for: subsidies and countervailing duties, technical barriers, government procurement, customs valuation, and antidumping duties.

25. GATT/L/6045, 8 September 1986.

26. GATT, BISD 29 Supp. 9, 10 (1981–1982).

27. GATT, BISD 29 Supp. 14 and 16 (1981–1982).

28. GATT, BISD 31 Supp. 10 (1983–1984).

29. GATT, BISD 33 Supp. 25 (1985–1986).

30. GATT, BISD 36 Supp. 61–67 (1988–1989).

31. GATT, BISD 36 Supp. 61 (1988–1989).

32. GATT, BISD 36 Supp. 61 and 66 (1988–1989).

33. Emphasis added. GATT, BISD 36 Supp. 63 (1988–1989).

34. Understanding on Rule and Procedures Governing the Settlement of Disputes ("Dispute Settlement Understanding (DSU)"), in WTO (1999, 354–379).

35. The process as fully elaborated in the DSU is much more complex, including rules on deadlines, multiple complainants, expert testimony, etc. Readers interested in a more thorough explication of the WTO dispute settlement system should consult Palmeter and Mavroidis (2004) and WTO (2004).

36. DSU, Art. 22, para. 1. For violation complaints, the DSU is emphatic that the withdrawal of offending measures if "the first objective" of the DSS. See DSU, Art. 3, para. 7. However, compensation can be used temporarily if immediate withdrawal is not possible. For non-violation complaints, a respondent is not required to alter its trade policies. However, a mutually satisfactory adjustment must be made. See DSU, Art. 26, para. 1(b).

37. The DSU contains some additional procedures that allow a respondent to challenge these requests. See DSU, Art. 22, para. 6–7.

38. See DSU, Art. I and Appendix 2.

39. The one exception involves claims filed under GATT Art. XXIII:1(c). For such cases, formation of a panel is automatic but all subsequent procedures must take place under the 1989 Improvements. See DSU, Art. 26, para 2. However, no dispute in the WTO has ever invoked GATT Art. XXIII:1(c) and there is no consensus on the substantive meaning and application of this GATT provision (WTO 2004, 34).

40. Under the DSU, panel formation, adoption of reports, and authorization to suspend concessions are all actions of the Dispute Settlement Body, not the General Council of WTO members. However, every WTO member has a seat on the Body and under current practice the General Council consists of the same individual diplomats as the Body.

41. Some are careful to note that the process is actually quasi-automatic since the complainant can stop the DSS proceedings if she wishes to do so.

42. DSU, Art. 21, para. 5, and Art. 22, para. 2.

43. For a comprehensive overview of GATT safeguards law, see Jackson (1997, 175–211).

44. Emphasis added. GATT 1947, Art. XIX, para. 1. For various historical reasons, this GATT provision is commonly referred to as the "escape clause." Since many different provisions of GATT allow

members to "escape" from their obligations without abrogating the treaty, I refer to Article XIX as the "safeguards clause."

45. For an extensive discussion of the negotiation draft text, see Glick (1984, 112–126).

46. GATT, BISD 26 Supp. 209–210 (1978–1979).

47. GATT, BISD 29 Supp. 11 (1981–1982).

48. For an overview of WTO safeguards law, see Lee (2005) and Van den Bossche (2005, 633–649).

49. Panel report of 27 March 1951, para. 29. The panel concluded in para. 30 that the United States is entitled to "the benefit of any reasonable doubt" and that Czechoslovakia had failed to prove that this injury was not serious.

50. Safeguards Agreement, Art. 2, para. 1.

51. Safeguards Agreement, Art. 4, para. 2(b).

52. GATT, Art. XIX, para. 1.

53. Safeguards Agreement, Art. 5, para. 1.

54. The GATT does allow MFN exceptions for preferential trade agreements.

55. GATT 1947, Art. XIX, para. 1.

56. Safeguards Agreement, Art. 2, para. 2. Some exceptions apply. See Article 5.2 (b) and Article 9.1.

57. GATT, Art. XIX, para. 3(a). The term "compensation" is not actually used in the text of Article XIX. However, this has become standard nomenclature and was formally adopted in WTO texts.

58. VERs were also commonly called: export-restraint agreements, gray-area measures, voluntary restraint arrangements, and orderly marketing arrangements.

59. Jackson (1997, 205). See also Jackson (2000, 69–86) for an overview of legal arguments about VERs.

60. Safeguards Agreement, Art. 11, para. 1(b) and para. 3.

61. GATT 1947, Art. XVI, para. 1.

62. CVDs are sometimes called "countervailing measures." For an overview on the law and economics of subsidies and countervailing duties, see Trebilcock and Howse (1995, 125–161).

63. GATT 1947, Art. VI, para. 3.

64. *Agreement on Interpretation and Application of Articles VI, XVI, and XXIII of the General Agreement on Tariffs and Trade* ("Tokyo Subsidies Code"), GATT, BISD 26 Supp. 56–83 (1978–1979). An extensive and detailed analysis of the Tokyo Subsidies Code can be found in Glick (1984, 208–235).

65. *Agreement on Subsidies and Countervailing Measures* ("SCM Agreement"), in WTO (1999, 231–274). The change in terminology from

"countervailing duties" to "countervailing measures" was semantic and does not reflect any substantive change. The internal text of the SCM Agreement exclusively refers to "countervailing duties."

66. GATT PPA, para. 1(b).

67. The main source of United States domestic CVD law was the Tariff Act of 1897, although additional rules were included in some pre-GATT bilateral trade agreements. See Jackson (1997, 285–287).

68. See GATT, BISD 26 Supp. 201 (1978–1979): "existing rights and benefits under the GATT of contracting parties not being parties to these Agreements, including those derived from Article I, are not affected by these Agreements."

69. *United States–Imposition of Countervailing Duty Without Injury Criterion* (Complainant: India). Discussed in Hudec (1993, 486–487).

70. GATT, BISD 9 Supp. 185–188 (1961). See also Jackson (2000, 94) and Jackson (1997, 285–286).

71. *United States–Suspension of Customs Liquidation* (Complainant: Japan). The definition of subsidy was key to this case, although exemptions under the grandfather clause of the GATT PPA also played a role in the dispute. See Hudec (1993, 468–469).

72. For export subsidies, see the Tokyo Subsidies Code, Annex. For domestic subsidies, see Tokyo Subsidies Code, Art. 11, para. 1 and 3.

73. According the SCM Agreement, a subsidy exists if two criteria are met. First, there must be "a financial contribution by a government or any public body within the territory...[or] any form of income or price support." Second, this action must confer a benefit. Any public policy that fails either criterion is not considered a "subsidy" by the WTO.

74. Quoted in Van den Bossche (2005, 553).

75. Emphasis added. GATT 1947, Art. XVI, para. 3.

76. The government agency was the Office National Interprofessionnel des Céréales.

77. Data from the GATT panel report for *French Assistance to Exports of Wheat and Wheat Flour* (Complainant: Australia), Adopted on 21 November 1958.

78. GATT 1947, Art. XVI, para. 3.

79. GATT 1947, Art. XVI, para. 3 and 4.

80. *European Economic Community–Subsidies on Export of Pasta Products* (Complainant: United States).

81. See panel report for *European Economic Community–Subsidies on Export of Pasta Products* (Complainant: United States), 19 May 1983, para. 4.4. GATT document number: SCM/43.

82. Agricultural subsidies are excluded from the SCM Agreement and are regulated under a different agreement.

83. SCM Agreement, Art. 3.1(b).

84. SCM Agreement, Art. 2.1.

85. SCM Agreement, Art. 5.

86. Article VI states that subsidies do not "result in material injury" if: (1) the exported price of a good is higher than the price of the like product in the exporter's domestic market; or (2) the subsidy does "not . . . stimulate exports unduly or otherwise seriously prejudice the interests of other [GATT members]."

87. However, the rise of preferential trade agreements, such as the North American Free Trade Agreement, has opened the door to new opportunities for forum-shopping (Davis 2009). This is discussed in the next chapter.

88. For an overview of the law and economics of antidumping duties, see Trebilcock and Howse (1995, 97–124).

89. GATT 1947, Art. VI, para. 1.

90. Emphasis added. GATT, Art. VI, para. 1. AD duties were also allowed if dumping "retards the establishment of a domestic industry."

91. *Agreement on Implementation of Article VI of the General Agreement on Tariffs and Trade* ("Tokyo AD Code"), GATT, BISD 26 Supp. 171–188 (1978–1979). This was an elaboration on the Kennedy Antidumping Code of 1967, contained in: *Agreement on Implementation of Article VI of the General Agreement on Tariffs and Trade*, GATT, BISD 15 Supp. 24–35 (1967–1968).

92. *Agreement on Implementation of Article VI of the General Agreement on Tariffs and Trade 1994* ("AD Agreement"), in WTO (1999, 147–171). A detailed account of the procedures and standards required by the AD Agreement is available in Czako, Human and Miranda (2003).

93. AD Agreement, Art. 2.4.

94. For example, see Jackson (1997, 256). Additionally, GATT members were not required to provide public notice or to allow foreign firm participation in dumping investigations.

95. The GATT did provide some limited examples of when states could not conclude that material injury had occurred.

96. See GATT, BISD 32 Supp. 186 (1984–1985).

97. AD Agreement, Art. 3.7.

98. I thank an anonymous reviewer for suggesting this argument.

99. See GATT 1947, Art. XIX, para. 3(a). This system was similar to retaliation in the dispute settlement system, but retaliation is permissible in the DSS only if a country has violated its trading obligations and refuses to remove the offending measure.

100. See Safeguards Agreement, Art. 8.3.

Chapter 6

1. Unilateral declarations can be denounced by notifying the UN Secretary-General (UNSG). Each treaty with a compromissory clause contains its own procedures for denunciation, but these procedures often require only that a treaty member notify the UNSG. For example, see Article 12 of the Optional Protocol to the International Covenant for Civil and Political Rights. On treaty termination more generally, see Shaw (2008, 945–952).
2. Alter (2012) counts eleven copies of the ECJ and four copies of the WTO DSS.
3. See also MacKinnon (2006, 942): "Rape under [ICTR and ICTFY] statutes is thus not a free-standing crime but must be charged as an act of war, genocide, or crime against humanity." Feminist legal scholars have tried to establish a history of treaty law and jurisprudence by scavenging through the records of post-World War II military tribunals and occupation laws (Askin 2003). However, many grand contemporary claims about the status of sexual violence in international law—such as Schomburg and Paterson (2007, 122): "Today it is firmly established that rape and other acts of sexual violence entail individual criminal responsibility under international law"—can be supported only by invoking ICTR and ICTFY rulings from the late 1990s.
4. See ICTR, *Prosecutor v. Akayesu*; and ICTFY, *Prosecutor v. Kunarac, Kovac and Vukovic.*
5. See Rome Statute, Article 7, para. 1 (g); Article 8, para. 2 (b)(xxii).
6. See Dawson (1999) for an overview of competing legal definitions of aggression.
7. See ICC Resolution RC/Res. 6, Adopted on 11 June 2010. See also Dawson (1999) and Ferencz (2007).
8. See Sornarajah (2004) for a discussion of the development of international investment law.
9. For example, see Blustein (2009), Dunoff (1994, 1999, 2009), and Guzman (2003, 2004).
10. Remarks by Robert Zoellick, former United States Trade Representative, at Princeton University on 29 November 2012.
11. See Davis (2009), Dupuy (1998), Pinto (1998), and Treves (1998). See also DiMascio and Pauwelyn (2008) on the interpretation of legal standards across different issue-areas.
12. See the panel report for *Turkey–Restrictions on Imports of Textile and Clothing Products*, DS34, para. 2.3. WTO Document: WT/DS34/R.
13. This example comes from Johns and Peritz (forthcoming). See Busch (2007) and Davis (2009) for other examples.

14. India invoked claims from both the GATT and the WTO Agreement on Textiles and Clothing.

15. See the Appellate Body report for *Turkey–Restrictions on Imports of Textile and Clothing Products*, DS34, para. 64. WTO Document: WT/DS34/AB/R.

16. See Allee and Peinhardt (2010), Allee and Peinhardt (2011), and Sornarajah (2004). ICSID was originally created in 1966, but did become a prominent component in BITs until the post-Cold War era.

17. For example, the 1991 BIT between Germany and Argentina requires a prior submission to domestic courts, while the 1991 BIT between Argentina and Chile does not. See *Siemens A.G. v The Argentine Republic* (ICSID Case No. ARB/02/8), Decision on Jurisdiction, 3 August 2004.

18. For example, see *Siemens A.G. v The Argentine Republic* (ICSID Case No. ARB/02/8), Decision on Jurisdiction, 3 August 2004, and *Salini Costruttori S.p.A. and Italstrade S.p.A. v The Hashemite Kingdom of Jordan* (ICSID Case No. ARB/02/13), Decision on Jurisdiction, 29 November 2004.

Appendix

1. Banks and Sobel (1987).

References

Abbott, Kenneth W. and Duncan Snidal. 2000. "Hard and Soft Law in International Governance." *International Organization* 54:421–456.

Abbott, Kenneth W., Robert O. Keohane, Andrew Moravcsik, Anne-Marie Slaughter and Duncan Snidal. 2000. "The Concept of Legalization." *International Organization* 54:401–419.

Allee, Todd and Clint Peinhardt. 2010. "Delegating Differences: Bilateral Investment Treaties and Patterns of Dispute Resolution Design." *International Studies Quarterly* 54:1–26.

Allee, Todd and Clint Peinhardt. 2011. "Contingent Credibility: The Reputational Effects of Investment Treaty Disputes on Foreign Direct Investment." *International Organization* 65:401–432.

Allee, Todd L. and Paul K. Huth. 2006*a*. "Legitimizing Dispute Settlement: International Legal Rulings as Domestic Political Cover." *American Political Science Review* 100:219–234.

Allee, Todd L. and Paul K. Huth. 2006*b*. "The Pursuit of Legal Settlements to Territorial Disputes." *Conflict Management and Peace Science* 23:285–307.

Alter, Karen J. 1998. "Who Are the 'Masters of the Treaty'?: European Governments and the European Court of Justice." *International Organization* 52:121–147.

Alter, Karen J. 2000. "The European Union's Legal System and Domestic Policy: Spillover or Backlash?" *International Organization* 54:489–518.

Alter, Karen J. 2001. *Establishing the Supremacy of European Law: The Making of an International Rule of Law in Europe.* Oxford University Press.

Alter, Karen J. 2003. "Resolving or Exacerbating Disputes? The WTO's New Dispute Resolution System." *International Affairs* 79:783–800.

Alter, Karen J. 2006. "Private Litigants and the New International Courts." *Comparative Political Studies* 35:22–49.

Alter, Karen J. 2012. "The Global Spread of European Style International Courts." *West European Politics* 35:135–154.

Alter, Karen J. 2014. *The New Terrain of International Law: Courts, Politics, Rights.* Princeton University Press.

Alter, Karen J. and Laurence R. Helfer. 2010. "Nature or Nurture? Judicial Lawmaking in the European Court of Justice and the Andean Tribunal of Justice." *International Organization* 64:563–592.

Askin, Kelly D. 2003. "Prosecuting Wartime Rape and Other Gender-Related Crimes under International Law: Extraordinary Advances, Enduring Obstacles." *Berkeley Journal of International Law* 21:288–349.

Axelrod, Robert. 1985. *The Evolution of Cooperation.* Basic Books.

Ayres, Ian and Robert Gertner. 1989. "Filling Gaps in Incomplete Contracts: An Economic Theory of Default Rules." *Yale Law Journal* 99:87–130.

Baird, Douglas G., Robert H. Gertner and Randal C. Picker. 1994. *Game Theory and the Law.* Harvard University Press.

Ballinger, Ronald B. 1964. "The International Court of Justice and the South West Africa Cases." *South African Law Journal* 81:35–62.

Banks, Jeffrey S. and Joel Sobel. 1987. "Equilibrium Selection in Signaling Games." *Econometrica* 55:647–661.

Barton, John H., Judith L. Goldstein, Timothy E. Josling and Richard Steinberg. 2006. *The Evolution of the Trade Regime: Politics, Law, and Economics of the GATT and the WTO.* Princeton University Press.

Baum, Robert Love. 1976. *Southwest Africa Under Mandate: Documents on the Administration of the Former German Protectorate of Southwest Africa by the Union of South Africa under Mandate of the League of Nations, 1919-1929.* Documentary Publication.

Bebchuk, Lucian Arye. 1984. "Litigation and Settlement Under Imperfect Information." *Rand Journal of Economics* 15:404–415.

Bello, Judith Hippler. 1996. "The WTO Dispute Settlment Understanding: Less is More." *American Journal of International Law* 90:416–418.

Benvenisti, Eyal. 2004. Customary International Law as a Judicial Tool for Promoting Efficiency. In *The Impact of International Law on International Cooperation,* ed. Eyal Benvenisti and Moshe Hirsch. Cambridge University Press pp. 85–116.

Bhala, Raj. 1998-1999. "The Myth about Stare Decisis and International Trade Law (Part One of a Trilogy)." *American University International Law Review* 14:845–956.

Bierwagen, Rainer M. 1990. *GATT Article VI and the Protectionist Bias in Anti-dumping Laws.* Kluwer Law and Taxation Publishers.

Bilder, Richard B. 1987. "International Dispute Settlement and the Role of International Adjudication." *Emory Journal of International Dispute Resolution* 1:131–173.

Blaydes, Lisa. 2004. "Rewarding Impatience: A Bargaining and Enforcement Model of OPEC." *International Organization* 58:213–237.

Bliss, Julia Christine. 1987. "GATT Dispute Settlement Reform in the Uruguay Round: Problems and Process." *Stanford Journal of International Law* 23:31–55.

Blustein, Paul. 2009. *Misadventures of the Most Favored Nations.* Public Affairs.

Bourgeois, H. J. 1988. The GATT Rules for Industrial Subsidies and Countervailing Duties and the New GATT Round — The Weather and the Seeds. In *The New GATT Round of Multilateral Trade Negotiations,* ed. Ernst-Ulrich Petersmann and Meinhard Hilf. Kluwer pp. 219–235.

Bown, Chad P. 2002. "Why Are Safeguards Under the WTO So Unpopular?" *World Trade Review* 1:47–62.

Bown, Chad P. 2009. *Self-Enforcing Trade: Developing Countries and WTO Dispute Settlement.* Brookings Institution Press.

Bradley, Curtis A. and Jack L. Goldsmith. 2000. "Treaties, Human Rights, and Conditional Consent." *University of Pennsylvania Law Review* 149:399–468.

Brewster, Rachel. 2003. "The Domestic Origins of International Agreements." *Virginia Journal of International Law* 44:501–544.

Brewster, Rachel. 2006. "Rule-Based Dispute Resolution in International Trade Law." *Virginia Law Review* 92:251–288.

Brewster, Rachel. 2009. "Unpacking the State's Reputation." *Harvard International Law Journal* 50:231–269.

Brewster, Rachel. 2011a. "The Remedy Gap: Institutional Design, Retaliation, and

Trade Law Enforcement." *George Washington University Law Review* 80:102–156.

Brewster, Rachel. 2011*b*. "The Surprising Benefits to Developing Countries of Linking International Trade and Intellectual Property." *Chicago Journal of International Trade* 12:1–54.

Bronckers, M.C.E.J. 1985. *Selective Safeguard Measures in Multilateral Trade Relations*. Kluwer.

Brownlie, Ian. 2008. *Principles of Public International Law*. Oxford University Press.

Burley, Anne-Marie Slaughter. 1993. "International Law and International Relations Theory: A Dual Agenda." *American Journal of International Law* 87:205–239.

Burley, Anne-Marie and Walter Mattli. 1993. "Europe Before the Court: A Political Theory of Legal Integration." *International Organization* 47:41–41.

Busch, Marc L. 2007. "Overlapping Institutions, Forum Shopping, and Dispute Settlement in International Trade." *International Organization* 61:735–761.

Busch, Marc L. and Eric Reinhardt. 2000. "Bargaining in the Shadow of the Law: Early Settlement in GATT/WTO Disputes." *Fordham International Law Journal* 24:158–72.

Busch, Marc L. and Eric Reinhardt. 2003. "Developing Countries and GATT/WTO Dispute Settlement." *Journal of World Trade* 37:719–35.

Busch, Marc L., Eric Reinhardt and Gregory Shaffer. 2009. "Does Legal Capacity Matter? Explaining Dispute Initiation and Antidumping Actions in the WTO." *World Trade Review* 8:559–577.

Busch, Marc L. and Krzysztof J. Pelc. 2010. "The Politics of Judicial Economy at the World Trade Organization." *International Organization* 64:257–279.

Cali, Basak. 2010. *International Law for International Relations*. Oxford University Press.

Callahan, Michael D. 1999. *Mandates and Empire: The League of Nations and Africa, 1914-1931*. Sussex Academic Press.

Callahan, Michael D. 2004. *A Sacred Trust: The League of Nations and Africa, 1929-1946*. Sussex Academic Press.

Carrubba, Clifford. 2005. "Courts and Compliance in International Regulatory Regimes." *Journal of Politics* 67:669–689.

Carrubba, Clifford J. 2009. "A Model of the Endogenous Development of Judicial Institutions in Federal and International Systems." *Journal of Politics* 71:55–69.

Carrubba, Clifford J. and Christopher Zorn. 2010. "Executive Discretion, Judicial Decision Making, and Separation of Powers in the United State." *Journal of Politics* 72:812 –824.

Carrubba, Clifford and Matthew Gabel. 2013. "International Courts and the Performance of International Agreements: A General Theory with Evidence from the European Union." Emory University book manuscript.

Cassese, Antonio. 2005. *International Law*. Oxford University Press.

Chayes, Abram and Antonia Handler Chayes. 1993. "On Compliance." *International Organization* 47:175–205.

Clark, Kim B. and Takahiro Fujimoto. 1991. *Product Development Performance: Strategy, Organization, and Management in the World Auto Industry*. Harvard Business School Press.

Conrad, Courtenay R. and Emily Hencken Ritter. 2013. "Tenure, Treaties, and Torture: The Conflicting Domestic Effects of International Law." *Journal of Politics* 75:397–409.

Czako, Judith, Johann Human and Jorge Miranda. 2003. *A Handbook on Antidumping Investigations*. Cambridge University Press.

Dai, Xinyuan. 2005. "Why Comply? The Domestic Constituency Mechanism." *International Organization* 59:363–98.

Dale, Richard. 1980. *Anti-dumping Law in a Liberal Trade Order.* St. Martin's Press.

D'Amato, Anthony. 1987. "Trashing Customary International Law." *American Journal of International Law* 81:101–105.

Davis, Christina L. 2003. *Food Fights Over Free Trade: How International Institutions and Issue Linkage Promote Agricultural Trade Liberalization.* Princeton University Press.

Davis, Christina L. 2006. Do WTO Rules Create a Level Playing Field for Developing Countries? Lessons From Peru and Vietnam. In *Negotiating Trade: Developing Countries in the WTO and NAFTA*, ed. John Odell. Cambridge University Press pp. 219–256.

Davis, Christina L. 2009. "Overlapping Institutions in Trade Policy." *Perspectives on Politics* 7:25–31.

Davis, Christina L. 2012. *Why Adjudicate? Enforcing Trade Rules in the WTO.* Princeton University Press.

Davis, Christina L. and Jennifer Oh. 2007. "Repeal of the Rice Laws in Japan: The Role of International Pressure to Overcome Vested Interests." *Comparative Politics* 40:21–40.

Davis, Christina L. and Sarah Blodgett Bermeo. 2009. "Who Files? Developing Country Participation in WTO Adjudication." *Journal of Politics* 71:1033–1049.

Davis, Christina L. and Yuki Shirato. 2007. "Firms, Governments, and WTO Adjudication: Japan's Selection of WTO Disputes." *World Politics* 59:274–313.

Dawson, Grant M. 1999. "Defining Substantive Crimes Within the Subject Matter Jurisdiction of the International Criminal Court: What Is the Crime of Aggression?" *New York Law School Journal of International and Comparative Law* 19:413–452.

Diehl, Paul F. and Charlotte Ku. 2010. *The Dynamics of International Law.* Cambridge University Press.

DiMascio, Nicholas and Joost Pauwelyn. 2008. "Nondiscrimination in Trade and Investment Treaties: Worlds Apart or Two Sides of the Same Coin?" *American Journal of International Law* 102:48–89.

Downs, George W. and David M. Rocke. 1995. *Optimal Imperfection? Domestic Uncertainty and Institutions in International Relations.* Princeton University Press.

Downs, George W., David M. Rocke and Peter N. Barsoom. 1996. "Is the Good News about Compliance Good News about Cooperation?" *International Organization* 50:379–406.

Downs, George W., David M. Rocke and Peter N. Barsoom. 1998. "Managing the Evolution of Multilateralism." *International Organization* 52:397–419.

Dugard, John. 1973. *The South West Africa/Namibia Dispute.* University of California Press.

Dunoff, Jeffrey L. 1994. "Institutional Misfits: The GATT, the ICJ and Trade-Environment Disputes." *Michigan Journal of International Law* 15:1043–1128.

Dunoff, Jeffrey L. 1999. "Rethinking International Trade." *University of Pennsylvania Journal of International Economic Law* 19:347–389.

Dunoff, Jeffrey L. 2007. "The Many Dimensions of Softwood Lumber." *Alberta Law Review* 45:320–356.

Dunoff, Jeffrey L. 2009. "Linking International Markets and Global Justice." *Michigan Law Review* 107:1039–1058.

Dupuy, Pierre-Marie. 1998. "The Danger of Fragmentation or Unification of the

International Legal System and the International Court of Justice." *N.Y.U. Journal of International Law and Politics* 31:791–807.

Elkins, Zachary, Andrew T. Guzman and Beth A. Simmons. 2006. "Competing for Capital: The Diffusion of Bilateral Investment Treaties, 1960-2000." *International Organization* 60:811–846.

Elkins, Zachary, Tom Ginsburg and Beth A. Simmons. 2012. "Getting to Rights: Treaty Ratification, Constitutional Convergence, and Human Rights Practice." *Harvard International Law Journal* 54:61–95.

Engle, Karen. 2005. "Feminism and Its (Dis)contents: Criminalizing Wartime Rape in Bosnia and Herzegovina." *American Journal of International Law* 99:778–816.

Falk, Richard A. 1967. "The South West Africa Cases: An Appraisal." *International Organization* 21:1–23.

Fang, Songying. 2010. "The Strategic Use of International Institutions in Dispute Settlement." *Quarterly Journal of Political Science* 5:107–131.

Fearon, James D. 1995. "Rationalist Explanations for War." *International Organization* 49:379–414.

Fearon, James D. 1998. "Bargaining, Enforcement and International Cooperation." *International Organization* 52:269–306.

Ferencz, Benjamin B. 2007. "Enabling the International Criminal Court to Punish Aggression." *Washington University Global Studies Law Review* 6:551–566.

Finger, J. Michael. 1993. The Origins and Evolution of Antidumping Regulation. In *Antidumping: How it Works and Who Gets Hurt*, ed. J. Michael Finger. University of Michigan Press pp. 13–34.

Fischer, Dana D. 1982. "Decisions to Use the International Court of Justice: Four Recent Cases." *International Studies Quarterly* 26:251–277.

Fiss, Owen M. 1984. "Against Settlement." *Yale Law Journal* 93:1073–1090.

Fox, Justin and Georg Vanberg. forthcoming. "Narrow versus Broad Judicial Decisions." *Journal of Theoretical Politics*.

Franck, Thomas M. 1998. *Fairness in International Law and Institutions*. Oxford University Press.

Fudenberg, Drew and Jean Tirole. 2000. *Game Theory*. MIT Press.

Gabel, Matthew J., Clifford J. Carrubba, Caitlin Ainsley and Donald M. Beaudette. 2012. "Of Courts and Commerce." *Journal of Politics* 74:1125–1137.

Gill, Terry D. 2003. *Rosenne's The World Court: What it is and How it Works*. Martinus Nijhoff Publishers.

Gilligan, Michael J. 2006. "Is Enforcement Necessary for Effectiveness? A Model of the International Criminal Regime." *International Organization* 60:935–967.

Gilligan, Michael J. and Leslie Johns. 2012. "Formal Models of International Institutions." *Annual Review of Political Science* 15:221–243.

Gilligan, Michael, Leslie Johns and B. Peter Rosendorff. 2010. "Strengthening International Courts and the Early Settlement of Disputes." *Journal of Conflict Resolution* 54:5–38.

Ginsburg, Thomas and Richard H. McAdams. 2003. "Adjudicating in Anarchy: An Expressive Theory of International Dispute Resolution." *Willam and Mary Law Review* 45:1229–1339.

Ginsburg, Tom, Svitlana Chernykh and Zachary Elkins. 2008. "Commitment and Diffusion: How and Why National Constitutions Incorporate International Law." *University of Illinois Law Review* 2008:201–237.

Glick, Leslie Alan. 1984. *Multilateral Trade Negotiations: World Trade After tthe Tokyo Round*. Rowman and Allanheld Publishers.

Goldsmith, Jack. 2003. "The Self-Defeating International Criminal Court." *University of Chicago Law Review* 70:89–104.

Goldsmith, Jack L. and Eric A. Posner. 2005. *The Limits of International Law.* Oxford University Press.

Goldsmith, Jack and Stephen D. Krasner. 2003. "The Limits of Idealism." *Daedalus* 132:47–63.

Goldstein, Judith and Joanne Gowa. 2002*a*. "US National Power and the Post-War Trading Regime." *World Trade Review* 1:153–170.

Goldstein, Judith and Joanne Gowa. 2002*b*. "US National Power and the Post-War Trading Regime." *World Trade Review* 1:153–170.

Goldstein, Judith L., Douglas Rivers and Michael Tomz. 2007. "Institutions in International Relations: Understanding the Effects of the GATT and the WTO on World Trade." *International Organization* 61:37–67.

Goldstein, Judith L. and Richard H. Steinberg. 2008. "Negotiate or Litigate? Effects of WTO Judicial Delegation on U.S. Trade Politics." *Law & Contemporary Problems* 71:257–282.

Goldstein, Judith L. and Richard H. Steinberg. 2009. Regulatory Shift: The Rise of Judicial Liberalization at the WTO. In *The Politics of Global Regulation*, ed. Walter Mattli and Ngaire Woods. Princeton University Press pp. 211–241.

Goldstein, Judith L. and Robert O. Keohane, eds. 1993. *Ideas and Foreign Policy: Beliefs, Institutions, and Political Change.* Cornell University Press.

Goldstein, Judith and Lisa L. Martin. 2000. "Legalization, Trade Liberalization, and Domestic Politics: A Cautionary Note." *International Organization* 54:603–632.

Goldstein, Judith, Miles Kahler, Robert O. Keohane and Anne-Marie Slaughter. 2000. "Introduction: Legalization and World Politics." *International Organization* 54:385–99.

Gowa, Joanne. 1994. *Allies, Adversaries and International Trade.* Princeton University Press.

Gowa, Joanne and Edward D. Mansfield. 1993. "Power Politics and International Trade." *American Political Science Review* 87:408–420.

Grieco, Joseph M. 1988. "Anarchy and the Limits of Cooperation: A Realist Critique of the Newest Liberal Institutionalism." *International Organization* 42:485–507.

Grossman, Gene M. and Elhanan Helpman. 1994. "Protection for Sale." *American Economic Review* 84:833–850.

Grossman, Gene M. and Elhanan Helpman. 1996. "Electoral Competition and Special Interest Politics." *Review of Economic Studies* 63:265–286.

Guillaume, Gilbert. 2011. "The Use of Precedent by International Judges and Arbitrators." *Journal of International Dispute Settlement* 2:5–23.

Gulati, Curtis A. and Mitu Gulati. 2010*a*. "Customary International Law and Withdrawal Rights in an Age of Treaties." *Duke Journal of Comparative and International Law* 21:1–30.

Gulati, Curtis A. and Mitu Gulati. 2010*b*. "Withdrawing From International Custom." *Yale Law Journal* 120:202–275.

Guzman, Andrew T. 1998. "Why LDCs Sign Treaties That Hurt Them: Explaining the Popularity of Bilateral Investment Treaties." *Virginia Journal of International Law* 38:639–6688.

Guzman, Andrew T. 2002. "A Compliance-Based Theory of International Law." *California Law Review* 90:1823–1887.

Guzman, Andrew T. 2003. "Trade, Labor, Legitimacy." *California Law Review* 91:885–902.

Guzman, Andrew T. 2004. "Global Governance and the WTO." *Harvard International Law Journal* 45:303–351.

Guzman, Andrew T. 2007. *How International Law Works: A Rational Choice*

Theory. Oxford University Press.

Guzman, Andrew T. and Beth A. Simmons. 2005. "Power Plays and Capacity Constraints: The Selection of Defendants in WTO Disputes." *Journal of Legal Studies* 34:557–598.

Hafner-Burton, Emilie M., David G. Victor and Yonatan Lupu. 2012. "Political Science Research on International Law: The State of the Field." *American Journal of International Law* 106:47–97.

Hafner-Burton, Emilie M. and Kiyoteru Tsutsui. 2005. "Human Rights in a Globalizing World: The Paradox of Empty Promises." *American Journal of Sociology* 110:1373–1411.

Hafner-Burton, Emilie M., Laurence R. Helfer and Christopher J. Fariss. 2011. "Emergency and Escape: Explaining Derogations from Human Rights Treaties." *International Organization* 65:673–707.

Halley, Janet. 2008. "Rape at Rome: Feminist Interventions in the Criminalization of Sex-Related Violence in Positive International Criminal Law." *Michigan Journal of International Law* 30:1–124.

Hathaway, Oona A. 2003. "The Cost of Commitment." *Stanford Law Review* 55:1821–1862.

Hawkins, Darren G., David A. Lake, Daniel L. Nielson and Michael J. Tierney. 2006. *Delegation and Agency in International Organizations*. Cambridge University Press.

Helfer, Laurence R. 2002. "Overlegalizing Human Rights: International Relations Theory and the Commonwealth Caribbean Backlash Against Human Rights Regimes." *Columbia Law Review* 102:1832–1911.

Helfer, Laurence R. 2005. "Exiting Treaties." *Virginia Law Review* 91:1579–1648.

Helfer, Laurence R. 2008*a*. "The New Innovation Frontier? Intellectual Property and the European Court of Human Rights." *Harvard International Law Journal* 49:1–52.

Helfer, Laurence R. 2008*b*. "Nonconsensual International Lawmaking." *University of Illinois Law Review* 2008:71–125.

Helfer, Laurence R. 2010. "Exiting Custom: Analogies to Treaty Withdrawals." *Duke Journal of Comparative and International Law* 21:65–80.

Helfer, Laurence R. and Anne-Marie Slaughter. 1997–1998. "Toward a Theory of Effective Supranational Adjudication." *Yale Law Journal* 107:273–391.

Helfer, Laurence R., Karen J. Alter and M. Florencia Guerzovich. 2009. "Islands of Effective International Adjudication: Constructing an Intellectual Property Rule of Law in the Andean Community." *American Journal of International Law* 103:1–46.

Henkin, Louis. 1979. *How Nations Behave: Law and Foreign Policy*. Columbia University Press.

Higgins, Rosalyn. 2003. "The ICJ, the ECJ, and the Integrity of International Law." *International and Comparative Law Quarterly* 52:1–20.

Hollyer, James R. 2010. "Conditionality, Compliance, and Domestic Interests: State Capture and EU Accession Policy." *Review of International Organizations* 5:387–431.

Hollyer, James R. and B. Peter Rosendorff. 2011. "Why Do Authoritarian Regimes Sign the Convention Against Torture? Signaling, Domestic Politics, and Non-Compliance." *Quarterly Journal of Political Science* 6:275–327.

Horn, Henrik and Petros C. Mavroidis. 2011. "The WTO Dispute Settlement Data Set, 1995-2011." Data available at the World Bank Data Archive.

Hudec, Robert. 1993. *Enforcing International Trade Law: The Evolution of the Modern GATT Legal System*. Butterworth Legal Publishers.

Huth, Paul K., Sarah E. Croco and Benjamin J. Appel. 2011. "Does International Law Promote the Peaceful Settlement of International Disputes? Evidence from the Study of Territorial Conflicts since 1945." *American Political Science Review* 105:415–436.

Jackson, John H. 1997. *The World Trading System.* MIT Press.

Jackson, John H. 1998. "Fragmentation or Unifications Among International Institutions: The World Trade Organization." *N.Y.U. Journal of International Law and Politics* 31:823–831.

Jackson, John H. 2000. *The Jurisprudence of GATT and the WTO.* Cambridge University Press.

Janis, Mark Weston. 1987. "Somber Reflections on the Compulsory Jurisdiction of the International Court." *American Journal of International Law* 81:144–146.

Jo, Hyeran. 2008. "Monitoring Compliance: The Design of Monitoring Institutions in International Cooperation." Ph.D. dissertation (Ann Arbor: University of Michigan).

Jo, Hyeran and Hyun Namgung. 2012. "Dispute Settlement Mechanisms in Preferential Trade Agreements: Democracy, Boilerplates, and the Multilateral Trade Regime." *Journal of Conflict Resolution* 56:1041–1068.

Johns, Leslie. 2007. "A Servant of Two Masters: Communication and the Selection of International Bureaucrats." *International Organization* 61:245–275.

Johns, Leslie. 2012. "Courts as Coordinators: Endogenous Enforcement and Jurisdiction in Adjudication." *Journal of Conflict Resolution* 56:257–289.

Johns, Leslie. 2014. "Depth versus Rigidity in the Design of International Agreements." *Journal of Theoretical Politics* 26:468–495.

Johns, Leslie and B. Peter Rosendorff. 2009. Dispute Settlement, Compliance and Domestic Politics. In *Trade Disputes and the Dispute Settlement Understanding of the WTO: An Interdisciplinary Assessment.*, ed. James C. Hartigan. Emerald Group Publishing pp. 139–163.

Johns, Leslie and Krzysztof J. Pelc. 2014a. "Fear of Crowds in WTO Disputes: Why Don't More Countries Participate?". UCLA and McGill University working paper.

Johns, Leslie and Krzysztof J. Pelc. 2014b. "Who Gets to Be In the Room? Manipulating Participation in WTO Disputes." *International Organization* 68:663–699.

Johns, Leslie and Lauren Peritz. forthcoming. "The Design of Trade Agreements." Commissioned for the *Oxford Handbook of the Politics of Trade.*

Kahler, Miles. 1992. "Multilateralism with Small and Large Numbers." *International Organization* 46:681–708.

Kelley, Judith. 2007. "Who Keeps International Commitments and Why? The International Criminal Court and Bilateral Non-surrender Agreements." *American Political Science Review* 101:573–589.

Keohane, Robert O. 1982. "The Demand for International Regimes." *International Organization* 36:325–55.

Keohane, Robert O. 1984. *After Hegemony: Cooperation and Discord in the World Political Economy.* Princeton University Press.

Keohane, Robert O. 1986. "Reciprocity in International Relations." *International Organization* 40:1–27.

Keohane, Robert O. 1989. *International Institutions and State Power: Essays in International Relations Theory.* Westview Press.

Keohane, Robert O. 1997. "International Relations and International Law: Two Optics." *Harvard International Law Journal* 38:487–502.

King, Gary, Robert O. Keohane and Sidney Verba. 1994. *Designing Social Inquiry.*

Princeton University Press.

Kingsbury, Benedict. 1998. "Foreword: Is the Proliferation of International Courts and Tribunals a Systemic Problem?" *N.Y.U. Journal of International Law and Politics* 31:679–696.

Kissinger, Henry. 2001. *Does America Need a Foreign Policy? Toward a Diplomacy for the 21st Century.* Simon and Schuster.

Koremenos, Barbara. 2007. "If Only One Half of International Agreements Have Dispute Resolution Procedures, Which Half Needs Explaining?" *Journal of Legal Studies* 36:189–212.

Koremenos, Barbara. 2008. "When, What, and Why do States Choose to Delegate?" *Law and Contemporary Problems* 71:151–192.

Koremenos, Barbara. 2013. "The Continent of International Law." University of Michigan book manuscript.

Koremenos, Barbara, Charles Lipson and Duncan Snidal. 2001. "The Rational Design of International Institutions." *International Organization* 55:761–799.

Kucik, Jeffrey and Eric Reinhardt. 2008. "Does Flexibility Promote Cooperation? An Application to the Global Trade Regime." *International Organization* 62:477–505.

Lauterpacht, Hersch. 1958. *The Development of International Law by the International Court.* Frederick A. Praeger.

Lebovic, James H. and Erik Voeten. 2006. "The Politics of Shame: The Condemnation of Country Human Rights Practices in the UNCHR." *International Studies Quarterly* 50:861–888.

Lebovic, James H. and Erik Voeten. 2009. "The Cost of Shame: International Organizations and Foreign Aid in the Punishing of Human Rights Violators." *Journal of Peace Research* 46:79–97.

Lee, Yong-Shik. 2005. *Safeguard Measures in World Trade: The Legal Analysis.* Kluwer.

Lorentzen, Peter, Taylor Fravel and Jack Paine. 2013. "Bridging the Gap: Using Qualitative Evidence to Evaluate Formal Models." Paper presented at the 2013 annual meeting of the American Political Science Association.

Lupu, Yonatan and Erik Voeten. 2012. "Precedent in International Courts: A Network Analysis of Case Citations by the European Court of Human Rights." *British Journal of Political Science* 42:413–439.

MacKinnon, Catharine A. 2006. "Defining Rape Internationally: A Comment on *Akayesu.*" *Columbia Journal of Transnational Law* 44:940–958.

Maggi, Giovanni and Robert W. Staiger. 2011. "The Role of Dispute Settlement Procedures in International Trade Agreements." *Quarterly Journal of Economics* 126:475–515.

Mansfield, Edward D. and Eric Reinhardt. 2008. "International Institutions and the Volatility of International Trade." *International Organization* 62:621–652.

Mansfield, Edward D. and Helen V. Milner. 1999. "The New Wave of Regionalism." *International Organization* 53:589–627.

Mansfield, Edward D. and Helen V. Milner. 2012. *Votes, Vetoes and International Trade Agreements: The Domestic and International Politics of Preferential Trade Agreements.* Princeton University Press.

Mansfield, Edward D., Helen V. Milner and B. Peter Rosendorff. 2000. "Free to Trade: Democracies, Autocracies and International Trade." *American Political Science Review* 94:305–322.

Mansfield, Edward D., Helen V. Milner and B. Peter Rosendorff. 2002. "Why Democracies Cooperate More: Electoral Control and International Trade Agreements." *International Organization* 56:477–514.

Martin, Lisa L. 2013. Against Compliance. In *Interdisciplinary Perspectives on International Law and International Relations*, ed. Jeffrey L. Dunoff and Mark A. Pollack. Cambridge University Press pp. 591–610.

McRae, D.M. and J.C. Thomas. 1983. "The GATT and Multilateral Treaty Making: The Tokyo Round." *American Journal of International Law* 77:51–83.

Mercer, Jonathan. 1996. *Reputation and Domestic Politics*. Cornell University Press.

Milgrom, Paul R., Douglass C. North and Barry R. Weingast. 1990. "The Role of Institutions in the Revival of Trade: the Law Merchant, Private Judges, and the Champagne Fairs." *Economics and Politics* 2:1–23.

Mitchell, Sara McLaughlin and Emilia Justyna Powell. 2011. *Domestic Law Goes Global: Legal Traditions and International Courts*. Cambridge University Press.

Moravcsik, Andrew. 2000. "The Origins of International Human Rights Regimes: Democratic Delegation in Postwar Europe." *International Organization* 54:217–252.

Morrow, James D. 1994. "Modeling the Forms of International Cooperation: Distribution Versus Information." *International Organization* 48:387–423.

Morrow, James D. 2001. "The Institutional Features of Prisoners of War Treaties." *International Organization* 55:973–993.

Morrow, James D. 2002. "The Laws of War, Common Conjectures, and Legal Systems in International Politics." *Journal of Legal Studies* 31:41–60.

Morrow, James D. 2007. "When Do States Follow the Laws of War?" *American Political Science Review* 101:559–572.

Norman, George and Joel P. Trachtman. 2005. "The Customary International Law Game." *American Journal of International Law* 99:541–580.

North, Douglass C. 1990. *Institutions, Institutional Change and Economic Performance*. Cambridge University Press.

Ostry, Sylvia. 1997. *The Post-Cold War Trading System*. University of Chicago Press.

Oye, Kenneth A. 1985. "Explaining Cooperation under Anarchy: Hypotheses and Strategies." *World Politics* 38:1–24.

Oye, Kenneth A. 1986. *Cooperation Under Anarchy*. Princeton University Press.

Palmeter, David and Petros C. Mavroidis. 2004. *Dispute Settlement in the World Trade Organization: Practice and Procedure*. Cambridge University Press.

Paulson, Colter. 2004. "Compliance with Final Judgments of the International Court of Justice since 1987." *American Journal of International Law* 98:434–461.

Paulus, Andreas. 2009. "Second Thoughts on the Crime of Aggression." *European Journal of International Law* 20:1117–1128.

Pauwelyn, Joost. 2002. "The Use of Experts in WTO Dispute Settlement." *International and Comparative Law Quarterly* 51:325–364.

Pauwelyn, Joost. 2004. "The Jurisdiction of the World Trade Organization." *Proceedings of the Annual Meeting (American Society of International Law)* 98:135–138.

Pauwelyn, Joost. 2005. "The Transformation of World Trade." *Michigan Law Review* 104:1–65.

Pelc, Krzysztof J. 2009. "Seeking Escape: The Use of Escape Clauses in International Trade Agreements." *International Studies Quarterly* 53:349–368.

Pelc, Krzysztof J. 2011. "How States Ration Flexibility: Tariffs, Remedies, and Exchange Rates as Policy Substitutes." *World Politics* 63:618–646.

Pelc, Krzysztof J. 2013*a*. "The Cost of Wiggle-Room: Considering the Welfare Effects of Flexibility in Tariff Rates at the WTO." *International Studies Quarterly* 57:91–102.

Pelc, Krzysztof J. 2013*b*. "Googling the WTO: What Search Engine Data Tell Us About the Political Economy of Institutions." *International Organization* 67:629–655.

Pelc, Krzysztof J. forthcoming. "The Politics of Precedent in International Law: A Social Network Application." *American Political Science Review*.

Pinto, Monica. 1998. "Fragmentation or Unifications Among International Institutions: Human Rights Tribunals." *N.Y.U. Journal of International Law and Politics* 31:833–842.

Pollack, Mark A. 2003. *The Engines of European Integration: Delegation, Agency, and Agenda Setting in the EU.* Cambridge University Press.

Pollack, Mark A. 2005. "Theorizing the European Union: International Organization, DOmestic Polity, or Experiment in New Governance?" *Annual Review of Political Science* 8:357–398.

Pollack, Mark A. and Gregory C. Shaffer. 2009. *When Cooperation Fails: The International Law and Politics of Genetically Modified Foods.* Oxford University Press.

Pomerance, Michla. 1997. The Advisory Role of the International Court of Justice and Its 'Judicial' Character: Past and Future Prisms. In *The International Court of Justice: Its Future Role After Fifty Years*, ed. A.S. Muller Muller, David Raic and J.M. Thurnszk. Martinus Nijhoff.

Pomerance, Michla. 1999. "The ICJ and South West Africa (Namibia): A Retrospective Legal/Political Assessment." *Leiden Journal of International Law* 12:425–36.

Posner, Eric A. 2006. The Decline of the International Court of Justice. In *International Conflict Resolution*, ed. Stefan Voight, Max Albert and Dieter Schmidtchen. Mohr Siebeck pp. 111–142.

Posner, Eric and John Yoo. 2005. "Judicial Independence in International Tribunals." *California Law Review* 93:1–74.

Posner, Eric and Michael de Figueiredo. 2005. "Is the International Court of Justice Biased?" *Journal of Legal Studies* 34:599.

Powell, Robert. 1991. "Absolute and Relative Gains in International Relations Theory." *American Political Science Review* 85:1303–1320.

Quigley, John. 2009. "The United States' Withdrawal from International Court of Justice Jurisdiction in Consular Cases: Reasons and Consequences." *Duke Journal of Comparative and International Law* 19:263–305.

Raustiala, Kal. 2000. "Compliance and Effectiveness in International Regulatory Cooperation." *Case Western Reserve Journal of International Law* 32:387–440.

Raustiala, Kal. 2005. "Form and Substance in International Agreements." *American Journal of International Law* 99:581–614.

Reinganum, Jennifer F. and Louis L. Wilde. 1986. "Settlement, Litigation and the Allocation of Litigation Costs." *Rand Journal of Economics* 17:557–66.

Reinhardt, Eric R. 1996. "Posturing Parliaments: Ratification, Uncertainty, and International Bargaining." Chapter 4, Ph.D. dissertation (New York: Columbia University).

Romano, Cesare P. R. 1998. "The Proliferation of International Judicial Bodies: The Pieces of the Puzzle." *N.Y.U. Journal of International Law and Politics* 31:709–751.

Romano, Cesare P. R. 2011. "A Taxonomy of International Rule of Law Institutions." *Journal of International Dispute Settlement* 2:241–277.

Rosendorff, B. Peter. 2005. "Stability and Rigidity: Politics and the Design of the WTO's Dispute Resolution Procedure." *American Political Science Review* 99:389–400.

Rosendorff, B. Peter and Helen V. Milner. 2001. "The Optimal Design of International Institutions: Uncertainty and Escape." *International Organization* 55:829–857.

Schneider, Christina J. 2007. "Enlargement Processes and Distributional Conflicts: The Politics of Discriminatory Membership in the European Union." *Public Choice* 132:85–102.

Schneider, Christina J. 2009. *Conflict, Negotiations, and EU Enlargement.* Cambridge University Press.

Schomburg, Wolfgang and Ines Paterson. 2007. "Genuine Consent to Sexual Violence under International Criminal Law." *American Journal of International Law* 101:121–140.

Shaw, Malcolm N. 2008. *International Law.* Cambridge University Press.

Simmons, Beth A. 1998. "Compliance with International Agreements." *Annual Review of Political Science* 1:75–93.

Simmons, Beth A. 2002. "Capacity, Commitment, and Compliance: International Institutions and Territorial Disputes." *Journal of Conflict Resolution* 46:829–856.

Simmons, Beth A. 2009. *Mobilizing for Human Rights: International Law in Domestic Politics.* Cambridge University Press.

Simmons, Beth A. 2010. "Treaty Compliance and Violation." *Annual Review of Political Science* 13:273–296.

Slaughter, Anne-Marie. 1992. "Towards an Age of Liberal Nations." *Harvard International Law Journal* 33:393–405.

Slaughter, Anne-Marie. 1995. "International Law in a World of Liberal States." *European Journal of International Law* 6:503–538.

Slaughter, Anne-Marie. 2003. "A Global Community of Courts." *Harvard International Law Journal* 44:191–219.

Snidal, Duncan. 1985. "Coordination versus Prisoners' Dilemma: Implications for International Cooperation and Regimes." *American Political Science Review* 79:923–942.

Snidal, Duncan. 1991. "Relative Gains and the Pattern of International Cooperation." *American Political Science Review* 85:701–726.

Sornarajah, M. 2004. *The International Law on Foreign Investment.* Cambridge University Press.

Staton, Jeffrey. 2004. "Judicial Policy Implementation in Mexico City and Merida." *Comparative Politics* 37:41–60.

Staton, Jeffrey K. and Georg Vanberg. 2008. "The Value of Vagueness: Delegation, Defiance, and Judicial Opinions." *American Journal of Political Science* 52:504–519.

Staton, Jeffrey K. and Will H. Moore. 2011. "Judicial Power in Domestic and International Politics." *International Organization* 65:553–587.

Stein, Arthur A. 1982. "Coordination and Collaboration: Regimes in an Anarchic World." *International Organization* 36:299–324.

Stein, Arthur A. 1990. *Why Nations Cooperate: Circumstance and Choice in International Relations.* Cornell University Press.

Steinberg, Richard H. 1997. "Trade-Environment Negotiations in the EU, NAFTA, and WTO: Regional Trajectories of Rule Development." *American Journal of International Law* 91:231–267.

Steinberg, Richard H. 2002. "In the Shadow of Law or Power? Consensus-Based Bargaining and Outcomes in the GATT/WTO." *International Organization* 56:339–374.

Steinberg, Richard H. 2004. "Judicial Lawmaking at the WTO: Discursive, Constitutional, and Political Constraints." *American Journal of International Law*

98:247–275.

Steinberg, Richard H. and Jonathan M. Zasloff. 2006. "Power and International Law." *American Journal of International Law* 100:64–87.

Steinberg, Richard H. and Judith Goldstein. 2008. "Negotiate or Litigate? Effects of WTO Judicial Delegation on U.S. Trade Politics." *Law and Contemporary Problems* 71:257–282.

Stiles, Kendall W. 2000. "U.S. Responses to Defeat in International Courts: A Contingent Model of Rule Compliance." *Political Research Quarterly* 53:401–25.

Stone, Randall W. 2011. *Controlling Institutions: International Organizations and the Global Economy.* Cambridge University Press.

Swaine, Edward T. 2006. "Reserving." *Yale Journal of International Law* 31:307–366.

Tomz, Michael, Judith L. Goldstein and Douglas Rivers. 2007. "Do We Really Know That the WTO Increases Trade? Comment." *American Economic Review* 97:2005–2018.

Trebilcock, Michael J. and Robert Howse. 1995. *The Regulation of International Trade.* Routledge Press.

Treves, Tullio. 1998. "Conflicts between the International Tribunal for the Law of the Sea and the International Court of Justice." *N.Y.U. Journal of International Law and Politics* 31:809–821.

Van den Bossche, Peter. 2005. *The Law and Policy of the World Trade Organization.* Cambridge University Press.

Vanberg, Georg. 2005. *The Politics of Constitutional Review in Germany.* Cambridge University Press.

Voeten, Eric. 2001. "Outside Options and the Logic of Security Council Action." *American Political Science Review* 95:845–58.

Voeten, Erik. 2008. "The Impartiality of International Judges: Evidence from the European Court of Human Rights." *American Political Science Review* 102:417–433.

Waltz, Kenneth. 1979. *Theory of International Politics.* Addison-Wesley.

Weiss, Stephen E., Mark T. Hogan, Jay W. Chai, Eugene J. Meigher, Edward F. Glynn Jr. and Dennis C. Cuneo. 1996. "The General Motors-Toyota Joint Venture, 1982-1984." *International Negotiation* 1:277–292.

White, Nigel. 1999. "To Review or Not To Review? The *Lockerbie* Cases Before the World Court." *Leiden Journal of International Law* 12:401–23.

WTO. 2004. *A Handbook on the WTO Dispute Settlement System.* Cambridge University Press.

WTO, World Trade Organization. 1999. *The Legal Texts: The Results of the Uruguay Round of Multilateral Trade Negotiations.* Cambridge University Press.

Index